THE **DIY** MUSIC MANUAL

Dedicated to musicians everywhere

THE **DIY** MUSIC MANUAL
RANDY CHERTKOW & JASON FEEHAN

EBURY
PRESS

1 3 5 7 9 10 8 6 4 2

A previous edition of this work was published under the title
The Indie Band Survival Guide in the US by St Martin's Press in 2008

This edition published in the UK in 2009 by Ebury Press, an imprint of Ebury Publishing

A Random House Group Company

The Random House Group Limited Reg. No. 954009

Addresses for companies within the Random House Group can be found at
www.randomhouse.co.uk

A CIP catalogue record for this book is available from the British Library

The Random House Group Limited supports The Forest Stewardship Council (FSC), the
leading international forest certification organisation. All our titles that are printed on
Greenpeace approved FSC certified paper carry the FSC logo. Our paper procurement
policy can be found at www.rbooks.co.uk/environment

Mixed Sources
Product group from well-managed
forests and other controlled sources
www.fsc.org Cert no. TT-COC-2139
© 1996 Forest Stewardship Council
FSC

Designed and set by seagulls.net

Printed and bound in Great Britain by Clays Ltd, St Ives PLC

ISBN 9780091927929

To buy books by your favourite authors and register for offers visit www.rbooks.co.uk

▶▶TABLE OF CONTENTS

▶▶INTRODUCTION

Welcome to *The DIY Music Manual*, a practical how-to manual to get your music heard, distributed, sold, booked, promoted and seen. In the past, you could only do all of this with the backing of a major record label but today you can now do it on your own. We'll tell you how to get started and walk you through the process.

This book is for all musicians, from hobbyists to professionals. It's also for managers, bookers, labels, promoters, recording engineers, music teachers, music video directors, filmmakers and anyone else that works with music. In fact, many of the methods we share here are useful for any creative endeavour; you don't have to be a musician to get a lot out of this *Manual*. But our focus is on how each topic relates to music. For instance, when we explain how to create websites, we specifically cover the creation of *music* websites, even though the principles of good website design we share are applicable to any site.

The information in this book is applicable to musicians of all ages, from teens starting their first garage band to retirees who have rediscovered their love of music and want to share it with the world. It will be indispensable to you whether or not you have a lot of experience with the Internet. The *Manual* will explain how to use all of the talents that you already have and supplement it with tools, techniques and a network of people to accomplish what was only possible for major label bands in the past.

More than anything, at the heart of this book are essential techniques for getting your music to the world.

▶▶WHO ARE 'WE' ANYWAY?

'We' are lead members of Beatnik Turtle, an indie band with over a decade of experience, over eighteen albums, a song that was licensed to Disney for a commercial campaign, years of live shows, college radio play, countless podcast plays (we'll explain podcasts, don't worry), theatre shows at venues such as Second City in Chicago, TV theme songs, music videos, websites and a completed Song of the Day project where we released one song each day for a year. In case you're curious, all things Beatnik Turtle can be found at beatnikturtle.com.

We are two working professionals – an IT expert and a lawyer – and we've brought all the knowledge and experience from our respective fields to bear on this book, just as you will learn to take advantage of your own skills in making your band a success. Thanks to our backgrounds, the two of us are just as inclined to discuss the state of the music industry or the future of independent music as we are to actually sit down and jam.

In the end, though, we are indie musicians with a band. We generated the material in this book by actually solving the problems we discuss here. In fact, this is the book we wish we'd had when we started out. For instance, when we wrote the section about how to submit your music to podcasts, we recorded the steps we'd been using for years and then did another round of submissions in order to test and refine the process.

So when we say 'we', we're talking to you as one musician to another.

▶▶WHAT YOU NEED TO GET STARTED

We're going to cover a *lot* of topics but we're going to take for granted that you know how to sing and/or play your instruments and that you have your own music to perform. You might do cover songs or you might write your own music, but, either way, we assume that you should already have that ready to go.

Finally, we assume you know how to use a computer and possess at least basic Web skills. We aren't going to spend a lot of time explaining what hyperlinks are or how to use a Web browser. Many of the opportunities that have opened up for musicians in the last few years are on the Web, so you'll be using it quite a bit to promote your music and get it heard by a worldwide audience. If you'd like to do some background reading, we suggest the book *Internet for Dummies* by John R. Levine, Margaret Levine Young and Carol Baroudi for a basic overview, as well as the book *Rule the Web!* by Mark Frauenfelder which can help you get the most out of the Internet.

▶▶ HOW TO USE THIS BOOK

This book is about *doing*.

In this book, we cover the theory behind how things work so you can navigate unfamiliar tasks (like publicity) but you should expect to *act* on these how-to steps and suggestions, not just think about them. In fact, this book will work best if you have a notepad next to you while you read so you can take notes on what to do next. We're big fans of *Getting Things Done*, a book by David Allen that provides an excellent system of organising your tasks and your time.

With the *Manual* in hand, you can shortcut the part where you are trying to figure out *what* you should do. In fact, that's what we struggled with for the past decade. We wrote it in this book so you can pick up where we left off.

Lastly, *The Manual* is not a book of lists and links. Although we have important links throughout this book, there are always new tools and services for musicians popping up (as well as ones that disappear). For this information, as well as a way to connect to other motivated musicians, head to DIYMusicManual.com.

Naturally, as a musician you'll want to improvise on what we suggest here. Go for it. As we like to say, these tools and lessons are no substitute for artful practice.

▶▶ TERMINOLOGY

Below, we provide our own definitions of a few music business terms to avoid any confusion about what they mean when we use them:

- **Unsigned:** Refers to a band or musician that does not have a contract with a music label for recording, production and distribution. Unfortunately, it seems to imply that being signed is the goal and that musicians that haven't been signed have a lower status than those that have. We will not be using this term and we suggest that indie bands skip it as well.
- **Independent ('indie'):** Used to describe a band, musician or label independent of the major labels no matter what style of music they play. We don't believe that musical success should be defined in the context of business contracts. The definition we use is: independent musicians are artists that handle their own music careers. It's something to be proud of.
- **The music industry:** The music industry has changed so much in recent years that a person in the business just five years ago would hardly

recognise it. While today the term still seems to refer to the monolithic music business, safer to say that there are many industries that are coming together around music. This term is in transition but we will use it to talk about the business of music.

Because the traditional players in the music business used to be gatekeepers for the distribution and sale of music, many of these terms defined music between what was inside of their system and what wasn't. This isn't surprising: in the past nothing outside the system would get heard by anyone but local bar crowds. What *is* surprising is that these terms are still used even though musicians now have access to almost all of the same recording and distribution channels that the traditional players use. When people talk about bands that are signed or unsigned, we ask them how they can hear the difference between a song that is owned by musicians or one owned by a company. Is there some magic way to analyse the audio signal to get an idea of who owns it?

Fortunately, music is music, no matter what contracts are signed and how the lawyers have chopped up the rights. Music fans don't care about contracts, they care about the music and the musician. And that's the point: there no longer needs to be a middleman between musicians and music fans.

This book will tell you how to reach them.

▶▶CHAPTER ONE

THERE HAS NEVER BEEN A BETTER TIME TO BE A MUSICIAN

'Less than ten years ago the "Holy Grail" for artists was to get a record or publishing deal. Today, many artists avoid these deals (especially record ones) at all costs.'
'The Record Biz Today: On Which End of the Food Chain?', National Association of Record Industry Professionals (5 June 2007)

There has never been a better time to be a musician.

The tools at your fingertips today were barely even dreams just ten years ago. Global digital distribution for music is simple to achieve and with it you can sell millions of copies of your album from one physical copy. There are more opportunities than ever before to get your music played and they are no longer exclusive to the major labels. The Web can get you a worldwide fan-base. And you can record your music at home with technologies and capabilities better than a professional recording studio could achieve a mere decade ago. The system, which used to be closed off, is now wide open for anyone who wants to participate. The traditional players in the music industry were like tollbooth operators and the price of admission was your music. Now, you don't have to ask anyone's permission and the cost is minimal.

We've entered a world where the musicians are in charge. The numerous middlemen who separated the musicians from their fans are falling away. In fact, musicians can stop wasting their time trying to appeal to the mainstream-minded music executives and focus on the people that really matter: the fans.

Unfortunately, the best techniques for taking your music into your own hands are scattered all over the Web or in books and courses oriented towards audio and computer professionals. Even more answers have existed only in the heads of musicians who have solved these problems from scratch but haven't yet shared how.

That is, until now.

You are holding a book written by two indie musicians who ran into those problems and who, by necessity, navigated and deciphered the confusing worlds of music copyright and licensing, CD replication, publicity, music video production and booking, to name a few. This is the manual that we wish that we had when we started our own band over a decade ago.

With this book, you'll learn how to win fans worldwide, achieve global digital distribution and sales, get your music heard on radio and the Internet, launch publicity campaigns and get yourself and your music noticed throughout the world.

In short, you now have everything you need to do it yourself.

▸▸ THE DEATH OF THE HIT-DRIVEN MUSIC INDUSTRY

THE LONG TAIL

The music industry has long focused on the hits. From the *Top of the Pops* to the focus on Gold and Platinum albums, the mark of success for music was based on the number of units sold. This industry is obsessed with popularity and sales numbers. This isn't surprising, since most of the sales came only from those hits. Why bother with any other music?

But that was in the days where music could only be sold as pieces of acetate or plastic and the only way to hear new music was to listen to the handful of radio stations in your town. At the heart of the titanic changes to the music industry is a concept called 'The Long Tail', a theory created by Chris Anderson, editor of *Wired* magazine, author of the book *The Long Tail*, and, incidentally, a musician.

His theory about what changed is simple: there has never been *room* for items that might sell just one or two units a week. But, with computers and the Internet, there is no end of shelf space. For example, if we look at music sales, it would resemble the graph on page 12. Most of the music industry focused on the head of the graph, which represents hit albums. But the grey part, the 'long tail', extends far beyond what the graph can even show.

Here's the surprising part: the combined sales of the Long Tail are *greater* than the combined sales of the Head (the 'hits'). The reason is simple: there's so much more that makes up the tail than ever can make up the head. And because people aren't limited to just buying their music from the head, they are travelling down the tail and buying what *they* want to hear, rather than what the industry has made available to them.

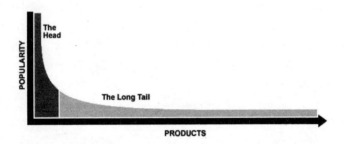

Are all of these so-called Long Tail songs, well, good? Naturally, not. But the amazing thing is that every single one of these tracks, good, bad and ugly, usually sell. In fact, this key paragraph from *The Long Tail* explains it best:

> ...for online retailers like Rhapsody the market is seemingly never-ending. Not only is every single one of Rhapsody's top 60,000 tracks streamed at least once each month but the same is true for its top 100,000, top 200,000 and top 400,000, even its top 600,000, top 900,000 and beyond. As fast as Rhapsody adds tracks to its library, those songs find an audience, even if it's just a handful of people every month, somewhere in the world.

This means that there's a market for all music thanks to high-speed Internet connections and dirt-cheap hard drive storage. The implications for your own music should be obvious: there's room for you in the pool. Hop in.

UNLIMITED CHOICES

In the recent past there were only so many radio stations, TV channels and shelf space.

Our audience's choices were limited. But today, there are unlimited choices. This changes everything.

Not all of it is good for the traditional media, the media that most musicians target to get their music played. A multitude of new entertainment options such as YouTube, podcasts, video games and the Internet have diluted their audience. In fact, according to *The Long Tail*, if you were to drop a television share sheet for the top television show on the desk of a TV executive from one of the three US networks of the 1970s, he would immediately cancel the show due to poor ratings. And with even more choices being offered to audiences, these numbers will possibly drop even further.

In the past, because the channels were so expensive, the gatekeepers focused on hit music or shows that maximised their audience share. Generations of people internalised this hits-only economic model and began to assume that there was 'a mainstream' that everyone liked. Anything that didn't make it past the gatekeepers had no value. But how much of this was caused by the fact that mainstream entertainment was the *only* entertainment available?

'Music is an industry grossly underserved by the blockbuster model', Chris Anderson told us in an interview. 'People don't realise how much music is out there. The vast majority of bands don't get signed to a major label and don't get sold in major record stores. Music is an example of the richness of culture and the violence that traditional distribution does to that variety.'

But as he explained in his book, the traditional distribution model is now being swept away. And this trend is good for indies. Plus, because the means of production and distribution are in the hands of people like you and me, more people are making music themselves. They have realised that they can find an audience on the Internet, even a big one. And so the irony is that the average person is not only spending less time consuming traditional mainstream media, they're actually competing against it.

With these trends dividing the attentions of the audience, the established players must change their business models. They are still focused on hits, with most of their income streams based entirely on the number of people watching and listening to their shows. As their audience continues to drop, the advertising money supporting film, TV show and major label album production is flowing elsewhere. The hit-driven producers of music – the major labels – are especially impacted.

NICHES

The limited number of channels of the past have exploded into a universe of niches. People can easily find others that share their interests no matter what that interest is and no matter where in the world those people are. But this doesn't mean niches are small. For example, there are millions of tennis fans.

Music works the same way. No matter what genre of music you play, fans of that style can find you and hear your music. All you need to do is reach out to them. You need only go to CD Baby (cdbaby.com), the world's largest independent music store, to find that the top sellers appeal to particular niches. Derek Sivers, the president and founder, shared his observation about this trend:

> Imagine an archery range with a target one hundred feet away that you're shooting at with your bow and arrow. For the last few decades that target has been two inches wide. And the only way you could hit it was aiming dead at the middle. If you had perfect aim, you could have a big hit. Otherwise, you'd have nothing at all. Now it's like that target is 100 feet across and it's easy to hit, except somebody did a little trick and cut out the middle. It's like a big giant doughnut. It's easy to hit but if you're still aiming at the middle, there's nothing there.

This trend is good for indies. There are people who want to hear your music. And, the goal of the rest of the *Manual* is to tell you how to effectively find your own niches.

HOME RECORDING AND ACCESS TO TECHNOLOGY

Distribution wasn't the only gated-off part of the hit-driven music industry, recording technology was also expensive and unavailable to most musicians. Recording used to require the financial resources and backing of a label. Today, access to this technology is within most musician's reach.

'Today's recording technology both equals that of the studios in the past, and at the same time is a fraction of the cost,' says Norman Hajjar, the Chief Marketing Officer of Guitar Center, the largest musical instrument retailer in the US. 'For less than $1000, you can be a bedroom rock star.' As Hajjar points out, this affordable recording technology and gear has 'unbottled the creativity that was always there; it was just inaccessible to most people. Musicians today have so many different and exciting ways to not only get access to the creative tools that allow them to express themselves, but also more ways to share their creativity with the world. Ways that were unfathomable in the past. I have zero doubt that we're hearing music today that would not have been created if it weren't for this access to technology.'

The recording capabilities that musicians have now are stunning, and are a whole world to explore itself. And it's even more powerful now that this music production revolution has been coupled with instant worldwide music distribution. It means that the musician's basic desire to make and record music that others will hear has now been fulfilled. And it's this new era that has brought a lot of people back to music, as well as enticing new people to explore it.

HOW THE DEATH OF THE HIT-DRIVEN MUSIC INDUSTRY AFFECTS YOUR MUSIC

Here's what it means to you:

- There is room for every artist
- You no longer need to go through gatekeepers to get your music to an audience
- Traditional mainstream media such as television and radio are no longer the only ways to get heard. There are more ways to win fans using a broad array of other media that don't have the same barriers to entry
- Music hits are never going to be as big as they were in the past, because people aren't forced to select their music from a small set of options. Astronomical hits were an artificial by-product of limited choices
- Because of the number of options that the audience has, you must compete for your audience's attention but there are countless niches for your music
- The distinction between being signed and being indie will not matter to fans. Instead talent, quality, publicity and genre will be all that matters
- Your band is a niche

▸▸MYTHS AND REALITIES OF MAJOR LABELS

Back when studio time was expensive and distribution and promotional channels were limited, musicians needed labels to record, distribute and promote their music. But this has changed. As Jeff Price says, a former indie label head and now founder of TuneCore (tunecore.com), a service that allows anyone to distribute their music digitally, 'Signing with a label is now just a choice.' And although many musicians still dream of getting signed to a label, it's no longer a take-it-or-leave-it proposition.

It's clear, from labels' history, that they have taken advantage of their powerful position in the past, as we discuss below.

MONEY PROBLEMS

As record producer, Steve Albini, revealed in a well-known essay called 'The Problem With Music' musicians in a moderately successful band signed to a major label with a US$250,000 advance (which is owed back to the label) can make as little as US$4000 per year. In the end, most albums never earn out their advance – the only money most musicians see.

This has caused established indie artists who already make a living off their music to look sceptically at signing when they're approached. The groups Hope & Social/Four Day Hombre (hopeandsocial.com) and Gavin Mikhail (gavin-mikhail.com) were both offered deals and both of them did what every musician should do before signing a contract: a simple cost-benefit analysis of the deal. Mikhail realised that the label that approached him would have to *triple* the amount of money that he brought in just to get back to the income level that he had already attained on his own. The band Hope and Social, formerly Four Day Hombre, and their manager Roo Pigott stayed DIY when offered a deal, because they found that the label was only going to do the same distribution, merchandise and PR that they were already doing for themselves at a very low cost (and which we discuss in detail in this *Manual*). In fact, they joined with their own fans to create a label of their own.

To get more insight into how record labels really work, we suggest *Confessions of a Record Producer* by Moses Avalon and *All You Need to Know About the Music Business* by Donald S. Passman.

CONTROL ISSUES

Labels wield a great deal of control over your creative work. In fact, they not only control the creative content of the work, they even control the release of the work itself. It's not unheard of for bands to go through the entire recording process only to find that the label has changed to a new management team that has decided to withdraw their support – leaving the band with an unreleased album and no recourse.

One story of how they can misunderstand the creative intent of an artist happened to Gavin Mikhail, before he decided to go on his own. He was approached by major labels, who liked the music he was making but told him that in order to pitch himself he needed to act dark and mysterious. They had him attend a gathering and go and brood in the corner in order to gain interest. This was the exact opposite of both Mikhail's personality and his music. After that bad experience, Mikhail passed on the offer and has since gone on to create a very successful independent career for himself.

For a more detailed look into what labels do and how they've treated artists, see *The Ultimate Survival Guide to the New Music Industry: Handbook for Hell* by Justin Goldberg.

SIGNING AWAY YOUR RIGHTS

Some of the rights that the label asks you to sign away never revert to the artist. For example, labels keep rights to the recording master of your album *for ever*. Even if the album goes gold and the band pays back all of the money owed to the label, that recording will still be owned by the label. It's theirs to exploit; not yours. A quote from Courtney Love said it best: '... the band owns none of its work ... they can pay the mortgage for ever but they'll never own the house'.

MORE BAD NEWS: CONSOLIDATION, COST CUTTING AND LAYOFFS

Labels and the *recording* music industry as it existed over the past half-century are in turmoil. They are losing money, cutting costs, laying off employees, suing its customers and consolidating in order to stay alive. As stated above, the music industry's business model is broken. They are still focused on hits and selling CDs. Each year, sales of CDs decline. Unsurprisingly, these sales declines are affecting those musicians who choose to sign with the labels:

- **Artist development:** Labels are spending less than ever on nurturing new musicians and bands and more on lawyers and law firms. In an article entitled 'Music Labels Might Still Be Shorts' (realmoney.com), Cody Willard writes: 'They can't just cut costs to boost cash flow forever. There's no fat left in those labels. They sure don't spend to develop talent over the years like they did back in days past.'
- **Turnover:** To compensate for lower revenues, the labels lay off employees. Musicians who do get signed can't be sure that the people they are dealing with today will still be there tomorrow.
- **Taking even more revenue streams:** Major labels are trying to get at even more of the artists' revenue streams. While they used to be limited to album distribution and ownership of the master recordings, they are now taking a cut of music publishing, merchandise, live shows and even sponsorship revenue in the guise of providing a one-stop holistic approach – something that a band can handle more profitably for themselves.

THE MAJOR LABELS' COLLAPSE AS AN OPPORTUNITY FOR INDIE MUSICIANS

The good news for indie musicians is that those people being laid off are experienced and talented music professionals, skilled personnel who are increasingly hiring themselves out to indies, charging by the hour or on a per-project basis. In fact, when we decided to get the help of a publicist for our CD release, we found one who had worked at Sony BMG promoting major groups for years, deeply experienced with getting albums in front of lots of reviewers. And we didn't have to give up the rights to our music to take advantage of that experience.

Even veteran artists are catching on to these trends. The ones that are popular enough to get out on their own are doing so now. In fact, many of them are bypassing the labels and going to banks and investors to raise the funds to record their albums. Artists that can show a steady income stream from prior releases have been able to raise serious money. The real question is, what role will the labels play now? According to Aaron O. Patrick in the *Wall Street Journal*:

> Big record companies say they aren't threatened by the efforts to produce music without them. Bands 'are not equipped with the necessary specialist skills to take care of business' such as hiring producers, designers, photographers and publicists, says Max Hole, an executive vice president at Universal Music Group International, the overseas arm of the world's largest music company by market share. 'We are experts in providing these services and skills, which allows the artist to create and make music.'

We find Mr Hole's suggestion that a band can't find their own photographer, publicist and designer to help them put together their own albums absurd, especially in the age of the Internet. And they're not going to ask you for the copyright to your music in return for their services. Furthermore, some tools, like a digital camera or a copy of Photoshop, are easily in your grasp. Whether the traditional players acknowledge it or not, we've entered a new era, one where musicians can do it themselves.

▶▶ THE NEW ERA OF MUSIC

Today's music world has entirely new concepts and terms that drive it, with audiences that have a completely different view of music than they have had in the past. You will need to take these into account in order to plunge forward into this world.

PRE-NET AND POST-NET

The heart of this new era for music is the Internet's capability for instantaneous transmission of music between people all over the world. Other factors include better encoding for small music file sizes, peer-to-peer file sharing, faster computers and broadband connections.

The **pre-net** era was one where limited resources meant limited access for audiences. It meant that there were few channels of distribution, with control concentrated among few players. These players decided what music would be distributed and where. It was a world of one-way communication – of broadcasting.

In the **post-net** era, barriers between artists and their audiences have fallen away. Post-net audiences are fickle and they expect to get most of their information and entertainment for free. Trends come and go quickly in this world. It's easy for something to 'go viral' because people spread the music they enjoy to people they know. In the Internet world, this can mean millions of people taking an interest in a short amount of time.

Perhaps the most interesting and relevant change to the post-net world is the cynicism of the public regarding the traditional media, especially when it comes to the music business. Today's audiences crave authenticity – a fact that isn't lost on the major labels. A *Wall Street Journal* article about YouTube singing phenomenon Marié Digby explains it best:

> Ms Digby's simple, homemade music videos of her performing popular songs have been viewed more than 2.3 million times on YouTube. Her acoustic-guitar rendition of the R&B hit 'Umbrella' has been featured on MTV's program *The Hills* and is played regularly on radio stations in Los Angeles, Sacramento and Portland, Ore. Capping the frenzy, a press release last week from Walt Disney Co.'s Hollywood Records label declared: 'Breakthrough YouTube Phenomenon Marié Digby Signs With Hollywood Records'. What the release failed to mention is that Hollywood Records signed Ms Digby in 2005, 18 months before she became a YouTube phenomenon. Hollywood Records helped devise her Internet strategy, consulted with her on the type of songs she chose to post and distributed a high-quality studio recording of 'Umbrella' to iTunes and radio stations.

This surprising development shows that it has become a *disadvantage* to be a major label act. According to the article, Digby's MySpace page had 'None' listed under 'Type of Label'. After enquiries from the *Journal*, it was changed to

'Major'. It's clear that Hollywood's approach catered to post-net expectations of authenticity.

Indies, on the other hand, don't need to manufacture it. They actually *are* authentic.

We will be using the terms pre-net and post-net to discuss differences between these two eras. We'll be comparing them often because there are still many commonly held pre-net conceptions that need to go.

The post-net world is truly exciting and it's only just begun. Those that choose to take advantage of these new changes rather than harking back to the pre-net era will find fans and experience success in new ways.

PRE-FILTERS AND POST-FILTERS

In the pre-net world, there are two layers of filters.

Pre-filters are the gatekeepers who decide what music will go into distribution channels such as stores, TV, radio and film. Examples of these are music executives, agents and A&R representatives. In the pre-net world, it was very tough to break into this system and only a minute percentage ever did.

Post-filters are the reviewers, newspapers, websites and other sources that people trust to filter through the sea of information and find the gems that match their tastes.

While the pre-filters still exist in the post-net era they can be ignored if someone wants to post their work for the world to see. There are no pre-filters on YouTube, for example. Anyone can post any video they want. But of that morass of videos, which ones are actually entertaining? That's where post-filters come in. Many people depend on sites like Milk and Cookies (milkand-cookies.com) to point out the good ones, which only posts links to videos that users in their community found amusing.

Also, even the role of post-filters has opened up. In the pre-net era, only a few people were empowered to review new works for the public. In the post-net world, anyone can blog their opinions or post a review on Amazon.co.uk. The traditional reviewers, who sometimes worked for publications that were funded by the major players' advertising, suddenly had unbiased, genuine competition from people who wanted nothing more than to share their opinions. This authenticity is the true currency of the Internet.

There are many types of post-filters:

■ **The traditional reviewer:** An individual who gives their personal opinion as to what is worthwhile. Some examples are music writers and movie reviewers. In the post-net era, it also includes bloggers and websites that post reviews.

- **Community-based filters**: Community-based filters are websites that let their own communities suggest and vote on what they consider to be the best content. With a large enough community, this can be a very powerful way to filter. Some examples of community-based filters are Digg.com and Reddit.com, which we discuss in Chapter 5: Your Web Presence.
- **Editor-based submission filters:** These combine elements of traditional reviewers with community-based filters. A website that has editor-based submission filters will accept submissions from anyone but an editor will sift through these and post what they think is worthwhile. One example of this type of post-filter is Slashdot (slashdot.org).
- **Aggregation filters:** Since there are now so many opinions to be found, some sites aggregate reviews to give a more accurate picture. For instance, Rotten Tomatoes (rottentomatoes.com) takes reviews from known movie reviewers and quantifies their opinions to find a combined approval percentage for each film.
- **Word of mouth:** The most important kind of filter there is. And one that becomes even more powerful online.
- **Advertising and marketing**: Advertising and marketing can have a powerful effect on what rises into people's consciousness.

Since pre-filters can now be avoided, the post-filters have become all-important.

They are the primary way that people will find out about your band. As Jim DeRogatis, music reviewer for the *Sun-Times* and co-host of National Public Radio's *Sound Opinions*, says, 'No matter how obscure a name I throw at you or you throw at me, the fact that we'll be able, in no time at all, to sample that band for ourselves is incredibly liberating. But you'd never know about [these groups] if I didn't mention it to you.' As an indie musician, you will need to target these post-filters. We will talk about how to influence them to cover your music in upcoming chapters.

THE BIG HIT VS THE LONG, SLOW BURN

Most major label bands are only profitable for a short time after they release, and so there was always an emphasis on the quick hit. And for some reason, musicians still think that it has to be true for them as well. But a sustainable music career is not built quickly – especially when you're independent and don't have the money for billboards and saturation of radio play. 'It requires a long, slow burn', as Gavin Mikhail says.

Fortunately, since the Internet is always on, you are constantly giving people a chance to discover your music, as opposed to the days when radio was the only significant way to get heard. Approaching your music with an eye on the long-term will result in greater successes than imitating the outdated hit model. Word of mouth and the recommendation of a friend has always been one of the best methods for fans to discover new music. Today, word of mouth and recommendations occur online as well as offline. But the great thing about it happening online is it's easily hyperlinked, shared, and for ever archived so others can stumble on the same recommendation in the future.

THE PEDESTAL VS THE ONE-TO-ONE RELATIONSHIP

If the prior music industry was all about putting the artist on a pedestal, the new one is about having one-to-one relationships with your fans.

As Andrew Dubber, Degree Leader in Music Industries at Birmingham City University, blogger (andrewdubber.com), and founder of Music Think Tank (musicthinktank.com), says:

> The new model is about starting an ongoing economic relationship with a community of enthusiasts. It's about attention and repeat engagement …. It's not a top-down, one-to-many distribution model. It's not a customer off the street happening by and exchanging money for a product. This is about trust, recommendation and reputation. This is a many-to-many dialogue, and the money goes where the attention lies.

Most all of the artists that we interviewed, as well as ourselves, all have developed personal connections with their fans and built a community. Both Gavin Mikhail and Jonathan Coulton talked about the eight- to ten-hour days they spent corresponding to individual fans through email. Our band has gone on to collaborate with fans on a their own projects – from writing music for live theatre to writing theme songs for podcasts and videos. The band Hope & Social/Four Day Hombre went even further, and ended up starting a music label with some of their biggest fans so that they could fund their next projects. And their music videos were all filmed by a fan, Mark Wordsworth, who turned out to be so talented, he ended up building a career as a music-video director.

▶▶DO IT YOURSELF

As an indie, making your music successful is now your responsibility.

Unfortunately, it's not enough to just post an MP3 on your MySpace page. Everything that a label would have done for you is now in your hands. You need to get yourself noticed, booked, distributed, played, seen and publicised.

Luckily, you have outstanding tools, services and resources at your fingertips to help you do it yourself. You have global distribution, unlimited promotional opportunities and countless new ways to get your music to millions of people all over the world. Stop worrying about a music *industry* and start focusing on music *fans*. They're out there. You just need to win them over.

That's what the *Manual* is all about. Read on to find out how.

▶▶CHAPTER TWO
YOUR NETWORK

Labels used to be the only way to get your music recorded, distributed and promoted. The entire game was all about winning over a few key people – businessmen, usually – who decided which bands got heard and which sat in obscurity.

That is no longer the case.

Rather than spend your time, money and energy on 'getting signed' you can now focus on winning over the people who really matter: the fans. Of course, the responsibilities, roles and costs that labels would have handled fall on you now. That's a lot to take on. Not only do you have to create all the music, you also have to design logos, book gigs, design a website and arrange publicity, to name just a few things. Although you can do it all yourself, it's hard to do it all well.

But doing it yourself doesn't mean doing it alone.

In fact doing it yourself in music isn't the same as doing it yourself in other areas. Even small labels don't do everything 'themselves'. They get graphic artists to design logos, album covers and posters. They get Web designers to create websites. They get publicists to convince the press to write about their bands.

You've heard the saying before: 'It's not what you know, it's who you know.' Or, as one of our friends puts it, 'It's who you get to know.' This is as true in music as it is in any other field. At the end of the day, despite all the advances in technology that have empowered the artist, it's not technology that will get your music noticed, booked, distributed, played, seen and publicised. It's people. People make things happen.

These are all real problems that you'll need to solve. Now your goal is to find the right people to help you do it.

▸▸THE ARM'S REACH LESSON AND NETWORKING

Networking scares most people. Maybe because they associate it with unpleasant tasks like 'finding a job' or because it can feel like a phony way to befriend someone. But networking doesn't have to be hard and, in fact, it shouldn't start with strangers at all. The people that you already know – people within your arm's reach – may be the ones who can help you achieve your band's goals.

We discovered some surprising talents among the people that we already knew which helped our band succeed, talents we didn't possess ourselves. For example, when we wanted to make a music video, one friend directed, others acted and we even got the use of another friend's professional video equipment. When we wanted to improve our website, we found graphic artists and Web programmers in our existing social network. Similarly, people within our arm's reach have given us opportunities. We performed at a college outdoor festival set up by a friend who worked there. We got great press for our TheSongOfTheDay.com project when a friend mentioned it to his buddies who wrote for a popular Chicago blog.

These opportunities arose because we made our goals and obstacles known to our friends, co-workers and families. If they didn't have the answers, we asked them if they knew anyone else who might. When they did know someone who could help, we asked them to introduce us so we could follow up. When people helped us, we made sure to repay them in some way – by giving them credit, assisting them in solving some problem of their own (even if it wasn't music-related) or simply by sending a thank you note.

We didn't realise it at the time but we were networking. While the traditional concept of networking put us off, it turned out it isn't that difficult when you begin with the circle of people you know. And as you expand your network, problems get easier to solve. The key is to understand what type of networks are available to you, how to use those networks effectively and how to reciprocate so that people feel appreciated.

▸▸TYPES OF NETWORKING

There are two general types of networking: skill networking and opportunity networking. A single person might be in both networks but thinking about each type of networking differently will clarify your approach.

SKILL NETWORKING

In a band, each member possesses skills beyond music. You might have a visual artist, Web designer and booker all within your band. Obviously, when available, you should do these things for yourselves. But you'll probably need more people involved to help out with all the other roles that a label tradition- ally filled. These roles include:

- Manager
- Booker
- Distributor
- Web designer
- Webmaster
- Graphic artist
- Publicist
- Photographer
- Recording producer
- Recording engineer
- TV/Film camera crew
- TV/Film editor
- Store clerk (for shows and events)
- Lawyer
- Accountant

If your indie band doesn't fill these roles from its skill network, essential tasks just won't get done. And yet, there are some that you just can't skip – espe- cially when it comes to promoting your band and getting your music heard. As Derek Sivers of CD Baby suggests, 'Whatever excites you, go do it and what- ever drains you, stop doing it as soon as possible. Because for everything you hate doing, there's someone else that loves it. Your goal should be to find those people and have them help you.' The goal of skill networking is to find those who can help you fill in the gaps you can't manage yourself.

OPPORTUNITY NETWORKING

Some people within your arm's reach will have access to opportunities for getting your band and music out there. In general, the people in your oppor- tunity network will have one thing in common: they'll have an audience. Some of these people include:

- Music journalists
- Bookers
- Venue managers/Bar owners
- Podcasters
- Radio hosts/DJs
- Bloggers
- Video game designers
- Film/TV/Video directors and music scouts
- Companies
- Theatre artists/Sketch comedy troupes

You might have some of these people in your arm's reach but these networking opportunities are typically harder to access at first. They require time and energy to cultivate. Sometimes they require credentials. The good news is, once you establish the necessary relationships, they will start coming to *you* with opportunities.

HIDDEN SKILLS AND OPPORTUNITIES

Many people have hidden skills or opportunities that you may not be aware of at first. For instance, when we were putting together the artwork for our second album, *Santa Doesn't Like You*, we lacked the software and know-how to get it in the format that the CD printing house required. We were stuck, until one of our friends – a neighbour, actually – revealed she was a graphic artist and had the necessary software to create the files. We'd had no idea she could do this. In fact, she was just someone we hung out with in our building from time to time. When we mentioned the problem, she offered to help. Since she was a friend, all she asked for in return was to get a credit in the liner notes so she could use it as part of her portfolio. We were happy to do that for her and we got the album art done in time.

You can also access networks online in innovative ways. When Brad Turcotte of Brad Sucks wanted a new logo, he turned to Worth1000.com, a contest site that challenges both professional and amateur artists to create (often humorous) photos, images, text and videos each week. Turcotte contacted the site owner to arrange a 'Design a Brad Sucks Logo Contest'. For only US$50 in prize money, he got the full rights to a logo he was pleased with. Hiring a graphic artist the normal way would have cost him much more than that.

▸▸ WORKING AND GROWING NETWORKS EFFECTIVELY

As George Hrab, a successful indie musician, puts it, the secret to networking is 'to find really talented people and be really, really, really nice to them'. If you can't pay them, you should find other ways to show your appreciation. Movies always end by rolling the credits. Indie bands can use this technique as well.

CROSS-PROMOTION

One way to acknowledge people who have helped you out is to expose *their* work to *your* fans. This can be as simple as linking to their website or mentioning them in a blog entry. For example, we have a special 'shout out' section at our TheSongOfTheDay.com site that lists every podcast that has played one of our songs. It's our little thank you. The most recent plays get a mention on our front page, with direct links to the episodes so that fans of our music can check them out. This results in more and more requests to play our music – not just from the same podcasters but from others who saw what we offered in return.

CELEBRATE AND ACKNOWLEDGE SUCCESSES

Theatre groups throw a cast party at the close of every run. We suggest doing the same for everyone who has helped you out whenever your band reaches a milestone like completing a tour, releasing an album or getting some great press. We've thrown parties, held barbecues and taken people out to dinner to show our appreciation and to celebrate. Usually, we end up talking about the next projects we want to work on and, because everyone's excited about what we've just achieved, they all usually offer to stay on board.

If you can't throw a party, at least send an email to everyone involved and acknowledge everyone who's played a part. Of course, it still helps to mention your next project...

THE WARM HAND-OFF

Sometimes, people in your network can help introduce you to people that you don't know but want to meet. It can be a big help to have a common connection refer you.

For example, for years we wanted to be part of the Chicago leg of the International Pop Overthrow Festival ('IPO') – a roving festival that showcases power pop-rock bands. We went the traditional route of sending in our CD and press kit to the festival organiser and never heard anything back. Months later when the festival came to town, we discovered our friend Yvonne Doll and her band The Locals managed to get in. When we told her we were hoping to be a part of the festival, she said she'd introduce us to the festival organiser, David Bash. The next day after their show, she introduced us to David who asked for a CD. The very next day he contacted us to help fill a last minute cancellation in the schedule. We had a great show and we thanked Yvonne for the warm hand-off. We've played the festival every year it's been in Chicago since and have also been included on a couple IPO compilation albums.

MANUFACTURING YOUR OWN OPPORTUNITIES

Sometimes you need to manufacture your own opportunities and expand your reach. At that point, the best thing to do is set your sights on someone who might be able to help you or provide an opportunity for your music and contact them. This is what most people think 'networking' is.

Sure, you might get a 'no' or no response at all but it's always worth trying because, often, people can surprise you. Although this can be the hardest way to expand your skill and opportunity networks, it can also be the most reward-ing when it connects.

Our band did this when promoting *The Cheapass Album* – an album of songs based on game titles from the trendy board game manufacturer Cheapass Games. At the time of the release back in 2004, we discovered a niche podcast that was created by Scott Alden and Derk Solko, the people behind BoardGameGeek.com (a website that gets over 600,000 unique visitors a month). It was immediately evident that the podcast didn't have a theme song. We didn't know Scott or Derk but we decided to make our own opportu-nity and offer to do a theme song for their show if they were interested. A few days later, after we sent them our albums, they agreed to let us write a demo and give it a listen.

Within a few weeks, they adopted the song for their podcast. We kept in contact with them and later took it a step further by doing more music, helping them with voice-over bumpers and creating some off-the-wall public service announcements. They talked about us in many episodes, which kept our name, our music and our website in front of hundreds of listeners. They even interviewed us in one episode. Scott and Derk became a big part of our opportunity network and we all became good friends. Their podcasts have been downloaded thousands of times and they continue to be downloaded years later by new visitors.

NETWORKING WITH OTHER BANDS AND MUSICIANS

As a musician, you're already a member of one of the most helpful networks you can access. In fact, you're holding a book by two of them right now. But we're not the only musicians willing to share what we've learned. As Brian Austin Whitney, the founder of the popular musician community, Just Plain Folks (jpfolks.com), said, 'There's musicians just getting started, there's those that are on their way and then there's those who have arrived. There's something to be learned and opportunities to gain from each of them. The key is to find these people.'

As the Just Plain Folks' motto states, 'We're all in this together.' When musicians cooperate and share resources, productive things happen:

- **Booking cartels:** Bands and musicians with a complementary sound can join forces for booking purposes. Being able offer an entire night of entertainment to a venue or bar makes their job easier and can get you more gigs in the long run.
- **Musician exchange programmes:** Team up with like-minded musicians in another city online. Each band can book a gig in their respective town and share the same bill. Both bands establish an out-of-town presence.
- **Substitutes:** Ever had a gig you just couldn't make? It's quite hard to find a substitute unless you know other bands and musicians in the area. Finding an appropriate substitute when you can't meet your commitment can save your relationship with the venue.
- **Cross-promotion:** Bands and musicians that work together can introduce their music to each other's fans.
- **Recommendations and referrals**: If you need to find someone who can help you or you need someone to hire, often other musicians can refer you to a trusted person or service.
- **Shared roles at gigs:** Bands can help each other out at shows. For instance, we once ran another band's store while they were playing onstage and they did the same for us while we performed.
- **Going beyond your arm's reach:** Each band has its own skill and opportunity networks and will often share and share alike. This can be a great resource for referrals of trusted freelancers and other services.
- **Newbies:** Don't forget that, as you progress, it's a good thing to offer guidance and assistance to other bands and musicians just starting out and add them to your own network. You never know if they'll return the favour someday.

Remember that you don't need to be in the same location to collaborate with other bands and musicians; it can happen online as well. Message boards, blogs, social-networking sites and our own site, DIYMusicManual.com, can help connect you to other bands and musicians. Often, a solution or opportunity are simply a few clicks away.

One unique example of musicians working together to help each other win fans is The Funny Music Project or The Fump (thefump.com). The Fump was created by a group of liked-minded comedy musicians as a way to help share and cross-promote each individual artist's fans to one another. As Amazon.co.uk would say, 'People who liked this band, also liked…' They created a website and posted original songs twice a week as a MP3 for free download or as a podcast.

But they didn't stop there. The higher-quality versions of the songs are available for purchase. There is a compilation CD created from this material, with extras, that they make available every two months. They even created a multi-level subscription model that gives subscribers access to all of the high-quality MP3s of the music or even automatic mailings of the CDs when they come out.

By banding together under a common theme, these musicians not only were able to cross-promote their music but also created a new business model. While The Fump is all about a certain segment of music comedy, this model could be replicated by any network of musicians for their own genre of music.

▶▶ YOUR FAN NETWORK

At the start, you and your band members will form the centre of your skill and opportunity networks but eventually your music will form your most powerful network. The network that should be your focus at all times: your fans. Winning these people over one by one is what the *Manual* is all about.

In the past, fans were little more than those people who liked a band's music, bought albums, purchased merchandise and came to shows. In other words, they were simply consumers.

That is no longer the case.

Thanks to the Internet, fans have also become empowered. They want to be treated as people. They are no longer limited to watching bands play on stage, they are now a part of that stage. They are part of the conversation. They feel entitled to a relationship with the musicians they like. They email, they download, they comment, they make mashups, they shoot videos, they record podcasts, they chat and they blog. Fans want a place to meet, discuss, collaborate and interact with you and other fans. Your fans form the most important and critical network your music will ever have. And it can grow or wither based on your involvement.

FANS AS CONTRIBUTORS AND COLLABORATORS

Fans today want to interact and participate – not just listen. Many are creative and can help you fill in gaps in your skill network. And when they do, good things can happen for both you and your fans.

Jonathan Coulton is an independent musician who makes a living writing and performing his own music. In September 2005, he challenged himself to write, record and release a musical 'Thing a Week' for free on his website (jonathancoulton.com). Midway through releasing the songs, a fan named Len Peralta emailed him and asked if he might create artwork to accompany each of the 52 songs. Coulton agreed. Soon, under Coulton's active encouragement, fans began making videos, animations and machinima (movies 'filmed' using video games) based on his songs. Coulton even asked fans to send in hand claps so he could include them in his final 'Thing a Week', a cover of Queen's 'We Will Rock You'. One fan created a Coulton card game. Coulton and Peralta later went on to sell the artwork as a book at Lulu.com and even created a colouring book. And then there's the fan that created karaoke versions of Coulton's songs...

A similar thing happened to Brad Turcotte, sole member of the band Brad Sucks (bradsucks.net), a band composed of 'one man with no fans'. However, his 'non-existent' fans have created tons of remixes of his debut album, *I Don't Know What I'm Doing*. After posting the original source tracks of his album at his website and encouraging his fans to remix it, Turcotte soon found himself overwhelmed with the response. Fans sent in *hundreds* of remixes – and they're still coming in. Turcotte decided to turn to his fan network for designing a logo and a week later picked out one that he liked. Then he did the same for album art – not just for his second album but also for a 'best of' compilation album culled from all the remixes his fans had created. He's even let fans come behind the curtain by making demos of his upcoming second album's songs available for their comments and feedback.

FANS AS PROBLEM SOLVERS

Although both Coulton and Turcotte use their blogs and forums to share their opinions, they also use them to ask their fans for help and direction. During the 'Thing a Week' project, Coulton regularly posed questions to his growing fan network to get their feedback on whether they thought he was giving away too much music for free and whether they thought it was hampering his ability to make a living as a solo artist. Fans responded to his request. Soon, his 'Thing a Week' became not only a creative challenge and an experiment in promotion, it became a public discussion of what it means to be a post-net musician. Fans offered up advice on his website design, his gigs and his merchandise. When the importance of promotion became a critical talking point, Coulton naturally enlisted his fans to help. After all, he's only one person.

Turcotte also regularly turns to his fans for help. He asks his fans for their opinions on new Web services, software and instruments. When Turcotte was researching digital download stores to use for his website, he asked his fans if they knew of others. They responded with alternatives (although he eventually built one of his own!).

FANS AS PROMOTERS

One of the more famous experiments in networking was Stanley Milgram's 'Six Degrees of Separation' which states that everyone is connected to everyone else within six people. What it means to you and your music in this connected world has been summed up by Eben Moglen, one of the primary lawyers and voices behind the free software movement:

> The result… is that twelve-year-olds do a better job of distributing music than the music companies. The music company continues to take ninety-four percent of the gross for promoting and distributing music and the twelve-year-olds who take zero off the top do a better job.

But as thought-provoking as this is, Moglen's 12-year-olds will only promote music that they've heard of. So rather than wait for a school-age street team to start promoting your music, you need to ask your fans to help promote you. Fortunately, people love to promote things they know and like. And some of your fans may be well connected and can help get you access to opportunities. Building an enthusiastic fan network to help spread the word about you is powerful. In fact, the best 'advertising' is trusted word of mouth.

Turcotte gave his music away for free to enable his fan network to become active promoters. Although he made his first album available for free download, people still bought his CD. Since CDs are harder to share than the MP3 files, he embedded the MP3 versions of his songs on the CDs to make it easy for his fans to continue to share his music. And as we mentioned above, he later released his source tracks for free to enable fans to remix his songs. This further introduced his music to others since the creators of these remixes actively promoted *their* remixes of *his* songs to other people.

Similarly, Coulton asked his fan network to spread the word and they did with so much enthusiasm, it surprised him. Fans would share his music with friends, play his music at parties and create CDs to give as gifts. Some realised they had press connections and opened those opportunities to Coulton. Others simply added a link to Coulton's website in their signature lines when they posted in forums or discussion groups.

Gavin Mikhail's fans created their own fan sites to promote his music. Many of these were created on free social-networking sites such as MySpace but some Japanese and Germans took it further – actually taking on the costs of hosting a site so they could promote and discuss Mikhail's music in their respective countries, in their own respective languages. For instance, the dedicated Japanese fan set up gavinmikhailjapan.com. The site is run by the fan and provides news, photos and Gavin's music (including links to where to purchase it). Given that Mikhail doesn't speak Japanese nor would he have the time to set such a site up, it's clear such generous fan promotion can add up.

FANS AS SOURCES OF OPPORTUNITIES

Fans can easily fall into your opportunity network, presenting opportunities to spread your music in ways you may not have imagined. Mikhail, Coulton and Turcotte have all had opportunities presented to them from fans such as blog write-ups, podcast plays and press mentions. You never know exactly who is listening and what opportunities they may offer. For instance, Coulton ended up getting a deal with Valve Software when a few of his fans – who worked at Valve – approached him at a show and asked if he'd be interested in writing a song for the end credits of their upcoming game, Portal. That was a great opportunity to land but it didn't stop there. The song he wrote for the game, 'Still Alive', was later licensed by Valve to Harmonix for their video game, Rock Band. This led to yet another opportunity as well: Harmonix worked with Coulton to make his song 'Skullcrusher Mountain' available for Rock Band as well.

FANS AS ORGANISERS

Your fans can even help you organise events or even help book your band. For example, fans are always demanding that Coulton tour in their hometowns. When he realised he had to travel halfway across the country to Seattle at the last minute for a personal matter, he blogged that he'd have one night free and could play a show if there was something set up. Fans in Seattle – who didn't want to pass up a rare opportunity to see Coulton live – immediately took up the challenge and, within twenty-four hours, had arranged a respectable venue. All Coulton had to do was contact the place to cement the details. Twenty-four hours later, he was on stage playing to a packed house.

FANS AS CONSUMERS AND SUPPORTERS

Your fan network will be the greatest source of revenue for your music. This can come both from playing live as well as from album and merchandise sales. It can also come from donations. Beyond selling their music, both Coulton and Turcotte have online 'tip jars' for those who have enjoyed the music they've given away for free. One of the side benefits of socialising with your fans is that it makes you and your band real people. There's a human face to the music. When you offer up albums and merchandise for sale or set up a tip jar and your fans feel connected to you, they're likely to support you by reaching for their wallets. Additionally, your involvement and interaction helps make it clear that the money they are spending is actually going to the artist, not some label.

►► YOU'RE NOT ALONE

The natural progression in this new world of music is to grow from doing-it-yourself to enlisting skill network help. Eventually, however, as you grow and win fans globally, certain tasks will become counterproductive. At that point – which is actually rather exciting and a testament to your efforts – you will need to consider whether it's best to graduate to hiring an expert or outside service such as a publicist, booker, video producer or other role you normally filled.

For instance, the UK band Hope & Social grew naturally from first doing everything themselves to enlisting help from talented friends and family – including a neighbour who helped create music videos on a shoe-string budget that eventually got pulled into rotation on MTV. Eventually, however, they needed to hire a manager and booker to handle their touring schedule, a radio plugger to promote their music and a publicist to broaden their efforts to capitalise on the initial buzz they had created. While such experts cost money, their expertise and relationships have helped grow Hope & Social to a size the original members could not pull off themselves and still give their all to their music.

As we said previously, the rest of the *Manual* will show you how to do all the things that a label would normally do for your music – on your own or by leveraging free or cost-effective Web or music services. It will also explore the roles of these experts, explain what they do and how, when the time comes, they may be able to assist you to grow further and win more fans than you imagined.

But first, it all starts with you in the next chapter.

▸▸CHAPTER THREE

YOUR BRAND

Pre-net, you had to build awareness of your music among those people you could physically meet or those who could see you play live. Post-net, you have the ability to share your music with more people than those pre-net bands could ever dream. Your arm's reach is no longer limited to where you're located.

Today, the people who have met you or seen you play live are likely to be a minority of the people who listen to your music. The majority will now be those who discover you online. To these people, your band will only be known through your music, name and the identity you convey through your website, logos, photos, blogs, videos, avatars, etc. Another way to say this is that they will only know you through 'your brand'. While you can't meet everybody, your brand will.

Because of this, whether you like it or not, you have a brand to manage. Ideally, you should not even start putting your music out into the world until you've come up with a clear and consistent brand identity. Skip this step and you'll have a haphazard brand that you don't control. If you have three different logos, a new slogan each month or otherwise portray an inconsistent online presence, it will confuse people.

You should take the time to accurately brand yourself. We'll talk about how to establish an effective brand in this chapter.

▸▸BRAND BASICS

WHAT'S A BRAND?

A brand is a communication of your band's identity. The key to effective branding is ensuring that your audience sees the identity you want to project.

Whether you're a solo musician or a large group, there's simply too much information about you and your music for new fans to easily digest. And let's face it, we all have very short attention spans. You have only a limited amount of time to compete against everything that's vying for people's attention to get your message out that you're a musician and your music is worth listening to. Branding is about distilling your identity into its key components. Some of these components are your name, your images (logo, album artwork) and your text (your story, your tagline). These components make up your Brand Toolbox but before we talk about these, we need to first understand what makes an effective brand.

BRANDS THAT WORK

There are four ingredients to an effective brand:

- **Accuracy:** Your brand should not be at odds with your actual identity. In other words, it should set accurate expectations and give people a clear sense of what your band and its music is about.
- **Impact:** Your brand should convey its message quickly and easily. When it comes to words, this means brevity (e.g. 'Have a Coke and a smile'); when it comes to graphics, it means having an image that 'pops'. It should be memorable. The cooler your logo, tagline and so on, the more likely your fans will promote it and purchase branded merchandise.
- **Repetition:** The key to an effective brand is to use it repeatedly. Repetition is necessary since it takes time to cement your identity in the minds of your fans. This can only happen at the individual level, so your brand only gets stronger each time a person encounters it.
- **Consistency:** Because repetition is the key to strengthening your brand, consistency is critical. Changing elements of your brand on a whim ruins the associations you've built up over time in people's heads. Your past branding work goes to waste every time you make dramatic changes.

ALWAYS BE BRANDING

Given these four ingredients, it's crucial you brand everything: your websites, your albums, your videos, your MP3s, your press kits, your posters and so on. Your brand is what fans will identify you with. After all, why else would anyone buy T-shirts from a *musician*? Your brand gives merchandise its value.

FINDING YOUR BRAND

You'll want to make sure you build a brand that's on target right from the start. You need to be comfortable with the words and images representing your band, both today and years down the road. Your brand should be rooted in your identity. At the heart of this is your music (style, attitude, lyrics) and your story (where you're from, your influences, your motivations, your goals). The best branding comes from these things because they're genuine. Plus, the more specific your brand is to you and your identity, the more distinctive it will be. Since branding is a long-term endeavour, the more in tune your brand is with your band's unique identity, the more durable it will be over time. Distilling your music and identity into a brand takes thought but we assure you that the time and energy you put in now will pay dividends in saved time and energy in the future.

▶▶ YOUR BRAND TOOLBOX

Your Brand Toolbox consists of your name, your images (logo, photos, artwork), your text (story, tagline) and your music. You'll be using these components over and over again for your websites, your albums, your videos, your MP3s, your press kits, posters and so on. You should have them ready before you even think of creating your first press kit or releasing your first track online.

YOUR NAME

More than anything, your band name will be the unique identifier of your music. If people hear your music, the first thing you want them to know is who you are. It's all about name recognition, so obviously you'll be associating your name with everything you do.

The second thing you want them to know is where they can go to find out about you. From a branding perspective, given the importance of the Web, it's an advantage to have a Web address that's the same as your band name. If you can do this, you'll have the further advantage of an email address that promotes your brand with each message.

If you don't have a Web address that matches your band name you'll need to include your Web address each time your band name is used. If you haven't picked a name, you're in luck and we have some suggestions as to how to pick one.

PICKING A BAND NAME, POST-NET

Your band name should represent the type of music you play and your energy and style as performers. You want a name that's memorable and unique.

When picking a name, follow these steps:

1. **Check a band database:** Check your name against a band name database to ensure that it's unique. We recommend Bandname.com, although there are also directories at Yahoo! and elsewhere that might be worth checking.

2. **Perform a Web search:** Use a search engine to ensure that your name isn't associated with something else that might confuse your brand. Don't name your band 'Google' for instance. Also, if you can, make up a word or choose a name that absolutely nothing else has so you can track any mentions of your band. For example, we know that 'Beatnik Turtle' is an unusual name, but we're the only ones with it.

3. **Check your trade mark office:** Check your local trade mark office to ensure that no one has trademarked your name. Owning a domain name does not automatically make you the owner of that trade mark. You can search all the European Community trade marks online via the Office of Harmonisation in the Internal Market's Community Trade Mark database (http://oami.europa.eu/CTMOnline/RequestManager/en_SearchBasic). Like a record label, you can hire a professional trade mark searching service, although this can be expensive. See Chapter 7: Your Rights for more information about trade mark law and how to register your band name as a trade mark.

4. **Check a domain registrar:** Check your name with a domain registrar such as GoDaddy.com. If the name is available, reserve it immediately.

YOUR IMAGES

Images are still worth a thousand words, particularly online. If you have someone in your band with some artistic ability, take advantage of that in crafting your images. Otherwise, turn to your skill network for help. To get started, you'll need a logo, an official band photo and a general colour palette. You may also need a mascot and/or an avatar.

IMAGE BASICS FOR MUSICIANS

When working with your brand images, keep these basics in mind:

COLOUR FORMATS

- **RGB:** This is the colour standard for computer monitors. Red, green and blue are blended to create all the colours of the spectrum. Files saved in RGB format are appropriate for anything that will be displayed on a monitor, including anything intended for the Web.
- **CMYK:** This is the colour standard for printing. It's the format that printers and merchandise manufacturers use. Cyan, magenta, yellow and black are blended together to achieve full-colour printing. If you intend to print any of your brand images – on a T-shirt, for instance – match the RGB number of each colour to a CMYK number so that the resulting ink colour matches what appears on your screen. See the textbox 'Mixing down your brand' for more information.
- **Black-and-white line art:** Some print media, such as newspapers, print only in black-and-white. Giving them your CMYK colour logo and letting them do the conversion to black-and-white line art may have disastrous results. A black-and-white, line-art version of your logo will also come in handy if you print a CD with one colour on the silkscreen.
- **Greyscale:** Greyscale printing allows shading, which is useful for photos that will appear in newspapers and other black-and-white media. Colour images convert more easily to greyscale than to black-and-white but those created specifically for greyscale will work better.

IMAGE STRUCTURES

Computers save images in one of two ways:

- **Rasterised:** Rasterised image files use a rectangular grid of pixels to capture the image information. The more pixels, the higher the quality and file size of the image. Digital photos are rasterised. Issues arise with rasterised images when resizing. In general, you can reduce a rasterised image in size without problems but if you expand the size you'll lose sharpness since the file replicates pixels to fill the extra space.
- **Vectorised images:** Vectorised image files use geometric objects such as curves and polygons to represent the data. Resizing vectorised images poses no quality issues since the image is mathematically recreated to fit any scale. Create your logo, mascot or any other line-art image in a vector image editor like Adobe Illustrator.

THE IMPORTANCE OF USING LAYERS

Many art programs, such as Adobe Photoshop and Illustrator and GIMP, allow you to create layers. Layering is the art world's equivalent to multi-tracking. Each layer is a complete and separate picture. This means you can make layers visible or hide them as you work, before 'mixing it down' or flattening them all into a final JPEG or GIF image. This flexibility allows you to test out different ideas quickly and easily. If you don't like one element, you can simply hide that layer from view. For instance, the source file for our Beatnik Turtle mascot is comprised of layers. We have the standard turtle as the basic layer, with additional layers for each type of hat he wears. This makes creating different versions with different hats a snap.

YOUR LOGO

Just as you want your band name associated with your music, you will want it associated with a logo. We recommend either setting your band name in an unusual typeface or using a combination of typeface and symbol. Whatever you create, it should be distinctive enough for a T-shirt or other merchandise. Line drawings and other symbols work better than photos because they can scale to small or large sizes cleanly. There's a reason the logos of major brands use drawn images.

The logo you choose will often suggest both the appropriate matching colour palette and font. A dynamic logo isn't easy to create, so enlist the help of a talented graphic artist in creating it. And make sure everyone in the band approves of the final version – you don't want to change it drastically once you start using it.

YOUR BAND PHOTO

Although your logo will represent your band and its music, people will still want to see the people behind the band. Your band photo will be used as the representative shot of your entire group in your press kit, in articles the press writes about you, on your website and on other promotional materials like posters and flyers.

Your band photo needs to be a group shot of all the members. Naturally, it should be clear, in focus and well composed, since this is the photo that will represent your band to the world and will likely be printed in newspapers, magazines and blogs when you get publicity.

Often, someone within your skill network will have the equipment and skills to help you and won't mind giving you the full rights to do whatever you please with the photo. However, if you end up hiring a professional photographer, keep in mind that they usually own the copyright. We discuss permissions in Chapter 7: Your Rights.

YOUR MASCOT

Your mascot refers to a character that represents your band. For instance, The Grateful Dead had its Dancing Bears, Iron Maiden has Eddie the Head and Beatnik Turtle has, well, its Beatnik Turtle. Your mascot is not the same as your logo, although your logo can incorporate your mascot. Having a mascot for your band is not necessary but it's useful for creating album artwork as well as for merchandising because it gives you more branding images to work with when creating products. Like your logo, it's best if your mascot image is line art, since the image will be resized depending on how it's used. Your mascot's colours should also match your colour palette.

YOUR AVATAR

You will be using your brand extensively on the Web. Services such as YouTube, MySpace, bulletin boards and so on, allow you to upload a profile image or avatar, to represent you. It can be used for other image identifiers such as the ID3 image tag embedded in an MP3. In general, these avatars are small, so your logo might not be clear enough. You can either create a special, stripped-down logo or use your mascot image. The main point is to create a profile image that can be applied consistently across Web presences. That way when people see your videos on YouTube, your comments on a bulletin board or chat with you over instant messenger, the avatar is the same.

YOUR COLOUR AND FONT PALETTE

Locking in a colour palette and limiting the fonts you use not only gives your brand a consistent look and feel, it's also a subtle and powerful way to evoke a mood that mirrors your music. Using the same colours and fonts will only strengthen this connection between your music and the identity you wish to convey to the world.

As you create your logo, mascot and other brand images, you should define and limit yourself to a set palette of complementary colours. And make sure you use the same colours in each instance. The green in your logo should be the same shade of green you use in your mascot, on your website, on CDs and so on. Of course, the colours you see on screen are not necessarily the same colours that print out on paper or on a T-shirt. To match colours on screen with those in print, it's a good idea to define your colour scheme using Pantone colours.

PICKING A CONSISTENT COLOUR PALETTE FOR SCREEN AND PRINT

Getting all your colours to match between screen and print is not difficult. The Pantone system matches print colours (CMYK) to screen colours (RGB) and provides an RGB number to use in your art software. Pantone's colour-matching system is widely used by printing houses, T-shirt printers and other merchandise manufacturers. To ensure a consistent colour scheme:

1. Go online and download a Pantone Colour Chart (pantone.com/downloads/inkjetsolutions/downloads/pdfs/ColourChart.pdf).
2. Pick each colour you want in your palette and note the RGB number and the CMYK number.
3. Use the RGB numbers to set the colours in your art software.
4. Give the matching CMYK numbers to your printer and merchandise manufacturer.

Taking this step at the outset will save you time, energy and aggravation down the road. Like your colour palette, consistency and repetition calls for you to define and limit the fonts you use as well. Consistent fonts among your logo, website, press material, merchandise and albums help tie all your materials and merchandise to your brand. You'll probably use three primary fonts: one for your band name, one for your tagline and one for standard text on your website and in print materials.

YOUR BANNERS AND PROMOS

Some websites may want to link directly to your site from one of your branded images. You should make these available from your website. Some sites even give their visitors the embed code, similar to the embed codes on YouTube, so that they won't even need to copy the images to their own sites.

YOUR TEXT

Your text is composed of the following: a description of your sound, your story, your slogan, your contact information and your writing voice.

A DESCRIPTION OF YOUR SOUND

You will need an accurate description of your music. This is never easy for any band. However, one of the best ways to describe your music is to talk about it in relation to well-known bands that you've been influenced by or bands you sound similar to.

Some musicians resent having their music compared to other groups but doing so accomplishes two things. First of all, by accurately referencing a few similar bands, you help set expectations for those people who have just discovered you and are curious about your sound. Second, by making these comparisons, you're leveraging the marketing efforts of those more popular bands. When people search for those bands – whether through search engines or through dedicated music services such as iTunes or Last.fm – your music might come up as a recommendation. Even better, because your band actually does sound like the comparison band, the people who discover your music this way will be just the sort of people who are most likely to become new fans.

Ideally, you should also compose a description of your music that does not rely on comparisons. This one should emphasise your style, genre and instrumentation. Again, it's better to go for an accurate description of your music rather than anything off-the-wall or tongue-in-cheek. Once you create these, keep them handy. You'll be using these just about every place you publicise your band.

YOUR STORY

You need an interesting and compelling way to introduce your band to people. You can't just write down the story of how you met. You need an angle. Once you find this, you need to be able to tell this story in multiple ways and in varying lengths. You should have a one-page version of your story as well as a one-paragraph version. Most importantly, you need an elevator pitch, a compact description of your band that must quickly categorise who you are and what you sound like – all within the time it takes to ride an elevator between floors. Ariel Hyatt from Ariel Publicity told us that her favourite pitch was from the bluegrass, rock, country, blues, jazz and Cajun/Zydeco band, Leftover Salmon. Their elevator pitch was that they played 'Polyethnic Cajun Slamgrass'. It was accurate, summed up their energetic live show and did it all with three words. Distilling your band and its sound down to an elevator pitch takes thought but if you create a good one for yourself, it can help define your identity.

Each of these versions – and parts of them – will come in handy in different circumstances when you need to explain what your band is all about, whether it's on your website, in your press materials or even in person.

YOUR SLOGAN

Not every group uses or needs a slogan but they tend to come in handy. This is especially true if you can create one that really captures the essence of your band and music. Your slogan is most likely to be used on the Web but can also become part of your logo, be included in your email signatures or be used on promotional materials. Web services such as YouTube, MySpace and Twitter typically provide fields for short taglines that are perfect for slogans. If you don't have one, you'll have to leave these empty or make up something on the spot, leading to an inconsistent Web presence.

YOUR CONTACT INFORMATION

Your band's contact information – phone number, email address and any other methods for contacting you – will appear in your press kits, on your website and perhaps elsewhere online. Changing it more often than absolutely necessary will result in out-of-date information leading to missed opportunities and connections. Additionally, you should use an email address at your Web domain (i.e. joe@beatnikturtle.com), instead of using a Gmail, Yahoo! or AOL address, since doing so reinforces your brand and leads recipients back to your website.

If the members of your band split the roles of booking, publicity and managing, then you'll need to make everyone's contact information available for all. But this arrangement can get confusing for those trying to contact you. Instead, we recommend designating one person as the main contact to simplify matters. One way to handle this is to set up your account to forward any incoming emails to multiple members of the band. It also helps to have a business card so that if you talk to someone in person and they want to contact you, you can easily hand them something with your contact information on it.

YOUR WRITING VOICE

Just as your colour palette and fonts evoke a mood or style, your writing voice reflects your band's identity to the world. This becomes a question of style and consistency. First, you need to make sure that whoever is writing for your band has a style that fits your music and one that everyone in the band is comfortable with. Ideally, the writing in your brand materials should evoke a singular tone and remain consistent throughout your story, website, newsletters, Web presence, blogs and any other text you share. In Beatnik Turtle's case, we chose a voice for the band that was a little tongue-in-cheek. Since our lyrics are typically upbeat and humorous, we felt our writing should be as well.

Additionally, this tone should be consistent throughout your branding materials. If you're a solo artist who is writing for him or herself, this should come naturally. With a band, however, this becomes a challenge. The band itself needs a singular voice – not individual voices. You don't want a voice that's at odds with the music and message you want to evoke.

Of course, your writing voice can change depending on the audience you're addressing. For instance, we adopt a more professional tone in our press and booking materials since we want potential bookers and music journalists to know that we take them and the opportunities they can present for our band very seriously. We also write more formally on our BackStage Blog so that our readers understand that we are sharing genuine information.

Related to your writing voice is your spokesperson, the person who represents the band with the press or other media. Again, if you're a solo artist, you speak on your own behalf. However, when there are several band members, it often helps to have one or two people in the group do the majority of the speaking. It doesn't have to be this way but if there are designated people doing the talking, it's easier to stay on message. We'll talk more about speaking to the press in Chapter 12: Get Publicised.

YOUR MUSIC

You should prepare a few tracks in MP3 format for your Brand Toolbox since your music is distinctive and forms the basis of your brand identity. Have some of your top songs – the ones that represent you the best – handy and available to send out to the press or anyone else who will be needing them.

MIXING AND REMIXING YOUR BRAND TOOLS

Think of it like this: the materials you create for your Brand Toolbox are the equivalent of the multi-tracked source files you create when you record a song. The public doesn't typically hear these individual tracks. Instead, the multiple tracks are mixed down to stereo for iPods or home audio systems. It's the same here: you'll be returning time and time again to all the source files of the images and text you've made to create different but consistent versions for your website, your Web presence, your albums and merchandise and your promotional materials.

For instance, you may end up mixing your logo with your slogan to create a Web banner in Photoshop and then flatten the result into GIF format for your website. Then, you might take this banner, resize it, combine it with your contact information and make a letterhead out of it for a Word or OpenOffice document. Later you might create a greyscale version for a show flyer. Eventually, you'll have quite a library of alternate versions, so when that newspaper writes a last-minute article about your band's show and asks you for logo in greyscale at a certain size and resolution, you'll be able to get it to them immediately.

Best of all, by working in this manner, you're not making up your brand on the fly. Given that consistency and repetition is the key to an effective brand, this process ensures that the mixes you make for public consumption are consistent with your brand.

MIXING DOWN YOUR BRAND – RECOMMENDED FORMATS FOR IMAGES AND TEXT

Since your brand source files are for your eyes only, you'll need to make mixdowns of your brand images and text for distribution.

IMAGES

Choose the appropriate format, size and DPI (dots per inch) of your images to maximise clarity and sharpness depending on where you intend them to appear.

FORMAT

- **Screen/Web:** For the Web, GIF and JPEG are the universal formats to use. The GIF format is best for line drawings and other simple graphics, while JPEGs are best for photos and other complex images. Most art programs allow you to optimise your GIF and JPEG settings for the Web to minimise file size, but as most of our audience has broadband Internet access, we use the settings for maximum quality (with correspondingly larger file sizes). Over a broadband connection, these images still download very quickly.
- **Print:** For print applications, the format depends on the recipient.
- **Press:** When the press wants photos, they typically ask for TIFF or BMP versions, which are uncompressed and therefore very large. When the press wants a logo, mascot or other line drawing, GIFs usually suffice, although they will sometimes request these in TIFF or BMP format as well.
- **Printers/Merchandisers:** For printers, T-shirt or other merchandise manufacturers, the source file will usually work, depending on what software you use. If not, they'll tell you whether they need TIFFs, BMPs, JPEGs or GIFs.

IMAGE SIZE AND DPI

- **Screen/Web:** Use 72 DPI for the optimal balance between quality and file size, regardless of the image size needed, which is usually measured in pixels. For example, avatars are generally 80 pixels by 80 pixels or 100 by 100. Album art for the iTunes Music Store needs to be 300 by 300. Either way, keep the DPI at 72.

- **Print:** Make your band photo, logo and other brand images available in print-ready form at your website for the benefit of the press. Flyers and posters should be available as well. To ensure that these print clearly, create these versions at 300 DPI at the physical size you intend them to print. For instance, a flyer should be 20x27cm. When creating images for a T-shirt or CD, the manufacturer will inform you of the exact standards they require.

TEXT

All your text, such as bios and other information, should be available to the public in Adobe PDF format as well as on standard Web pages so the press can copy and paste when necessary. The text source files – Word documents, OpenOffice documents and so on – should only be available to you for editing.

ACCESSIBILITY

At the end of the day, you'll have source files and mixdowns of your branded materials. As a band, you'll want to access both at a moment's notice. However, only the mixdowns – the finished logo in JPG or GIF format, the band bio in PDF format (see 'Mixing down your brand', above) – should be made publicly available. For the sake of convenience, we recommend that you save your source files privately online for easy access by all members of the band, either at a password-protected section of your website or on a storage and sharing service like Box (box.net) or Amazon's S3 (aws.amazon.com/s3).

Mixdowns, of course, should be made public. After all, this is the brand you're promoting. Bookers, the press and fans may want to have access to these branded images and text. We'll talk more about setting up a Press/ Booking page and its importance in Chapter 4: Your Website.

▸▸ CHAPTER FOUR

YOUR WEBSITE

Besides your musical instruments, your website is the most important tool that you have as a musician. It's the Web that took the decision of whether you will get heard out of the hands of music executives and back into the hands of musicians.

There are hundreds of millions of people on the Web and if you have a website, any one of them could be discovering your music at this very moment. Your website is your best promoter, salesperson, agent, publicist, distributor, disc jockey, news reporter and more. It's the centre of your fan network and a store that never closes. Even if people meet you or see you play live, if they can't find you later on the Web, you might as well not exist.

Web technology changes quickly and is a broad topic that could fill many books, so we're going to stick with concepts that don't change and others that are specific to music websites.

▸▸ DON'T RELY SOLELY ON SOCIAL-NETWORKING SITES

Thousands upon thousands of musicians have chosen social-networking sites like MySpace and Facebook to represent their brand and music to the world and then called it a day. And why not? It's quite simple to set up a presence at their sites and it's free. While there are a few advantages to doing so – simple tools to stream music, write blogs and post videos – they don't approach the real benefits of having your own website that you control.

You should definitely have a profile on those sites and use them to build Web presence. In fact, we're going to tell you the best way to use them in the next chapter – but don't rely on them exclusively. Here's why:

- **Limited songs:** Typically these sites limit the number of songs you can make available.
- **Lack of creative control:** Social-networking sites force you to conform to their limited options for format and design. Their priority is branding themselves and generating revenue through your content, which is why you're limited to *their* choices, not yours.
- **Advertising:** Your content must compete with their advertising.
- **Strange domain name for your brand and merchandise:** You will have to print *their* website name on *your* T-shirts, stickers, posters and other branded materials. Additionally, your email address won't be from your own website. Nothing beats having your own Web domain that you control.
- **Poor Web statistics and trackback:** Aside from the 'number of views', these sites typically provide very poor Web statistics for gathering information about when visitors arrived, how long they stayed, what they read, what they listened to and who referred them to your site. All this information is critical to understanding your audience. Having access to these stats is extremely important, as we describe in detail later in this chapter.
- **Poor place to host critical information:** These sites are a poor place to host important information about your band such as press releases, stage plot and microphone layout or effectively promote your albums and merchandise.

Although these are significant disadvantages, this is only a partial list. Social-networking sites are intended for just that – building relationships and brand presence; they are not meant to be a substitute for a fully featured website.

▶▶ STARTING A NEW WEBSITE

DOMAIN NAMES

The first thing you'll need is a unique Web address or domain name. As we said in Chapter 3: Your Brand, your domain name is extremely important because it conveys the most information about your band. When we say 'beatnikturtle. com', we've given you everything you need to know to access our music, videos, podcasts, show information, photos, press materials, and more.

If you haven't registered a domain name, be careful about letting your Web hosting company do it for you. Some Web hosting companies will register your domain in *their* name, which means you may have a legal battle on your hands if you need to move to a different Web host. Avoid this at the start by registering the name yourself with a reputable domain registrar. That way you control your domain and can take it with you if the Web host you originally choose doesn't work out.

Domain names are inexpensive and should cost between £2 and £20 a year to maintain. Once you have your domain, your Web hosting company should advise you on how to configure it for their services.

WEB HOSTING

After you get a domain, you will need a Web host for your site. Web hosts typically charge a monthly or annual fee to host your site, make it available for the public and provide email addresses with your domain name.

Because you will have a music website, your needs are slightly different from most website customers. Bandwidth, which is the amount of data that gets transferred to and from your website, becomes expensive if you get popular. So review any Web host's bandwidth charges carefully and use hosts with high limits.

You can use any Web hosting company but there are a few that are geared towards musicians. Often Web hosts that specialise in music sites provide functionality other Web hosts don't – tools and resources that make designing and updating content for your band website quicker and easier. Some of these include easy-to-use flash music players; RSS-enabled blogs, news pages and forums; robust gig calendars; integration with social networking and media sharing sites; mailing list programs; and other important features we'll be discussing below. Obviously, if you're going to pay for a Web host, quality tools and resources are an extra benefit that can save you time and energy which are better suited for music-making, music promotion and winning over fans – not being a Web developer. So, it's worth giving specialised Web hosts a look.

There are a ton of Web hosts, however, including some that are free such as FreeWebs (freewebs.com). One Web host that specialises in sites for musicians is Hostbaby (hostbaby.com) which provides tools such as mailing lists and music players as well as high bandwidth limits streaming music needs. Hostbaby.com is associated with CD Baby; CD Baby will even waive their CD registration fees if you subscribe, which can save you money – especially if you have multiple CDs.

WEB DESIGN TOOLS

Now that you have a Web host, you need to design your website. There are two main methods of creating a custom website: website Creation Software and Content Management Systems. Naturally, if you decide to work with a

Web designer from your skill network, you should defer to whatever tools that person is comfortable with.

WEBSITE CREATION SOFTWARE

If you use a software package on your own computer, use a full-featured package such as Adobe DreamWeaver. The advantage to using tools like this is that you have complete flexibility in your design. The downside is that updates to your website can be difficult, since you are limited to making changes from home or even just from the designer's PC. This doesn't seem like a big deal until you realise that changes happen often, including adding a news story, adding a new show listing or even just fixing some spelling mistakes. This becomes a pain quickly, so we recommend a CMS instead, which is what we use.

CONTENT MANAGEMENT SYSTEMS

A Content Management System (CMS) can be thought of as a website creation program that exists at your website – not on your local computer. Because of this, you can update your site using any Internet browser. Most of these systems, such as WordPress (wordpress.org) or Movable Type (movabletype.com), have WYSIWYG editors that work just like a word processor, which you can use to write text for your site without learning HTML. Most allow you to keep a blog, as well as make updates easily whenever and wherever you'd like to do so – at home or from any Internet connection. And because it's so accessible, multiple band members can update. You don't need to rely on one band member to do all the work. Since you should be updating your website often with news, fresh tracks and upcoming shows, these features are advantageous.

The best part of a CMS system is that it separates the site's design from its content, allowing you to update each separately. With a few clicks, your designer can change the look of your website without affecting the content you posted. And your less technologically savvy band members can post new entries without fudging the design.

Web hosts often feature built-in CMS software. And, typically, Web hosts specialising in music sites feature CMS software designed specifically for the needs of bands, which may make creating your site easier. If you go with a standard Web host, our favourite flexible and free CMS tool to use is WordPress (wordpress.org). The power of WordPress lies in thousands of free themes you can choose that change the look and design of your site (wordpress.org/extend/themes/). It also has thousands of plug-ins that extend the functionality of your WordPress-based website very easily (wordpress.org/extend/plugins/).

For example, we recommend using the PodPress plug-in which makes it simple for you as a band to publish podcasts with minimal effort. We also recommend GigPress, StatPress, Akismet and All In One SEO pack. It's used by many bands, including our own and others mentioned in this book.

⏩PLANNING YOUR WEBSITE

KNOWING YOUR WEBSITE'S AUDIENCE: AUDIENCE PROFILES

Before you can design your website, you need to decide what content you'll offer. Most band websites we surveyed were either designed around the assumption that only fans visit or, worse, designed as ego-trip billboards that focus only on the people in the band. Instead, you need to determine who your audiences are and design it for *them*.

For example, imagine that a booker or talent buyer is visiting your site. Can they immediately tell what you sound like? Is it apparent whether or not you've played other gigs? Can they easily find your stage plot and microphone layout? Most importantly, can they find your contact information right away? If your website can't meet this audience's specific needs, you should adjust the design and content accordingly.

Thinking from each audience's viewpoint doesn't only affect the type of content you provide and where it's located, it also affects your navigation structure. After all, you don't want audiences finding themselves in the wrong section of the website, lost and with no idea what to do next. They should always be able to find what they want.

Fortunately, band website audiences aren't too complicated to unravel. But remember, catering to each of the audience profiles is only half the story. The other half is to steer them where you want them to go.

DESIGN YOUR WEBSITE TO CONVERT VISITORS

Visitors come to your website for their own reasons but the site should also actively steer their decisions and make it as easy as possible to do what you want them to do. You want a new visitor to join the mailing list, participate in your forum and buy your albums and merchandise. You want the press to find information about your band to help them write a great (and accurate) article about you. You want a booker to contact you with that gig. This means that your website should balance its content and design between giving each audience what they want and leading them to take those actions you want them to take.

Conversion can be encouraged in the design by limiting choices and making them simple to spot and navigate. Conversion can also be driven by content. For example, if one of your goals is to build your mailing list, repeat the 'join the mailing list' message in your news updates, blog entries and elsewhere on your site, where appropriate.

PROVIDE CONTENT FOR EACH OF YOUR AUDIENCES

To help you, we've put together a table of the eight audience profiles a typical band website should be designed for. We've outlined what each of these audiences want out of your website and what it is you want out of them. Lastly, we've outlined a few of the key website sections in play at each instance. Additionally, we've put together a table of feature content for a typical band website. This table is useful as you set out to create the content and should be used in conjunction with the audience profile table to help reinforce the idea that content needs to speak to various audiences.

PUTTING IT ALL TOGETHER: YOUR AUDIENCES, WHAT THEY WANT AND WHAT YOU WANT THEM TO DO

Audience	Expectations	Conversions	Site Features
All fans	Finding tour dates. Finding upcoming shows. Discovering latest projects. Buying your albums and merchandise. Listening to your music. Viewing photos and videos. Participating in the fan community.	Joining the mailing list. Subscribing to the blogs. Participating in the forum. Buying the albums and merchandise. Coming to shows. Telling friends about the band.	News. Blog. Forum. About the Band. Music. Photos. Videos. Store. Calendar. Mailing List.
Fans coming to a show	Finding an address, directions, map and phone number for the venue. Finding the time of the performance and the acts going up before and after. Determining the cover charge and any drink minimum.	Coming to the show. Bringing friends. Promoting the event. Discussing the event in the forum.	Calendar. News. Blog. Forums. Mailing List.

Audience	Expectations	Conversions	Site Features
Bookers and talent buyers	Locating the band. Contacting the band. Learning about the band's performance history. Reading fan and venue testimonials. Downloading flyers, bios and other text and images.	Hiring the band.	Testimonials. Booking Information. Calendar. Music. Photos. Contact Us.
The press and journalists	Downloading the press kit and press releases. Contact the band for interviews. Finding images and credit info for the article. Reading testimonials.	Writing articles about the band. Reviewing the latest album. Featuring the latest project. Contacting us.	Press Information. News. Music. Photos. Contact Us.
Sound people	Determining the style of music and instrumentation. Preparing for any special sound needs. Viewing stage plot and microphone layout.	Contacting us. Making the band sound right on stage.	Sound/ Performance Information. Music. Contact Us.
Potential song Licensees	Listening to songs. Requesting high-quality versions. Determining licensing requirements. Finding non-commercial use requirements. Determining podsafe status.	Contacting us to license our songs. Requesting high-quality versions. Commissioning custom music.	Copyright Information. Music. Contact Us.
Web surfers who stumble onto your website	Finding instant gratification.	Listening to music. Watching videos. Buying albums and merchandise. Joining the mailing list. Subscribing to the blogs.	Music. Photos. Videos. About the Band. Store. News. Blog. Forum.

SITE FEATURE CONTENT FOR MUSIC WEBSITES

Content	Description
About the band	Basic information about your band: name, style of music, similar bands, members and bios, instrumentation, hometown and band history.
News	Latest news on your band. Place the latest story on the front page with older stories cycling to a separate news page. If possible, offer an RSS feed.
Blog	Offer one or more band blogs with more personal perspectives on the band.
Show calendar	Upcoming shows as well as a catalogue of past shows you've played.
Music	All the music you've made available to the public as well as samples of those available for purchase. Ideally, provide an embedded player to listen immediately.
Store	All albums and merchandise available for sale with photos and descriptions of each or links to the appropriate vendors such as CD Baby, iTunes, SpreadShirt.com, etc.
Album information	Information on each of your albums including lyrics, liner notes and possibly guitar tablature or full sheet music.
Photos	Albums of photos of your band, recent performances and other events.
Videos	Music videos or videos of the band performing.
Information for the press	The band bio, press releases, press-ready photos, logos and other images, contact info including the band press representative's email and phone number and press clippings.
Information for bookers	Band contact info including the band representative's email and phone number, booking information, stage and microphone plot and press-ready photos and images.
Testimonials	Quotes from fans, bookers, venues and satisfied customers from corporate events, festivals, weddings and parties.
Stage and performance Information for sound people	Stage and microphone plot, band instrumentation and any other information a sound person might need.
Forums	A place for fans to meet up, arrange shared rides to your performances, coordinate grassroots promotion and so on.
Mailing list information	Information about your mailing list and an easy sign-up process.

Contact us	Usually a Web contact form but can be as simple as a band member's email address.
Sitemap	A map of the entire site to help people find what they want.
Legal information	Any legal information such as the copyright or Creative Commons license, privacy policy statement (for your mailing list) and so on.
Links	Links to external sites such as individual band member pages, other bands, favourite venues and so on.
Band-only area	Password-protected section to store Brand Toolbox source files for access anywhere.

GIVING THEM A REASON TO RETURN OR KEEP CONNECTED

While it's often possible to get people to come to your website, the hard part is getting them involved – to come back repeatedly or to stay in touch via your mailing list or RSS feed. Think about the websites you check regularly. What do you like about these sites that keeps you coming back? What made you subscribe to their feed, join their mailing list or discuss things in their forums?

Usually, the secret ingredient is fresh, updated content that people *want*. News sites constantly post new stories. YouTube constantly features new videos. Blogs like BoingBoing.net always have a new blog entry. Daily deal sites like Woot (woot.com) and Tanga (tanga.com) always have a new product.

As a musician, here is what you can offer at your music website to keep people coming back:

UPDATED BAND CONTENT

Writing new blog entries and keeping people informed on what you're doing as a band is a big part of getting people invested and cultivating your fan network. Fans, after all, want to feel involved.

You can document life in your band by writing, taking photos or shooting videos. Many bands post daily tour blogs when they're out on the road. Some solo musicians use their blog as a personal journal, sharing their thoughts not only on music but also about their day-to-day life.

Naturally, the more entertaining these updates, the better. Our friend Pete Shukoff, of the band Nice Peter, is a natural at this. He frequently updates his blog with humorous observations about what's going on in his life. He'll discuss anything: drunken audience members at shows, playing 'You Are My Sunshine' twenty times to the delight of seniors at the old folks' home (they didn't know any of his own songs) or interesting graffiti he's seen scrawled on venue toilet walls while touring.

EPISODIC PROJECT RELEASES

Jonathan Coulton episodic project, 'Thing a Week', promised fans one new song a week from September 2005 to September 2006. The lure of weekly updates kept people coming back for more. During the process, his forums took off and became extremely active. Fans were always eagerly anticipating the next 'thing' to come along.

We did something similar at TheSongOfTheDay.com by releasing a new song for every day of 2007. Visitors returned on a daily basis to hear each new song. Over the year, more people kept visiting and interest in our band and its music grew.

Brad Turcotte got people returning to his website by posting the source tracks to the songs from his debut album. Each month he would post one of the tracks and then fans would download and remix them. Turcotte actively promoted any remixes people made of his music, creating an incentive for people to join the forums and share their results.

One added benefit of an episodic project is that it tends to generate material for your blog and news feeds. Coulton would regularly blog about the new 'thing a week' he was writing and has kept this level of involvement by blogging regularly since. Turcotte maintains a very active blog as well, posting not only about his music and upcoming projects but also on topics related to his music, like the software and equipment he uses, as well as commentary on the music industry – which leads us to a third method.

UPDATED NON-MUSIC CONTENT

You can use your website to cover topics beyond the scope of your band, too. These topics should be related in some way to what your band is all about but by widening your focus a bit you can piggyback on the popularity of a larger topic (we'll talk about the concept of piggybacking in Chapter 8: Get Noticed). For instance, if your music speaks of social or political activism and there's an issue that your band feels passionately about, then dedicating a section of your website to that issue would be a natural fit.

Marc Gunn and Andrew McKee of the Brobdingnagian Bards (thebards.net) did this years ago when they used their site to collect and catalogue the lyrics and tabs of traditional Irish folk songs. Adding this section to their band's website was natural since the band was rooted in traditional Irish music. This section not only helped them catalogue songs for their own repertoire, it also became a destination among search engines – sending people directly to their site whenever they searched for information about- or lyrics to- an old Irish folk song. This piggy-backing worked in their favour given that their own music aligned with the music people were searching for. Many new fans discovered the Brobdingnagian Bards simply by searching for their favourite Irish song. The Bards thought correctly that searchers would want to hear a rendition of the Irish song so they provided their own renditions as song samples as well as a link to purchase it.

We did this when we wrote and self-published the online precursor to this book, *The Indie Band Survival Guide* at our band's website. We wanted to share everything we had learned from nine years as an indie band with other indie musicians. Because there were no books that spoke directly to us as indies and because we felt strongly enough about the subject to research and write *The Indie Band Survival Guide* over two years, we felt it would be a natural complement to our band's website. Once released, the online version got caught up in the blogosphere and the traditional press including *Billboard Magazine*, the Associated Press and Reuter's. Interest in our site, band and music grew as a result. So did sales.

There are more ways to encourage people to return to your site beyond announcing news of a new album for sale or a show next Saturday. The more regular, relevant content you can offer at your site, the more reasons people will have to stay tuned to your website and, ultimately, your music.

▶▶WEBSITE DESIGN AND CONTENT

Knowing what your audiences want and knowing what you want them to do will help keep you focused as you start branding, designing and creating content for your website.

Rather than try to teach a mini-course in the subject of Web design, we simply recommend one book: *Don't Make Me Think: A Common Sense Approach to Web Usability* by Steve Krug. It will help you create an effective website with a design, navigation and structure that's intuitive and accessible. If you're tackling your website on your own, this book is well worth your money and time. Even if you have a Web and graphic designer in your skill network or one that you're ready to pay, understanding the concepts in this book will help you relate to what your designer will be doing.

There are a few general concepts to consider as you're putting together a design:

- **Always be branding your website:** All aspects of your website need to be branded. You need to keep your identity in front of your audiences at all times while they visit your site.
- **Lead with your best music:** In our opinion, it's so difficult to even get a person to listen to an independent band's music in the first place, you shouldn't shoot yourself in the foot by leading with anything but your best music. You are better off winning a new fan than worrying about phantom lost sales.
- **Make it a multimedia experience:** People now expect interactive and engaging content on the sites they visit.

DESIGN CONCEPTS
BILLBOARDS

One of the best ways to design and lay out your Web pages is to think of them as billboards. People don't spend a lot of time on websites, so if you have a message to get across, use images and just a few words. In fact, your entire website should be easy to understand, easy to navigate and easy to use.

For example, when we initially launched a streaming radio player that streamed hours of Beatnik Turtle music we had a news story about it (text), hyperlinked to the feature (again, text) and promoted it in our newsletter (once again, text). But what got visitors to finally click on it was a big, bright banner with a drawing of a radio and the words 'Beatnik Turtle Radio–Click Here!' right in the middle of the page.

YOUR FRONT PAGE

Web designers usually leave the front page until last. It's the hardest page to create because it performs many functions beyond being the hub of navigation. Some websites try to cram all of their content on the front page. We're embarrassed to say that we subscribed to this misguided idea for years. But we've learned some things since and we have the following suggestions:

- **Brand:** Have we emphasised this enough? Beyond having a branded Web banner, logo, colour scheme, font, etc., your front page needs to clearly inform the visitor what your site's about and what they can expect from it.

- **What's new:** Your latest news update and/or blog entry should be clearly visible since this is where you'll be telling audiences what you're currently doing and what you're planning to do.
- **Make your music player readily accessible:** You're a band, so make your music the focal point of your site. Your music player should be readily accessible on the front page – either embedded or one click away. Don't make them search for it. (We'll discuss everything you need to know about music players below.)
- **Focus on one or two additional content items:** This took our band years to figure out. At first we thought we needed to include all our content on the front page so visitors would know how much there was to do at our site. But this only confused and frustrated our audiences. We've learned to emphasise only a few key content items – things we want visitors to see if they only have a few seconds to look around. For us, this means our albums (displayed in a column along the right side of the screen) and our latest video. Both are presented as billboards – images with big play buttons (YouTube does this naturally) – not text.
- **Ditch the splash page:** Many bands insist on a splash page welcoming people to the site. Although it may seem cool to have a page like that, it's totally unnecessary. It violates an important rule of human nature: instant gratification. Throwing up a splash page acts as a road block, creating one more click between people and their destination.

YOUR CONTACT US PAGE

No matter what content you put up, you have to have a 'Contact Us' page. Almost all of Beatnik Turtle's best opportunities have come through the site this way. Gigs, music licensing opportunities, press articles, interviews and song-writing commissions have all come to our attention via the Web form and email address on this page. We can't imagine what we would have missed out on if we hadn't made it easy for people to contact us. You may include a phone number, too, if you're comfortable releasing it. For instance, when ABC Family/Disney wanted to license one of our songs for a commercial, they left multiple voicemail messages with all of the numbers we had posted in addition to emailing because they were under a deadline.

You should have the 'Contact Us' link at the top or bottom of each page and built into your template so that any new pages feature it automatically. If you use a Web contact form rather than a direct email address, verify that it works properly. We've had more than one Web contact form fail on us. It's hard enough creating opportunities for yourself; you don't want to block the ones that come knocking. In fact, we've configured our Web form to send all submissions to multiple members of the band.

YOUR STORE PAGE

Your store page should contain all of your albums and merchandise. This page should be easy to navigate with links to all the services handling distribution of your music and products. To encourage sales, you will want to include direct links to songs sold at digital distribution stores (iTunes, Rhapsody, Napster, etc.) and wherever your CD is sold (CD Baby). Direct links to your merchandise is also a must. We'll talk in detail about getting your music in these stores in Chapter 10: Get Distributed and Sold.

DONATIONS, SPONSORSHIPS AND MEMBERSHIPS

Donations are an alternative way for fans to support a band, particularly if you share free music on your website. If you share free music, we recommend putting the donation link near where users download songs. Of course, some bands put their tip jars on every page of their site.

When accepting donations, it helps to give fans something in return as a thank you. Some musicians email free songs, others send buttons or stickers. Some musicians take a cue from US National Public Radio and US Public Television by offering sponsorships with different levels of benefits depending on the amount donated. Jonathan Coulton did this at his site by offering his fans a chance to post a short message on his site. A donation buys you a 50-word message alongside an icon of a banana (US$5), monkey (US$10) or robot (US$25).

Most bands use PayPal (paypal.com) for this because they offer embeddable tools to seamlessly integrate donation boxes into your website design. If you have an account on PayPal, search their help centre for 'donations' for instructions. You can use other methods for accepting payments, such as credit card merchant accounts, but PayPal boasts a trusted brand name and a streamlined payment process for users.

Finally, some bands sell memberships rather than sponsorships. Members get access to parts of their website that has special songs or other content. Most Web hosting solutions will have an option to password-protect parts of the site that can be used for this. An alternative is to use services like AMember (amember.com) which is a tool that costs money but nevertheless allows you to control access to parts of your website. It handles a login system for your users, expires users who haven't renewed their membership and more.

YOUR PHOTO ALBUM

When we designed our first website in January 1998, we sat behind our friends and watched as they tried to use it. Their initial complaint was that it had no photos. When we revamped the site, we made sure to include a photos page. When we watched people use the new site, *it was the first thing they clicked on*. Not the music. Not our bios. The pictures.

You should take new pictures of the band frequently. And you don't want to lump all your photos on one page. You want a solution for organising images effectively that handles time-consuming tasks such as creating thumbnail images and slide shows. Your Web host or your CMS might offer a solution but alternatively there are specialised programs that allow you to host your photos on your own server.

Although you'll have a dedicated photo album page, you'll want to incorporate your best shots in other areas of the site: blog entries, news stories and so on. We'll discuss photos and photo sharing sites further in the next chapter which you can embed in your site to serve this purpose.

YOUR MAILING LIST

Joining your mailing list should be convenient and simple because the goal is to cultivate and grow a fan network. Include a link to your mailing list form on each page and build it into your standard template, just like your 'Contact Us' link.

Feature the mailing list link wherever your visitor takes a conversion action on your website such as downloading a song or joining your forum. At that point, you'll know they're interested in your band and music, so it'll be especially likely that they'll take the time to sign up for your newsletter as well.

Almost all of the mailing list software available will deliver a special welcome message to new subscribers. Don't use the default text for this message; this is a rare opportunity to send a direct message to an interested fan and feature your albums, merchandise and other conversions on your website. If your program allows you to write welcome messages in HTML, you should even include pictures and images.

We discuss mailing list software and newsletters further in the next chapter.

INTEGRATING WEB PRESENCE GADGETS AND TOOLS

Social networking and media sharing sites often allow you to embed features on your website. YouTube allows you to embed videos, Twitter allows you to embed your latest update, Flickr allows you to embed your most recent photos.

As you design your site, be sure to anticipate using these tools. We'll talk more about these social and media sites and integrating some of the widgets they provide in the next chapter.

TESTING YOUR SITE

Designing your site to speak to the various audiences is difficult. If you didn't use a Web host specialising in music sites or take advantage of a Web designer, your site will probably need tweaking. You need to test it – from each of the eight audiences' perspectives. Pretend you're a booker, a journalist, a fan and so on and see if you can find the information they would each be looking for quickly and easily. Browse your site as one of these audiences and purposefully put yourself in the wrong place on your site. Can you find your way back to the information they need easily? A general rule of thumb is, if it takes more than two clicks to get back to where you should be once you've become lost, you need to redesign.

After you've test-driven your site, get your friends and family to try it out. Stand over their shoulders as they click around. Don't lead them or answer any questions they have, because you won't be standing over the shoulder of any visitors to your site. Can they find your music easily or do they get lost? Do they learn what your band is up to or are they distracted by other things? Are they confused and frustrated? If your friends and family are, you can bet others will be as well. And others won't have the patience to keep clicking to find what they need. Take this feedback and make the necessary changes. Then test again, until you get it right.

CONTENT CONCEPTS AND TECHNIQUES

As you build your site, keep the following techniques in mind. Many of these will also apply to any content you create – including your press materials, posters and flyers.

DRAW THEM A MAP

One of the most useful lessons we've learned about writing content for our website came from the book *The Tipping Point* by Malcolm Gladwell, an examination of how and why trends are started. We call it 'Draw Them a Map'. In *The Tipping Point*, Gladwell tells the story of an experiment performed at a college campus attempting to boost the rate of students getting tetanus shots. The researchers showed the first group photographs of the devastating effects of tetanus and gave the second group a written description. The expectation was that the grotesque visual images would better inspire students to get their shots. Counterintuitively, both groups came in at an almost identical (and very low) rate. They decided to run a second experiment but this time gave one of the groups a map to the student health centre, even though every student knew where the health centre was. This time, more students in the group with the map got their tetanus shots.

What's the lesson here? We've drawn four from it and we use them whenever we write for our websites:

1. **Get to the point.** The content is less important than the message you want to convey. You can write paragraphs about why people should buy your album but the only important sentence is: **'Click here to buy our album right now.'**
2. **Direct people to act.** Insert a concrete 'call to action'. Write, 'Call 555-2983 and book Beatnik Turtle today', not, 'If you are interested in booking Beatnik Turtle, you should call us at 555-2983'. Direct readers to do the action that you want them to do.
3. **Keep it simple.** Anything you tell readers to do should be convenient. If you want them to buy an album, don't make them click ten times to do it.
4. **Be explicit even when it's obvious.** The map in the experiment was unnecessary yet effective. On your website, it may seem unnecessary to write 'click on the button to buy the album', if the button says 'buy now' but it can eliminate any shred of confusion (and it acts as a call to action).

AIDA

An old marketing acronym reinforces these ideas: AIDA. It stands for four concepts that marketers use when drafting advertising or marketing material.

Attention
Interest
Decision
Action

Take your readers through all four of these steps if you want them to respond to a call to action.

Make your message flashy to get their attention. Once you've got their attention, get them interested in what you want them to do, whether it's listening to your latest track or buying a ticket to your next performance. Then, give them a reason or two to make the decision you want them to make, like a discount on merchandise or the fact that time is running out. Finally, make your call to action: *click here now*. Every advertisement, billboard, TV ad, radio spot and movie trailer follows this formula. Obviously, AIDA helps direct your website audiences to actions you want them to take but it's also useful for posters, flyers and any other marketing materials that you create.

REPETITION AND CONVENIENCE

Repetition is also important when influencing people to take action. If you want people to do something, keep repeating that message. Of course, this doesn't have to be done with words. For example, we have images of our albums throughout our site, each of which links to its respective ordering page. Featuring album artwork is one form of repetition. Try to think of as many different ways as you can to repeat your call to action.

SALTING

Would you like to learn a technique that will make people take notice and pay attention to whatever you say? What if you could do it right now, in one easy step?

You would? Great. This technique is called 'salting'. Effective salting piques a reader's curiosity and creates a knowledge gap that only you can satisfy. Once you've 'salted' their desire to know something, you're the only one who can quench their thirst. This technique is useful for sales but it can also be handy for conveying information you want people to retain.

Radio stations use this technique all the time before a commercial break. They announce which songs will be coming up after the break so listeners stick around. Magazines do this by asking questions on the front cover, with a promise that the answers lies within.

USE IMAGES FOR EVERY STORY

Include an image wherever text appears. The Web is a visual medium. And less is more. The adage 'a picture speaks a thousand words' rings true because people love looking at photos first rather than the captions. Create your content, your blog entries and news stories with this psychology in mind. Use graphics and photos to break up long blocks of text.

ROYALTY-FREE IMAGES

It's often helpful to have a set of royalty-free images and photos handy. Here are some suggestions:

- **Photo and clip art libraries:** You can buy archives of stock photos or clip art on CD or DVD.
- **Clip art subscriptions:** You can subscribe to services that will give you access to thousands of images such as clipart.com.
- **Government archives:** Anything created by the US government such as space photos taken by NASA or other US departments (.gov) is in the public domain and copyright-free thanks to US taxpayers. You can join the free ride.
- **Photo sharing sites:** There are many photo sharing sites like Flickr and Photobucket that allow you to copy photos but most of them don't allow you to use their images for commercial purposes such as your band. Note that if you use images from members of these sites, depending on the licence they have, you'd have to ask permission. See Chapter 7: Your Rights for more information.

▶▶GETTING INTO SEARCH ENGINES

People will find your website in a variety of ways. They may learn your domain at a performance or get it off your CD or other branded material. But many will discover you either through referrals or searches. You want your site to feature prominently in searches at Google and other major search engines whenever anyone searches for your names, your band name, your albums or your song titles.

SUBMITTING TO SEARCH ENGINES

Once your site is launched, submit it to search engines to make sure they pick it up. See the table below for submission URLs. Although there are more search engines than these, most simply license and repackage the results of this small set.

SUBMITTING TO SEARCH ENGINES

Search Engine	Submit Link
Google.com	http://google.com/addurl/?continue=/addurl
Yahoo.com	http://search.yahoo.com/info/submit.html
Live.com	http://search.msn.com/docs/submit.aspx

SEARCH ENGINE OPTIMISATION

Search Engine Optimisation, often called SEO, is the art of engineering a website and its content to achieve higher rankings in a search engine. The higher the ranking, the more likely you'll be at the top of the search list when the appropriate search terms are entered. Getting a high ranking in search engines can mean serious money so, unfortunately, you'll be competing against experts who get paid to optimise their client's websites for the highest rankings possible. The good news is, search engines don't want to be manipulated and are constantly sifting through the results for sites engineered to be popular without actually being relevant or genuine. Simply creating a genuine band website with frequently updated content often helps. After a while, your site should naturally rise to the top of the search results for your band and your music.

SEO is an ever-changing topic. Search engines continuously modify the mechanisms they use to calculate rankings. They adapt their algorithms in an endless battle to keep SEO companies from exploiting their systems. So, techniques to keep your band's website on the cutting edge of SEO don't belong in the *Manual*. However, there are a few general principles that stay constant and, if you follow them, you will improve your ranking.

The following should be kept in mind as you design your website:

- **Title each Web page:** Be sure to title each page you create. The title gives search engines the best clue to the topic of the page. Even more importantly, when your page does come up in a search, it's the page title that is displayed and highlighted as a link. People looking over their search results will only have this to go by. So, your page title should entice people to click it.
- **Remember text:** Search engine results are based on text, not images. Although it's important to have images and be brief with text, be sure to include all search-relevant text on your site. For instance, we display lyrics for all of the songs on TheSongOfTheDay.com, and as a result, there have

been a lot of searchers who ended up there based on a snippet of text that happened to be a lyric.

■ **Intra-site linking:** When external sites link to your site, it increases your rankings. Although you can't control what external sites do, the linking between pages within your own site can affect your page ranking as well. Cross-link where appropriate.

■ **Flash, video and graphics don't count:** Flash, video and words in graphics aren't readable by search engines and therefore don't appear in the search rankings. A site that uses a lot of these doesn't tend to do well in search results. Always offer alternative text for every image file and create text captions for your flash animations and videos so that the search engines know what they're looking at.

■ **MP3 search engines:** If you're comfortable sharing your music without restrictions, make your MP3s downloadable to the user's PC, not just available as a streaming feed. Doing so will allow those files to be picked up in MP3 search engines. These search engines link to your MP3 files directly. Our Web statistics show that MP3 search engines send us far more visitors than text search engines. And, when MP3s are tagged properly, those listeners will know where to find your band's site if they want to know more about your music.

TRACKING WHO'S TALKING ABOUT YOUR BAND

You can also use search engines to discover who's talking about your band and music and who's linking to your site. This can be very useful information.

To track mentions of your band and find out the rank of your website, you will need to do the following:

1. **Search on your band name:** Search on your band name to track the overall number of search results and to find all pages that mention your website. Make sure to search on common misspellings. Enclose multiple words in quotation marks and use the OR operator, which works in most engines. For example, we search on **'beatnik turtle' OR 'beatnick turtle'**.

2. **Search on other terms associated with your band:** Additionally, you'll want to search on other terms associated with your band such as the names of your albums and songs.

3. **Use the following search engines**
   ■ **Standard search engines:** Search Google.com, Yahoo.com and Live.com. Each engine also offers real-time alerts (google.com/alerts,

alerts.yahoo.com, alerts.live.com), which will notify you when new mentions of your search terms are indexed. We often use these to find mentions of our band name.

■ **Blog search engines:** Although the standard search engines search blogs, we also recommend Google Blog Search (blogsearch.google. com) and Technorati (technorati.com), a specialised blog search engine.

4. **Check your PageRank:** Check your Google PageRank by installing the free Google Toolbar (toolbar.google.com). The higher your PageRank, the higher up your page will appear in the search results.

Tracking your band on a regular basis will give you valuable information – information you can use to fine-tune your SEO strategies. We'll be using this technique in Chapter 12: Get Publicised to track the progress of your media campaigns and to reach out to those who are talking about you in order to network and explore other opportunities for your music.

▸▸WEB TECHNOLOGY FOR MUSIC WEBSITES

Next we're going to cover all of the key Web technologies that you will be using on your band's website. These include RSS, flash music players, MP3 encoding, ID3 tagging, Web statistics and more. Rather than go into great detail about each of these topics, we're going to tell you what you need to know from a musician's standpoint, with more specific information available from any of a number of Web design books and websites. While some of these topics might seem obscure or technical, we actually use all of these technologies for Beatnik Turtle *every single day*. No band website should be without them. It's even better if your Web host provides these features as part of their package.

REALLY SIMPLE SYNDICATION (RSS)

The Web is drenched in information. In the early days, when you wanted to keep up with a website, you had to bookmark it and remember to return on a regular basis. Developers created 'What's New' pages and encouraged visitors to 'check back often'. With the advent of blogs, podcasts, media sharing sites, news aggregators and other frequently updated websites, developers evolved a new communications standard to make it easy for people to follow their favourite sites. The most popular standard invented to solve this problem is called Really Simple Syndication (RSS). Another standard is called Atom but it's not as widespread, so we recommend sticking with RSS.

Although the term 'syndication' implies the broadcast of information, RSS doesn't quite work that way. An RSS file is simply a text file: a date-organised list of entries. Let's take a blog as an example. Once you publish a new post on your RSS-enabled blog, the software automatically appends a new entry to the RSS file. This entry contains the title of the entry and the content of the post or perhaps only an excerpt. When the RSS file is updated, it doesn't alert those who have subscribed to the RSS feed. All your blog software does is add the new entry to the file and call it a day.

The real work is done by the programs that subscribe to the feed. Blog readers and podcast players will typically check all the RSS files they are subscribed to periodically and pulls the latest RSS file. By comparing the new RSS file with the previous ones, it figures out which entries are fresh and pulls the new information to the subscriber's reader or player. For instance, if you subscribe to TheSongOfTheDay.com's daily podcast feed through iTunes, the next time it launches, it will conveniently download the latest podcasts to iTunes.

Because RSS makes it simple to inform fans of updates, your blog, news, forums and all other regularly updated content should be RSS-enabled. We'll discuss how in the next chapter.

One RSS service that you may want to explore is Feedburner (feedburner. com), which makes it simpler for your users to subscribe to your feeds.

PASSWORD-PROTECTED WEBPAGES

One advantage to having your own website is that you can protect parts of your site so that only you, or people you approve, can access files in that section. Password protection methods vary and depend on your Web host and possibly the technology that you use for your website.

The following material should be password protected and reserved for your band's own use:

- **Brand Toolbox image source files:** Source files of your Brand Toolbox for easy access and sharing between band members. This usually consists of layered Photoshop and Illustrator files but can also include special images you use only in certain circumstances. Final, mixed-down images should be available for any visitors to your site.
- **Brand Toolbox text source files:** Word processor files (Word documents, OpenOffice documents, etc.) with your press releases, bios and so on, should be protected because they are easily edited. Final versions should only be distributed in Adobe PDF format.

■ **Song files:** Songs that you don't want released to the public but want to have on hand for press campaigns or for exclusive release to other music sites, should be protected as well.

SOUND ENCODING

Sound encoding is the process of turning analogue sound waves into digital information. A particular encoding method is called a codec. There are many different codecs that you can use. Of course, the most famous and universal codec is the MP3. We'll discuss everything you need to know to prepare music for distribution on your website below.

SOUND ENCODING FORMATS AND TERMS

Before we talk about the formats, there are terms we need to introduce to help you understand how they work. Audio formats can be either uncompressed or compressed:

■ **Uncompressed:** Uncompressed formats keep sound information in its raw form, without trying to shrink or otherwise modify the file. Uncompressed formats leave the audio data unchanged but result in very large file sizes.
■ **Compressed:** Compressed formats use mathematical or audio approximation techniques to shrink the size of an audio file.

There are two types of compression you can use:

■ **Lossless compression:** Lossless compression shrinks the size of an audio file without degrading sound quality. It does so in a variety of ways. For example, it might encode four seconds of silence by inserting a time marker that essentially tells the player to play silence for four seconds, ditching the actual silence you recorded. These techniques result in a smaller file size and don't degrade sound quality.
■ **Lossy compression:** Lossy compression reduces the file size by removing or approximating some of the original sound information. For example, these methods may drop certain sound frequencies that are beyond the range of human hearing. Whether you notice the effect of the compression on the sound quality of the recording depends on the type or amount of lossy compression applied to the file. Applying lossy compression to a file that's already been compressed will lead to greater sound degradation.

Now that you know the types of compression, we can discuss the most common codecs useful for Web distribution:

- **MP3:** MPEG-1 Audio Layer 3 was created by an organisation called the Motion Pictures Expert Group. This is the most common music codec and it's the one that people are most likely to be able to play on their computers or portable players. There are both lossless and lossy compression versions of this format but the most common ones are lossy. You can adjust many settings while encoding an MP3 file which alter the sound quality of your music and we'll recommend how to best do so for Web distribution in a later section. Additionally, MP3 files contain a layer of information that allows text to be embedded that audio players can display such as the song title, band name, copyright and lyrics. It even allows an image such as an album cover. Inserting this information is called ID3 tagging and we'll discuss this below.

- **WAV:** The WAV codec is one of the best formats to use to preserve sound quality. Although there are compressed versions of this codec, the most common forms of WAVs are uncompressed. Uncompressed WAV files are usually quite large and as a result are not ordinarily used on the Web to distribute music. They are more appropriate when sound quality is critical, such as when used for TV, film or podcast purposes. Media projects that incorporate music are often themselves compressed which can make the final version sound bad and unfortunately reflect badly on the band rather than the producer of the programme. It's usually up to you to convince the producers to use the WAV file instead.

- **AAC:** Advanced Audio Coding is Apple's proprietary audio codec. It's used by iTunes and is not universally handled by all players like MP3 and WAV are. AAC allows tagging much like an MP3. It also allows Digital Rights Management (DRM) technology to prevent unauthorised use.

- **WMA:** The Windows Media Audio format is Microsoft's proprietary audio codec and is the second most popular format. It can support a range of encoding quality and is playable on many devices but not all. Like Apple's AAC, WMA allows the use of DRM to control distribution.

- **OGG:** The Ogg Vorbis codec is a high-quality open-source standard. Many of the other formats, such as MP3, ACC and WMV, are patented but OGG technology is free to developers and users alike. OGG files have encoding settings that can affect the size and quality, similar to MP3 files. They also allow ID3 tagging.

■ **FLAC:** The Free Lossless Audio Codec or FLAC, is a lossless compression format. The tools to compress audio to a FLAC format are free and open-source versions exists for them. Sites like ETree (etree.org), the live music archive, use FLAC exclusively in order to get the highest quality audio with the smallest size.

OUR RECOMMENDED METHOD FOR ENCODING MUSIC FOR WEBSITES

Below is the Windows encoding method that we used for releasing over 365 songs over the Web. This method ensures the most reliable playability and quickest download times across multiple platforms:

1. Export a file from your final mixdown with the following settings:
    Stereo
    16-bit
    44.1 kHz
    WAV file.
2. Install the free audio tool Audiograbber from audiograbber.com-us.net.
3. Download the free Windows binary version of the LAME encoder from lame.sourceforge.net. Unzip the files into the same directory as Audiograbber, by default, C:\audiograbber.
4. Start Audiograbber and click the MP3 button. Change your settings to the following.
    Grab to: MP3 file via intermediate WAV file. Keep the WAV file
    Use ID3v1 Tag
    Enable the Internal Encoder Tab
    Choose the LameEnc DLL
    Choose Constant Bitrate and set the slidebar to 128
    In the Quality box, select Joint Stereo and Normal
    In the Bitstream flags, click only Original
    In the Encoder priority, choose Normal
    Click OK when your screen has these settings
5. After you have changed these settings, drag your WAV files from a file window into Audiograbber. Audiograbber will begin converting them into MP3s at these settings. You can also use the browse button on the MP3 screen.

PREPARING YOUR MUSIC: OPTIMAL MP3 ENCODING FOR YOUR BAND WEBSITE

While there are many ways to encode your music, you want everyone to be able to play your files and the MP3 standard is the most widely used and play-able standard. While you may prefer certain MP3 encoding settings for your own music collection, there are special considerations you should take into account for your music website. Unfortunately, many different settings and methods to encode an MP3 file are incompatible with some players. It's critical to encode your songs in a format that is playable by as many different set-ups as possible.

See 'Our recommended method for encoding music for websites' above for recommendations for encoding your music in MP3 format for distribu-tion on your site. These suggestions were born out of trial and error as we encoded hundreds of our own songs. If you're a techie or audiophile and want a detailed technical explanation of how each of the MP3 encoding options work, visit DIYMusicManual.com.

ID3 TAGGING

An additional benefit of MP3s is the ID3 tagging feature. That allows you to embed text in your MP3 files to display the song title, band name, copyright and lyrics in music players. It even allows an image such as an album cover. As we noted in the previous chapter, this functionality allows you to brand your MP3s properly.

There are two versions of ID3 tags: ID3v1 and ID3v2. ID3v1 is older, crude and limited in scope. ID3v2 is a much more useful and descriptive format and is the most common standard today. We used to fill in both ID3v1 and ID3v2 tags on all of our MP3 files to be safe. Occasionally, though, some media players would display the more limited ID3v1 tags, ignoring the ID3v2 tags, resulting in truncated titles and less information than we'd actually embed-ded. Therefore we recommend using only ID3v2 tags (id3.org/Frames) since all modern media players support the newer standard.

There are plenty of free software programs including iTunes and Windows Media Player that you can use to quickly and easily tag your MP3 files. You can also purchase ID3 tagging software to help you manage large numbers of songs. If you have to handle a lot of song files, we recommend purchasing the one we used for tagging all the songs we posted at TheSongOfTheDay.com: Tag & Rename from Softpointer (softpointer.com/tr.htm).

Make sure to fill in the tags as consistently as possible. Be careful to spell your band name, album and song title correctly. Since this is a branding opportunity, we recommend including your website, the copyright information and any other relevant information. Lastly, you'll want to insert an image for media players to display. Usually, musicians opt for inserting the album artwork but you can use your logo or another branded image instead. For example, for the songs we released at TheSongOfTheDay.com we used our Brand Toolbox to create an image with our mascot, band logo, the logo of TheSongOfTheDay.com and our tagline.

MP3 FILE-NAMING STANDARD

Always name your audio files consistently, because you never know where they might end up, such as a huge folder of song files. Make sure the file name emphasises your band's name. We suggest putting your band name first: Band Name – Song Title.

Due to the way most computers read files, omit punctuation marks such as question marks, apostrophes and quotes. For maximum compatibility, replace spaces with underscores. Also, the shorter, the better. And make sure you've spelled your band name and song title correctly!

- Bad Examples:
     PizzaTheRockOpera.mp3
     PizzaTheRockOpera–BeatnikTurtle.mp3
     beatnikturtlepizzatherockopera.mp3

- Good Example:
     Beatnik_Turtle-Pizza_The_Rock_Opera.mp3

PLAYING MUSIC FROM YOUR WEBSITE

Once you've encoded your music into MP3 format, tagged the file and named it, it's time to make it available on your website. One of the reasons MySpace.com and similar social-networking sites have done so well with musicians is the ease of uploading music and using their audio players. Unfortunately, the players are typically inflexible and limit the amount of music you can make available.

Today, there are multiple technologies available for playing your music from your website and we are going to cover each method, as well as giving practical examples of how to use each.

UPLOADING YOUR MUSIC

Now that you have your MP3 files ready, you will need to upload them to your website. First, create a directory on your Web server called 'music' or 'MP3' that can be accessed from a browser. (It needs to be inside your Web directory, which might be called 'public_html', 'Web' or ask your Web host for specifics.)

Once the files are uploaded, protect the directory from being listed so that visitors can't download all of your MP3 files at once. See the documentation from your Web hosting provider for information on how to do this.

There are three ways to upload your MP3 files to your website:

- **File Transfer Protocol (FTP) or Secure Shell (SSH).** Your Web host should give you an FTP or SSH account for you to upload files to your server. In order to use these methods, you must use a program on your computer. We recommend WS-FTP (ipswitch.com) or the free and open source WinSCP (winscp.net). For Macintosh, Transmit (panic.com/transmit) and Cyberduck (cyberduck.ch) are both good choices.
- **Web-based upload solution.** Your Web host may provide an uploading solution for you to transfer files to your website through its CMS. If one is available, you'll need to follow the instructions they provide.

DOWNLOADING, STREAMING, SHARING AND PODCASTING

Each method of delivering music to visitors has its own advantages and disadvantages. We use all of four of the following methods to distribute our music to people based on the circumstances.

- **Downloading.** Downloading lets a user copy the file on to their computer. Once it's downloaded, the file is available to them for their own use.
- **Streaming.** Streaming works like radio. Although the sound data gets sent to the user's computer, streaming players are usually configured to prevent the user from saving the file locally. However, determined people can always get around this limitation, so do not depend on this to protect your music.
- **Sharing.** Sharing a file is similar to downloading but allows a user to get the data from multiple sources in addition to your website. We talk about file sharing your own music in the Web Presence chapter.
- **Podcasting.** Podcasting lets users subscribe to a feed and automatically download songs when you publish them. This is only appropriate for songs that you wish to give away. We cover this in the next chapter.

DOWNLOADING

The simplest way to share music from your websites is to upload MP3s to your website and provide direct links which visitors can use to download the entire file. There are a few advantages to this simple method of distribution. First of all, visitors can keep the file and add it to their iTunes or Windows Media Player playlists. Second, if you post direct links to your MP3s, they'll be indexed by MP3 search engines. We get a large number of plays from these engines.

While this method is simple, it can confuse some users. When visitors click on the link, Quicktime will most likely launch in their browser and play the file. To the uninitiated, it may appear as if the song can only be listened to and they might believe that they can't download it. Users can right-click the link (or shift-click on a Mac) and choose to save the file locally but not every user knows this technique. So, some people won't figure out how to save the file. To avoid confusion, remind visitors that they can 'right-click or shift-click to save'.

ONLINE PLAYLISTS (STREAMING)

Another method is to create an online playlist and post it at your site. This allows visitors to stream your MP3s rather than download them. In principle, online playlists work the same way they do with almost any audio player you might have on your computer except the one difference is that the MP3s are being accessed from your website rather than locally. Although this is a streaming method, it's very easy for people to open up the playlist and download the songs directly if they want to. Some sites still use this format, although we don't recommend this if you can use any of the other methods that we list below.

There are two major formats that you can use for this:

- **M3U:** This format was originally developed for Nullsoft's WinAmp player and has been adopted as a fairly universal standard. Almost every MP3 player handles playlists created in this format. There are two types: M3U basic and M3U extended format. We recommend using the M3U extended format because this format includes information about the songs that the player can display, such as the song title, artist, etc. Some players will pick up the ID3 tags and display it. Some though, may not.
- **PLS:** The PLS format compatible with many players including Nullsoft's WinAmp player and iTunes. It is not compatible with Windows Media Player, however, because Windows doesn't associate the file extension PLS with any media player. Because of this, we do not recommend using this standard.

If you want to know how to make an M3U playlist for your site, we have a sample at DIYMusicManual.com.

FLASH MUSIC PLAYERS (STREAMING)

We recommend using Flash players above any other delivery mechanism for music. Most players let you control exactly how you want to deliver your music (downloading or streaming), change the look and feel (brand your player) and link directly to your store pages (which encourages sales). Your visitor needs Adobe Flash Player installed on their computer for any Flash players to work but this software is nearly ubiquitous and available for all major platforms (Windows, Mac, Linux). Still, there are always a few people that might not have it and may not be able to hear your music.

Flash players vary. Some are simply play buttons (like the one we use at TheSongOfTheDay.com), while others rival any audio player software you might have on your computer – boasting playlist functionality, EQ controls, volume, balance and other standard features. Here are three recommended flash players: Wimpy Player (wimpyplayer.com), JW MP3 Player (jeroenwijering.com/?item=jw_mp3_player), XSPF Web Music Player (musicplayer.sourceforge.net) (an open source and free solution).

PLAYING VIDEO FROM YOUR WEBSITE

Hosting videos from your website may raise your Web hosting rates – especially if any videos you post become popular. There are a variety of formats that you can use for your videos, with some of the better known ones being Quicktime, WMV, Real, MP4, AVI, DivX and Flash. Unfortunately, each one of these has its own associated player and not all of your visitors will have the means to play it. This can frustrate viewers. To resolve this, you may want to encode your video in a variety of formats.

Web hosting sites such as YouTube (youtube.com) and Blip TV (blip.tv) have become an extremely popular way to solve video hosting problems. Not only do you take advantage of their bandwidth, their sites are so prevalent that in many respects they have standardised video. Nearly every Internet surfer can play a YouTube video, for instance. We'll talk about these video hosting sites in Chapter 5: Your Web Presence.

WEB STATISTICS

One of the biggest advantages of having your own website is full access to Web statistics. Your Web host will probably provide some Web statistic programs by default but there are free options you can install such as AWStats (awstats. sourceforge.net) or Webalizer (mrunix.net/Webalizer). Additionally there are solutions for sale, such as Mint (haveamint.com).

Many people ignore their stats but that's a big mistake. Statistics are an incredibly powerful technique for understanding how people actually use your website and gauging interest in your band 'out there'. Also, Web stat analysis is crucial for publicity purposes. There is no more important technique for tracking your media campaigns – your statistics that will clue you in to who's talking about you and who's sending visitors your way, identifying the blogs, podcasts, news sites and other websites directing traffic to you.

STATISTICS ARE PEOPLE

There are hundreds of millions of people on the Web and any one of them might be discovering your music at this very moment. While these people may only show up as numbers in your Web stats, they are people nonetheless. For instance, at one point Gavin Mikhail was getting 15,000 plays of his songs *a day*. While that's a huge number, it's still abstract and can lose some meaning. But you have to keep in mind what's actually generating that number is people. As Mikhail puts it, 'I realised that I would have to be playing to a stadium to get that much exposure for my music and yet, here I was playing to that many people without even leaving my house.' Mikhail's comment in many respects sums up the Internet. And it's only getting bigger.

As you review your stats, fight the abstraction and visualise a venue you've played at. If 1,000 people listened to one of your songs on the Web, for example, imagine all of those people standing in that venue, listening to you play. We've found this technique helps put your statistics in perspective and while you might not get the same rush out of reading your stats as you would if you were playing live for a massive crowd, it still means your music is being heard by 1,000 people.

WEB TERMINOLOGY

Once you start getting into the back-end of a website, there's a new set of terminology to learn. These terms have specific meanings that aren't always straightforward, so we're going to define them here so that we can use them in our discussion later.

■ **Hits:** A hit is a request to the Web server where your website is hosted. Many people still equate hits with popularity. This is not the case.

Whenever a person browses one of your Web pages, each image, frame and page element counts as a hit from a visitor. Ignore this statistic. Although it used to be the major statistic people tracked because of the way browsers originally worked, it's useless today. Visits and Unique Visitors are more useful statistics.

■ **Visits:** A Visit is a complete session spent at your website by one user. It can last seconds, minutes, hours or days and is determined by the continuous presence of a Unique Visitor at your site.

■ **Unique Visitors:** This is the number of distinct visitors to your website. This is usually calculated on a monthly basis. For example, a single Unique Visitor might visit every day but would only be counted as one Unique Visitor that month, even though they were responsible for 30 Visits.

■ **Visits Per Visitor:** Combining Visits and Unique Visitors, you get an average Visits Per Visitor. This tells you how often people return to your website. You want this number to be as high as possible since it means you have regular visitors. If this statistic is close to one, your website does not bring people back.

■ **Pages:** This is how many separate Web pages are requested from your website, total. This is also expressed as Pages Per Visit, which can be an interesting statistic. If the Pages Per Visit stat is close to one, your visitors are looking at just one or two pages before exiting.

■ **Bandwidth:** This is the amount of data people have transferred from your site. Because of the file size of your MP3s, you can use this to determine if the average visitor is listening to your songs. This is also expressed as Bandwidth Per Visitor.

■ **Visit duration:** This is the average amount of time that a user spends on your site.

■ **Referrers (or referring sites):** Referrers tell you who has linked to your website. This can be used to identify each site that links to you and also how many people have clicked those links. This is one of the most useful statistics. You can see, for instance, if the music blog that reviewed your latest album actually sent any new listeners your way.

■ **Referring search engines:** This statistic tells you which search engines sent visitors to you.

■ **Search Terms:** This statistic tells you what search terms are sending people to your site and how many visitors each one sent.

■ **Viewed files:** This statistic will display a list, usually sorted from high to low, of the number of times each file is requested from your website. This shows you what your most popular files are. This statistic can help you gauge how many times one of your MP3s was listened to by visitors.

NOTHING IS AS IT SEEMS

Unfortunately, nothing about Web statistics is straightforward. Web stats can be both inflated or deflated depending on factors you can't control. The biggest factor is something called caching. Caching occurs when large Internet Service Providers (ISPs) make a copy of your website to their network so that they can serve it to their users more quickly. Some of your visitors will visit these cached pages instead of your site itself and as a result your Web server won't be able to count them, even though, in essence, they were visitors.

Another issue is that the Unique Visitor statistic is based on unique IP addresses. However, unique IP addresses don't necessarily mean unique people. Multiple visitors can come from the same IP address, in some instances (e.g. different people visiting your site from the same office network), while one visitor may come from multiple IP addresses (e.g. while checking your site from home and at work).

The lesson here is that these statistics can only give you a general sense of what's going on at your Web site. They shouldn't be read as absolutes.

REFERRERS

Possibly the most useful information you'll get from your stats is a list of all of the websites that have referred visitors to you and how many visitors they each sent. We watch these statistics every day for our own websites and visit each new page that pops up to see what they're saying about us and why they're linking. This is called trackbacking. Using this, you can find out trends related to your band *as they are happening*.

Contrary to popular belief, not all websites are catalogued in search engines and some of them may be talking about your band. Using your stats to trackback can often fill in the gaps searching doesn't capture. For example, forums and message boards might link to your site. These sites are often located behind a login screen that search engines can't get past. (We recommend signing up for accounts on these sites to see who's talking about you.)

Also, some bloggers may spontaneously link to a file or image on your site in passing while discussing something unrelated and without typing a single word that you would ever search for. The referrer page is the only way to find out about these links.

Trackbacking is also the best way to find out how well your media campaigns are working. Once you get media coverage, one way to gauge its impact is to see how many people stories that link to you are sending to your site. This can help you refine your media campaign. In fact, trackbacking can even help you find media coverage that you didn't know you had. Many times, the media doesn't even inform you when they've published a piece – even if you did an interview with them. Fortunately, any coverage you get on the Web often provides a link to your site and the referred visitors will clue you in to when and where you've received publicity.

FINDING 404 ERRORS USING STATISTICS

404 errors occur when you have a bad link on your site or when a visitor is sent to a page that does not exist. One of the common statistics that is provided by most stats engines is the number of 404 links that your site has and which links are 404 so that you can fix them.

SEARCH ENGINE TRACKING

Your Web statistics are the only way to track how many links you get from each search engine as well as which search terms people used to wind up on your site. Web statistic tools not only track standard search engines but also social bookmarking sites such as StumbleUpon, Digg and other such sites.

YOUR GLOBAL AUDIENCE

As we mentioned in previous chapters, fans can and do come from all around the world. Your Web statistics can track this and tell you which country each visitor came from. In one month alone, TheSongOfTheDay.com had visitors from New Zealand, Morocco, Poland, Vietnam, Brazil, United Kingdom, Finland, Spain, India, Chile, Israel, Canada, Macedonia, Sri Lanka, Iceland, Saudi Arabia, Australia, France and others; 78 countries in all. The world is listening and the impact of global listeners will only grow as the Web does. It's good to know where your fans are.

CLICKPATH TRACKING

Your basic stats help a lot but they won't tell you the paths people take while they visit and click around your site. This information is valuable for measuring how well your design and content is leading visitors through your site. Basic Web statistic programs cannot capture this. You also need a clickpath tracking program.

With a clickpath tracking program, you will be able to find out such things as:

- What links your users are clicking
- How long they remain on each page
- The individual paths each user takes as they travel through your site
- The most common entry and exit pages
- The times of day that people tend to visit

There are a number of clickpath tracking solutions that vary in power and accuracy. The better ones use cookies and embedded graphics as mechanisms to track users as they surf your site. Some programs can even recognise a returning visitor and assign a name to them if they join your mailing list or otherwise enter their email address on a site.

The information clickpath tracking programs provide can be invaluable. Using Google Analytics (google.com/analytics), for instance, you can track your conversion rates by entering specific actions for it to watch for such as the purchase of an album or the download of a song.

FREE CLICKPATH TRACKING

If your Web host hasn't already integrated these solutions within your site, we recommend the following free clickpath tracking software. As with Web statistic programs, you can always use more than one to analyse what's going on at your site:

- **Google Analytics (google.com/analytics/):** We highly recommend Google Analytics. They offer detailed instructions on implementing on your website.
- **TraceWatch (tracewatch.com):** Although Tracewatch is not as easy to install as Google Analytics, it is still worth implementing because instead of consolidating the data, it lists each visitor to let you see how *individuals* are clicking through your site. This can tell you how easy your site is to navigate. But unless you're an experienced website administrator, you will need help from your skill network to get it working.

DON'T RELY SOLELY ON SOCIAL-NETWORKING SITES (REPRISE)

Based on all the information these statistics can provide about your site and more importantly how your band and music is being received in the world, you should take a moment to feel sorry for the bands that rely solely on social-networking sites as their main website. Those tools are better used to help bolster your branded Web presence (and boost your SEO), not replace it. We'll talk more about establishing your Web presence in the next chapter.

LEARNING MORE

There's a lot to having a website but as we've seen there's plenty of tools and services that can help. We keep track of all the best of these resources at DIYMusicManual.com for you. DIYMusicManual.com is a free and open community for indie musicians and we'll discuss it more in the next chapter.

▶▶ CHAPTER FIVE

YOUR WEB PRESENCE

The Web allows you to reach people in new ways beyond playing live shows – whether it's through social networks, message boards, podcasts, blogs or even virtual online worlds. You'll be able to target your message and get your music in front of the people most likely to enjoy it based on their interests and tastes – not just their locale. Even better, the Web makes them easy to find. There are millions of potential fans out there who should know about your music and you need to put your band and your music where they are.

The Web started out as a new way to *broadcast* information to people. Today it has grown into a *conversation*, where you can interact with anyone who shares the same interests. But more importantly, it's become a *collaboration*, enabling people all over the world to socialise and work together. This chapter will explore each of these activities – broadcasting, conversing and collaborating.

While we're going to mention a lot of websites and technologies by name, keep in mind that the Web is fluid and some sites that we mention might even disappear before this book goes to print. Rather than dwell on particular sites, we'll instead focus on the underlying concepts behind them. Our goal isn't just to show you the latest useful tools; it's to prepare you to recognise and take advantage of new ones when they come out. Also, keep in mind that some of the services that you use and rely on today might even disappear in the future. To help keep you up to date, we will maintain a listing of the current useful tools for musicians at DIYMusicManual.com.

▸▸ BEFORE YOU START

Before you begin broadcasting, conversing and collaborating, there are a few things to keep in mind when establishing your Web presence: setting up your profiles, doing self-promotion and dealing with user agreements.

KEEP TRACK OF YOUR LOGINS AND PASSWORDS

Because you will be joining many different sites for your band, you will need a way to keep track of the websites, logins and passwords and perhaps even share it with other members of your band. We recommend doing this in a spreadsheet or on Google docs online (docs.google.com), although you should password protect the files themselves. For a very secure solution, we like Password Gorilla (fpx.de/fp/Software/Gorilla), a free tool that allows you to track all of it in one convenient place with a single password.

ALWAYS BE BRANDING: YOUR ONLINE PROFILES

As we learned in Chapter 3: Your Brand, an effective brand is consistent and repeated. As you build your Web presence, you'll create accounts at multiple sites, each of which will ask for personal information. So, you'll be making heavy use of the images and text in your Brand Toolbox.

Given the number of tools out there, you're going to want to divide the job of maintaining each one among your band members. We recommend having your branded images and text ready to go at your website so anyone in the band can access them. Some of what you'll need includes:

- **Avatar:** Upload the same avatar representing your band anytime you register an account. In our case, we always use our turtle mascot.
- **Tagline:** Many sites ask you for a pithy saying or short description of yourself. We suggest making a tagline out of your elevator pitch.
- **Description or bio**: Many sites allow a more detailed profile description. Our advice is to keep it short. Use your elevator pitch or short bio (with a link to your website for more information).
- **Links:** Most profiles allow you to link to your website. We recommend copying and pasting your website in full from your browser's address bar, since there's nothing more embarrassing than mistyping your own website's URL.
- **Footer or signature line**: Some sites allow you a footer or signature line that displays when you make posts or leave comments. Use this footer as

another opportunity to promote your band. We get a lot of visitors from posts that we make because of footers.

■ **Your contact information:** Keep your contact info consistent. You'd be surprised at how many people contact you using your profiles.

SELF-PROMOTION (AND STEALTH-PROMOTION)

If you believe in your music, you shouldn't be ashamed to promote it, especially when you're first starting out and your music needs the biggest boost. There's nothing wrong with self-promotion, but when you promote yourself you want to do it appropriately. That means that you shouldn't just push your music at people. As Chris Anderson says in his interview for the book *Blogging Heroes*:

> Bloggers shamelessly self-promote but they do it in an appropriate way. They email people they know, regarding things that really are of interest to those people and ask for links [back to their own blogs]. They're not just begging for a random link – they're actually adding value, because this link is in fact complementary to something the blogger they're emailing has already done.

This isn't just true for blogs, it's true for anything that you do online that you wish to self-promote. In fact, we recommend the following:

■ Carefully target the people that you wish to get your message to.

■ Think of their point of view when you promote yourself, for example, give them links to a song of yours that relates to a topic that they cover in their blog.

■ Remember there are real people behind the posts, blogs and messages on the Web. No one likes another sales pitch. You might want to wait until you've exchanged some emails before even bringing up your music.

■ Do some research on who you're contacting or the group you're targeting. This means actually reading their posts and blogs.

■ In your messages to those you target, be sure to focus on *them*. Talk about recent entries in their blog, podcast or profile as it shows that you are aware of their own work. That way, they're more likely to pay attention to you

■ Don't forget that all of the general concepts covered in Chapter 2: Your Network apply to self-promoting online as well. Also, we go into more detail on promotion in both Chapter 8: Get Noticed and Chapter 12: Get Publicised.

That said, keep in mind that there are some sites where you won't want a branded online profile. Instead, you'll just want to be yourself or an anonymous user. Sites that ask for user submissions of news stories or links to interesting websites, such as Digg.com, Slashdot.org or BoingBoing.net, typically frown upon blatant self-promotion. For example, those with editors often reject stories about an 'amazing' new song or video if they sense that they were submitted by the band itself. And sites like Reddit.com, which are judged by the site's online community, can often be harsher in public about you and your story than any editor.

Record labels don't let this stop them. They still shamelessly self-promote, by using pseudonyms or paying third parties to post stories on their behalf. For sites such as these, we recommend creating pseudonym profiles yourself. Eventually, your fan network will be the ones to promote you spontaneously by submitting stories, links and posts about your music. In the meantime, you'll have to be your own fan.

For example, we wrote a song dedicated to the Battle of Denmark Strait and the HMS *Hood* for our Song of the Day project. We made a very simple post to a message board at an HMS *Hood* website and provided a link to the song, saying that it was a tribute to the battle. The members of the message board loved it but it was a very low-traffic forum and we only got a handful of hits. To our pleasant surprise, one of the people on that board posted the link to a website about model warships and another about ships in general. Those additional posts got us hundreds of additional plays. This was about 10 minutes work for that exposure.

USER AGREEMENTS

Almost every website where you create an account will have a user agreement. When you signed up for these sites as an individual, you probably didn't bother reading them. Unfortunately, with your band and its music at stake, you need to start paying attention to these, since some may require you to give up certain rights.

You must make sure that these agreements don't overreach and hamper any plans you have for your music, videos or other content you upload. For example, the user agreements for music sites can be especially aggressive about copyrights, sometimes dictating that you give them the right to sell your music on compilation albums or use it in other ways you might find objectionable. We routinely skip websites that have user agreements that claim overbroad rights to the material that we upload. You can check DIYMusicManual.

com to see what other indie musicians have said about the site's user agreement and whether they found it fair. But if you're ever uncertain about the meanings behind any agreements, you should consult your solicitor.

⏩ BROADCASTING

In this section, we'll talk about technologies you can use to broadcast information to your fans. Technologies in this category include emails (your mailing list), blogs, podcasts, video blogs, photo sharing and more. Broadcast tools are often incorporated or embedded directly into the design of your website.

MAILING LISTS

Do you know who your fans are? You should and your mailing list is the best way to do so. People who sign up for your list are most likely the loyal fans that come to your shows and buy your albums. Much of your success depends on your ability to inform and motivate them.

You should ask for contact information whenever possible. While your website should elicit contact information at multiple points (when they download a song, purchase some merchandise, etc.), you should mention the mailing list whenever you interact with them. Have a piece of paper out and add newcomers to the list when you see them in person, such as when you run a merchandise table.

Collecting a mailing list serves many purposes but here are some of the most important ones:

- It tells you who's in your fan network.
- It lets you broadcast and announce your latest albums, videos and news directly to your fans.
- It lets you broadcast show information to fans to boost live show attendance.
- It boosts sales by allowing you to advertise and pitch your albums and merchandise.
- It helps with branding by reminding your fan network about your band.

Of course, any time you're dealing with a lot of information, it helps to have software to do the heavy lifting. You may need to track thousands of names or even tens of thousands (or, if you're successful, millions, although at that point you'll need more than software).

You should build an email list and a traditional mailing list as well. Both come in handy at different times for different purposes. We'll talk about both below.

PRIVACY POLICY

Many people are concerned about giving away their private information. With identity theft and spam on the rise, it's not hard to understand why. To set them at ease, you should post a policy for how you plan to use, safeguard and handle the personal information you collect from them and adhere to it. The idea, after all, is to build trust with the fans that are willing to give you their information so you can contact them. Plus, in the EU, it's the law.

The European Union has some of the most comprehensive data privacy rights granted to their citizens. Member States like the UK have adopted many of these legal principles. Under the EU Data Protection Act, you need to safeguard any personal information you store on a person. This includes your fans' email addresses.

Keep in mind that, once you post a privacy policy, you have to abide by it and allow your users the right to know what you maintain on them (their email address), the right to correct this information if it's wrong and the right to have you delete it. We therefore suggest you keep your privacy policy straight-forward and set a policy that all personal information you collect from others will only be used for the purpose of keeping the band in contact with those who sign up. In other words, don't sell or otherwise give your fans' personal information to any third parties for other purposes (such as sharing your list with another band).

You should create a page at your website where you announce your policy. It doesn't have to be in legalese. Plain English will do. You should link to this page from all pages related to your mailing list.

One way bands inadvertently violate their privacy policies is by sending email to their lists by using the **To:** or **CC:** field to send emails to multiple members of their mailing list. These fields expose everyone's email address to everyone else on the message – and anyone the initial recipients forward the message on to. To avoid this embarrassing mistake and breach of agreement, put the band's email address in the **To:** field and place everyone else's in the **BCC:** field. There are two practical benefits of doing so. First, by addressing it to your band email, you'll know if your email went out correctly once you receive it. Second, if anyone accidentally hits 'Reply All' in response to your newsletter, they'll only end up writing to your band address, not to everyone on your mailing list.

For more information about the EU Data Protection Act, see http://ec.europa.eu/justice_home/fsj/privacy/index_en.htm.

EMAIL LISTS

An email list will be one of your primary methods for broadcasting information directly to your fans. You need consistent and regular contact with your fans. In fact, as Ariel Hyatt of Ariel Publicity (arielpublicity.com) says, 'No list, no band'. Fortunately, it's simple, inexpensive and fans expect to sign up for them.

Unfortunately, email is not as reliable as it once was, thanks to spam. Most email spam filters are very aggressive. Your newsletter, which likely contains hyperlinks and images, will probably trigger some of your fans' spam filters even though they've signed up for it legitimately. Although this may occur here and there, enough newsletters should reach their intended recipients to make it worthwhile to use this method to broadcast to your fans.

To increase the odds in your favour, you will want to encourage those who sign up to add the incoming email address of your newsletter to their spam whitelist, so it's sure to go through.

Additionally, you'll probably want to reproduce the content in your newsletters on your blog or elsewhere on your website. Since your site should be RSS-enabled, this will doubly ensure your fans are getting your message.

Although email is inexpensive, you shouldn't bombard your fans' inboxes with newsletters whenever you have news. Doing so will surely annoy even your biggest fans. We suggest limiting the frequency of your newsletters to no more than twice a month. Of course, special announcements, such a last-minute gig or major media coverage, are exceptions. However, they really should be special and make sure the subject line of your email conveys the unusual circumstances – be clear that you aren't normally going to overwhelm their mailboxes.

BRANDING YOUR EMAIL LIST

You should brand every newsletter that you send. Each one should have a consistent look and feel and should appear as a natural extension of your website. In our case, we actually named our newsletter, *TurtleShell* and it was created out of items from our Brand Toolbox. Once we'd created a template for the newsletter – the design, structure, fonts, use of images – we stuck to it.

WHAT TO WRITE ABOUT

Sometimes, the hardest hurdle to overcome is coming up with what to write about for your newsletter.

Here's a list of ideas:

- List upcoming shows
- Mention new songs, albums or merchandise
- Trumpet recent successes (a well-attended show, a positive music review, etc.)
- Link to media coverage you've received
- Highlight recent mentions in blogs or podcasts (and be sure to cross-promote)
- Feature photos from recent shows, both of the band and of the fans
- Announce upcoming projects (see the 'Stay Tuned Lesson' in Chapter 8: Get Noticed)
- Quote interesting or funny questions or comments from fans

Whatever you decide to write, make sure it's fresh news. It shouldn't be anything too old or something you've previously mentioned in an earlier newsletter. Also, be sure to use your band name frequently in your stories. Although it'll be your fans reading, seeing your name repeated always helps with name recognition.

WHAT TO INCLUDE
In addition to fresh content, each newsletter should contain the following:

- **Subject line:** Typically your subject line will be the name of your newsletter. If it's a regular mailing list, you'll want to denote the edition (the month or issue number). For *TurtleShell*, we would make the subject line: 'TurtleShell-The Beatnik Turtle Newsletter-[Month, Year]'. Of course, if the reason behind emailing your list is to announce something special, it helps to tell them this here.
- **How to subscribe/unsubscribe:** Include information on how recipients can subscribe and unsubscribe to your newsletter and provide links. Telling readers how to subscribe is important in cases where one fan forwards your newsletter to another person who isn't on your mailing list but then wants to join.
- **Basic information about who you are:** Beyond branding the entire look and feel of your newsletter, we suggest including your website, contact information (you may want to create a separate forwarding email address for replies to your newsletter), who you are (the elevator pitch version) and links to where they can purchase your music and merchandise (your store page).
- **Copyright information:** Don't forget to add any copyright or information about the newsletter. We suggest using a Creative Commons licence to

make it clear that people can share or post your newsletters if they like, as long as they attribute you and as long as it isn't for commercial purposes. Of course, by the same token you'll need to clear any copyrighted graphics or photos you plan to use.

With the exception of the subject line, we suggest including the rest of this information in the footer. In our design, we adjusted the footer font to be slightly smaller than that of the body text. Additionally, to ensure consistency, we built this footer into the template of the design. Once we'd written it, we never needed to deal with it again.

▸▸WRITING GOOD COPY

Writing newsletters can be time-consuming. However, keeping your fan network up to date is vital. It keeps your name in front of them, reminds them that you're doing things and keeps them involved. Don't make this into an overwhelming task. And since we'd all rather be making music than studying for our journalism degree, stick to the following rules of thumb:

- **Be brief.** Keep your articles short. Write headlines and blurbs that effectively convey the main message.
- **Who, what, where, why, when and how?** Begin each story by answering all of the above questions in the very first paragraph, like a good newspaper article.
- **Use pictures.** Try to include pictures with every story.
- **Direct people to act.** Insert a 'call to action' in your stories if you want your fans to do something. Don't assume they'll 'get it' from context. For example, 'Buy our new album today by clicking on this link.' Or, 'Come to our show on Saturday.' See Chapter 8: Get Noticed for the most effective ways to do this.
- **Salt your stories.** Throw in a teaser promise or question at the top of a story to arouse curiosity and draw the reader through to the end. For more on salting, see the previous chapter, Your Website.
- **Check spelling and grammar.** Obviously.
- **Get an editor.** Pass your newsletter to at least one other person with a knack for words to look it over for obvious mistakes before hitting Send.

EMAIL LIST SOFTWARE

Email list software simplifies the entire process of subscribing, unsubscribing, drafting and sending bulk emails to fans. You do not want to do this manually or use your personal email account. Fortunately, you have many options when it comes to this kind of software. First, your Web host may provide you with a ready-made system that can be easily integrated into your website. If not, then there are Web services, desktop programs and open source programs that run on a Web server that can do this for you. We've used PHPlist (PHPList.com), which is free and runs off our own server. We've had some people recommend the pay service EZine Director (ezinedirector.com) but there are quite a few services out there. We'll list the features you will want in an emailing list program if you are going to evaluate one:

- **Subscription form that integrates with your website.** The email list program should provide a sign-up form solution that embeds easily into your website.
- **Automatic unsubscribe.** Your program should let users unsubscribe auto-matically via a link in the newsletter. You do not want to manually manage this process.
- **Dead email address functionality.** You'll want the program to remove dead or bouncing email addresses in an automated fashion.
- **Template functionality.** The program should allow you to create templates. This saves time and allows you to brand consistently.
- **Archive content.** It should keep an archive of all of the messages you've sent.
- **Ability to send text and HTML versions**. Some people don't want newsletters full of photos and images and prefer the text-only version. Sophisticated email list programs allow the subscriber to decide what type of email they'd like to receive, automatically converting the HTML newsletter you create into text for those users.
- **Click tracking.** The program should perform click tracking so you can tell whether readers are clicking on links within your newsletter.
- **Postal mail integration.** Ideally, you'll want this program to be your one-stop shop for managing all the mail you send, whether electronic or postal. It should be able to manage both and have the ability to interface with printing programs so you can use it to send postal mail such as postcards.
- **Multiple and separate list capabilities.** Your program should handle multiple lists and let single users subscribe to multiple lists at once. This may be useful later if you create more than one newsletter.

USING YOUR EMAIL LIST SOFTWARE

Mailing list software combines the features of a word processor, database and email program in one package, handling all aspects of creating, managing and administering your list.

CUSTOMISING YOUR EMAIL SOFTWARE

Mailing list software should be highly customisable and easy to integrate within your website. For example, add a 'Join Our Email List' box in the sidebar of all your Web pages. Also, anytime a visitor performs a conversion action – buys merchandise, downloads a song – you should ask them to join while you have their interest.

Another way to entice people to join your mailing list is to offer something free for signing up or provide something exclusive to those who receive the newsletter. One year, we decided on the latter for Beatnik Turtle by giving them one free song each month.

Be sure to customise the default confirmation message. Typically, when someone signs up on your list, the program emails them a confirmation email. This message is customisable and should be branded and, more importantly, offer links to your albums and merchandise, perhaps with a special discount for having subscribed to the newsletter.

POSTAL MAILING LIST

Now that we have email, it's become rare for musicians to use postal mail to communicate with their fans. After all, it's relatively expensive and time-consuming. However, you may want to take this step for special occasions. For example, a CD release show may warrant a mailing.

If you do a postal mailing, we suggest using postcards. It's cheaper, more likely to be 'accidentally' read by the recipient (even if it's floating through the air as it heads into the bin). It also forces you to be brief and think 'billboard' when you create it. To make your postcards as effective as possible, give them some value by making them coupons for a discount ('Bring this postcard to the show for £X off the new CD') or a free gift (a button, poster, special CD, etc.). Encouraging people to bring in their postcards in this manner will give you valuable feedback as to whether this expensive way of contacting your fans was effective.

GOING MOBILE

As the Web goes mobile, so can your presence. This is a growing field and yet another avenue for building your presence and connecting to your fans. There are tools and services that will allow you to blast text or multimedia messages to your consenting fan network through their mobile phone. For example, you can send digital flyers to targeted fans reminding them you're playing in their area the day of the show. There are a number of mobile content providers that will allow you to broadcast your audio, graphics and video content available to mobile users – either freely or for sale – such as BroadTexter (broadtexter.com) and Myxer (myxer.com). A list of available services can be found at DIYMusic-Manual.com. We'll talk more about these mobile content services as a method to sell ringtones and music in Chapter 10: Get Distributed and Sold.

BLOGS

Blogs have changed the nature of how people communicate and interact with each other and have even changed the nature of journalism itself. Originally coined from the terms 'Web' and 'log', early blogs were essentially online diaries. Although such online diaries still exist, blogs soon evolved into a communication form to rival the popularity and quality of print media.

It seems that everyone has a blog. In fact, many expect every business and organisation to have one. This includes your band. But that's not the only reason you should consider starting one of your own. Most communication with your fans is impersonal. For instance, your news stories, newsletters and press releases will tend to be factual: we have a show, we got some media coverage, our new album is out, our drummer exploded. These are not typically places to be casual. In your blog, you can (and should) promote your latest albums, releases, merchandise and anything else that you've been up to but do so from a personal angle. The strange thing that happened on your tour, the wild events of last night's show, the fact the T-shirt manufacturer misspelled your band name and has to do a second run, all make great blog fodder though they may not be suitable for your news section.

As we said in the previous chapter, Nice Peter's blog is a great example of how to use blogs to humanise yourself and entertain your audience. They start to feel like they're part of what you're doing.

Better still, because of the informal tone band members should feel comfortable blogging. In fact, most blog software allows the creation of multiple author accounts and automatically identifies the author of each post.

CREATING A BLOG

There are two ways to create a blog: a self-hosted blogging program you can install on your own website or a Web-based blog hosting service that will serve up your blog for you. Before we go into these two options, let's look at the must-have features of your blog solution:

- **Rich text editor:** Your blog should have the option of working like a word processor when editing entries, with buttons for bold, italics, etc. You should have the option of blogging without knowing any HTML.
- **Embedded HTML:** YouTube, Flickr and other sites allow you to embed their videos and images into your blog. Make sure your blog allows embedded HTML.
- **Sound player:** You'll want the blog to feature a built-in music player. If you link to one of your songs, it should be able to embed a player right there in the post.
- **RSS-enabled:** Make sure that the blog you choose generates RSS feeds.

SELF-HOSTED BLOGGING PROGRAMS

It's now very simple to set up and update a blog. In fact, your Web host should provide blogging software for free. Of course, if your host doesn't or provides blogging software that is not RSS-enabled, you may want to install one yourself. Also, if you've decided to use a CMS to create and manage your website, then it's likely that the CMS will feature a built-in blogging module that will allow you to add one to your site quickly and easily.

Blog program features vary, so before you integrate one into your site, confirm that it contains the must-have features listed above. We suggest using WordPress (wordpress.org), which you can also use to create the rest of your website.

WEB-BASED BLOG HOSTING SERVICES

The other method of creating a blog is to register with a blog hosting service such as LiveJournal or Blogger. Many hosts are free but even those usually offer a pay version that adds extra features like more storage space. There are two advantages to using a blog host: they take care of the software back-end for you and they tend to have built-in blogging communities who will come and read your blog if it matches their interests.

However, because your blog is such a powerful way to personalise yourself, it really should be hosted on your website and incorporated into the design. For branding purposes, if you use a blog hosting service based elsewhere, you should embed it within your website. That way, you're not sending people away from your music, albums, mailing list and merchandise, to read your blog.

SOME BLOG HOSTING OPTIONS

- **Livejournal.com:** LiveJournal is more than a blog, it's a set of online social communities as well. As a result, we keep a LiveJournal account even though we have our own blogging software.
- **Blogger.com:** Blogger.com is owned by Google and is a solid blogging engine.
- **Wordpress.com:** Wordpress.com uses Wordpress but allows you to just create an account and start blogging rather than needing to set it up on your server.

GETTING INTO BLOG SEARCH ENGINES

You should get your blog into the blog search engines such as Technorati. com. Although you can let it 'find you', we recommend informing sites like Technorati initially when you launch your blog to get it in their system.

BLOG PINGS

Blog pings will inform blog search engines that you've updated. You should add the following blog pings to your blog software so that what you write will appear immediately in their search tools. There are numerous services but we recommend these three at a minimum:

http://rpc.pingomatic.com/
http://rpc.technorati.com/rpc/ping
http://api.feedster.com/ping

PODCASTING

We'll discuss other people's podcasts in detail in the Chapter 11: Get Played and Heard (including how to get your music played on them). In this section, we want to explain podcasting as a method to broadcast to your fan network.

Although every band should have a blog, starting a podcast is optional. Creating and recording a podcast episode is more time-consuming than writing a blog entry. That said, if there's anyone who knows how to produce one, it's musicians, since most of us are familiar with recording. You may want to reserve this method for special occasions such as while touring (there's always a lot of time to kill while travelling in the van) or as a lead-up to a special event.

There are two general types of podcasts that you may want to create. In a talk-radio-style podcast you can talk about what's going on behind the scenes with your band or cover other topics that interest you – while interspersing your music throughout. In a music-only podcast, you simply feature music you're willing to share. You can podcast live performances, alternate mixes or demos. For TheSongOfTheDay.com, we did both types – a daily music-only podcast featuring a new song and a weekly talk podcast where we discussed the songs we'd created that week, that is until work and time pressures led us to drop the weekly podcast since the editing took so much time. George Hrab manages to combine both talk and music in his *Geologic Podcast* (http://geologicpodcast.com) often adding new songs in between sketches and talk segments. For some musicians, podcasting can lead to entirely different projects such as Grant Baciocco of The Throwing Toasters who has gone on to produce the multiple-award-winning podcast 'The Radio Adventures of Dr Floyd' (http://doctorfloyd.com).

Like blogs, podcasts should be RSS-enabled. Without RSS, you're merely posting an MP3 file to your site for download. In essence, delivering music to your fans via RSS allows those who subscribe to get the latest episode downloaded automatically to their computers or MP3 devices. And every time they see a new episode, they will think of your band.

If you create a podcast, all the rules of branding still apply. Include an opening theme (or an abbreviated version of one of your signature songs) and an outro to end each episode. The outro should state what the listener just listened to, provide your website address and state any copyright or Creative Commons information.

Creating your own podcast goes beyond the scope of this *Manual* but there are several good books that can walk you through the steps and show you the techniques of great podcasters.

RECOMMENDED PODCASTING BOOKS & RESOURCES

If you want more information about podcasts, including how best to start your own, we recommend the following:

- *Podcasting for Dummies* by Tee Morris and Evo Terra.
- *Podcasting Bible* by Mitch Ratcliffe and and Steve Mack
- *Tricks of the Podcasting Masters* by Rob Walch and Mur Lafferty
- *Expert Podcasting Practices for Dummies* by Tee Morris, Evo Terra and Ryan Williams.

Additionally, podcast411.com is an excellent Web resource (and podcast!) run by Rob Walch that educates people about podcasting as well as interviews other notable podcasters for insights and other podcasting lessons.

MUSIC PODCAST TECHNIQUES FOR MUSICIANS

Although we recommend other books to learn the intricacies of podcasting, we've learned a few things ourselves by applying our musician instincts to the medium. In fact, some of these techniques will be at odds with what the podcasting books suggest but they will result in higher-quality audio that will help your podcast stand out:

- **Apply your mixing and mastering skills:** Treat it just like any song. Even the simple use of EQ and compression on all of your voice tracks will set you apart from every other podcast. Sound quality tends to be something that most podcasters, who have little other audio experience, neglect.
- **Use WAV:** When you create the sections of your podcast (songs, talk, sound effects, etc.) work with them in WAV format. Once you've assembled the entire podcast as a WAV, mix it down, compressing and limiting for clarity and punch. *Then* encode the WAV into MP3 format.
- **Sound encode for high quality:** Apply the sound encoding techniques from the previous chapter: encode your podcast at 128Kb at minimum. If your bitrate is too low, your audience will think that the podcast *and your songs contained within it* were recorded poorly. We found most podcasting books suggest bitrates as low as 96k or even 56k. This is only appropriate for talk-only podcasts. Don't do this to your music.
- **Respect your audience's time and edit:** Trim your podcasts mercilessly. Take out silences, awkward moments or boring ones.
- **Caffeinate beforehand:** If you talk during your podcasts, make sure that whoever is doing the speaking does so with energy and gusto. Keep your audience engaged with what you're saying.
- **Emulate radio shows and podcasts you enjoy:** There are good reasons you enjoy listening to what you do. Beyond the content, the best shows usually sound great, pace well, don't drag and have plenty of energy. Copy that.
- **Syndicate your podcast:** Don't just post the MP3 file to your website for people to download. Do it like any podcster would and syndicate it automatically using one of the syndication sites like Liberated Syndication

(libsyn.com), Podpress (podpress.org) or others suggested by the recommended podcasting books.

MEDIA MANAGEMENT SITES

Media management sites host your videos, audio, photos and other media and let you share them with the world. These external sites usually allow visitors to make comments and receive automatic updates whenever you add new media. The best media sites allow you to freely embed the media you post within your own website. This gives you powerful options for handling bandwidth-eating media and saving you money with your Web host. In this section, we'll cover each type of media-sharing site and how you can use it to expand your Web presence and leverage their services for your band's benefit.

PHOTO-SHARING SITES

If you're taking a lot of pictures of the group, you may want to use photo-sharing sites which specialise in displaying your photos on the Web such as Flickr (flickr.com), Photobucket (photobucket.com) and Webshots (webshots.com). These sites vary in functionality but they can help you group your photos into albums, present them on your website and handle time-consuming details such as resizing to create thumbnail images without affecting the original files.

Photo-sharing sites are generally easy to use and have nifty features. You can take advantage of their storage and bandwidth and save yourself the trouble of installing and managing photo gallery software on your own website. Most, however, begin charging money for additional storage space or advanced features such as when you reach a photo or photo album threshold limit.

VIDEO-SHARING SITES

To the extent that your band creates videos, they can be a major part of your Web presence. The enormous traffic generated by video sites such as YouTube is reminiscent of the initial rush that occurred when people realised they could get music downloaded directly to their computers. The same technological advances that made it so easy to record music at home has had the same effect for video. Because of this, the days when musicians are to be heard but not seen are long gone.

Even though video is better at getting a listener's attention, it has some shortcomings. For one thing, video has a lower replay value. People are more willing to watch a video they've never seen than listen to a song they've never heard but if they like the music they will listen to that song over and over again. Videos are lucky to get watched more than once. The goal is to use the video to introduce people not just to the song in the music video but also to lure people to your website so they'll discover what else you offer. In other words, it's critical to brand your video so that they can find out more about you. This is especially true since you can never be sure where your video is embedded on the Web.

Most music videos follow the MTV standard by featuring a brief flash of credits (band name, song title, director, etc.) in the lower corner of the screen. But you don't have to follow this standard. We begin our videos with a splash screen featuring our logo, band name and the title of the song. We also end it with quick, branded credits to thank everyone who participated in making it. You can also add a 'bug', which is a small logo that sits in the corner of the screen throughout the video. TV stations use bugs so viewers are reminded what channel they're watching and there's no reason you can't use the same technique with your logo or mascot. Keep in mind, however, that video sites often have their own bug, so make sure to place yours in another part of the image, otherwise it will be covered up.

Note that these video sites use compression which can affect the quality of the video and reflect poorly on your band. We have found that to get the best quality video, the format that you choose to upload is critical, as are the height and width. All of these affect the final presentation, sometimes drastically. Since these sites compress video in different ways, you should refer to them to see what they suggest for best results. You can also go to DIYMusicManual.com where we have information on the best formats and techniques for uploading music videos to these services.

An additional disadvantage is that these services include ads. Worse, these embeddable players often suggest other videos within the player itself. YouTube's player, for instance, displays related videos after yours has finished playing. These are clickable and can send your hard-earned visitor to YouTube to watch other videos. This doesn't help keep your visitors on your own website, which is preferred.

Be aware that if you upload a video with any copyrighted content that you do not own (including a cover song), you need permission. If you do this at a video site, such as YouTube, you will be violating the user agreement and, should they find out, your account might be suspended. Even if you host the video at your website, you are still at risk of infringement. For more information, see Chapter 7: Your Rights.

▸▸AUDIO-SHARING SITES

Audio sites have a very mixed history. They range from the success of the early incarnation of MP3.com to outright scams that do nothing more than try to take a musician's music as well as their money. Because of this chequered history, you should take particular care to read the agreements of all audio-sharing sites you sign up with. Do not risk losing the rights to your music.

Nevertheless, some audio sites are worth working with. For example, Last.fm (last.fm) is a site that allows users to track and share the songs they are listening to on their computers and music players. If they search on your band name, they will find other users that have played your music, as well as give you suggestions about other similar groups to look for. If you fill in a band profile, your band logo will get associated with your page. We will talk about these sites in detail in Chapter 11: Get Played and Heard.

SOCIAL-BOOKMARKING SITES

Managing bookmarks nowadays is a big job and it's not surprising that a lot of sites have grown up around tracking and filtering links. Some merely keep track of your own bookmarks but the better ones are geared towards sharing bookmarks with the community, using 'the wisdom of the masses' to help filter links for quality and context. You can set up accounts on all of these types of sites as they're free, easy to use and might help drive traffic to your website.

There are two types of social-bookmarking sites: non-voting and voting.

NON-VOTING SITES

By far, the most popular non-voting social-bookmarking sites are Delicious (del.icio.us) and Magnolia (ma.gnolia.com). Both sites allow you to enter your favourite bookmarks and tag them with one-word descriptions. Links can have multiple tags. Since these links are social, if other people post the same link, you'll see how many others have bookmarked the site, who they are and how they tagged the site. We recommend signing up for an account at both of these sites.

You can also use these sites to track how many people are bookmarking *your* website and who they are. Since most people's links are public, you can find out interesting information about your fans' personalities and taste in music by looking at the other links that they post. Finally, you can also use these sites to search on terms like 'music', 'indie band' or other terms to find useful links or Web tools.

VOTING SITES

Vote-based social-bookmarking sites let their user communities decide which links are worthwhile. Anyone who registers can post new links. Then it's up to the other users to decide whether to vote for them. The links with the most votes make it to the 'Most Popular' pages of these sites, which subsequently get a lot of traffic.

Not everyone who uses these sites votes. Voting is not a requirement. In fact, the links that make it to the top pages of these sites often get far more visits than the number of votes would suggest. Only those who care enough to do so will add their votes and even fewer will add comments. But if your website ever makes it to the front page, it'll generate a lot of traffic.

These voting-based social-bookmarking sites usually have a music category as well as a video category. If you write a song with a great hook or one that ties in somehow to a current event or Web meme, the community may take notice and vote on your page. The same goes for a compelling video. The best part is these sites generate quality hits – visitors tend to be people genuinely looking for music to listen to and music videos to watch. Also, these sites allow comments on every link, so read them for some unvarnished opinions about your music, video or site. The largest and most active vote-based social-bookmarking sites are Digg (digg.com) and Reddit (reddit.com).

A special class of voting sites will install a voting toolbar in your browser. These sites function like voting social-bookmarking sites with the convenience of voting buttons at the top of every page, as well as an additional button that will take the user to a randomly chosen, highly rated link. The more popular the link, the more likely that the toolbar will send users there. These toolbar sites also allow users to comment on the links, although the way the functionality is set up, users don't read those comments until after they've visited the recommended site. The comments posted generally are as honest as you'll see about your music, video or site.

The most popular toolbar-based site is StumbleUpon (stumbleupon.com), which has a toolbar that is easy to install and use. We suggest that you give it a try before submitting your site, in order to get a feel for it. It can represent a lot of traffic, so we believe that it's well worth your time to explore this tool. To our pleasant surprise, we ended up getting over 20,000 visitors to TheSongOfTheDay.com this way shortly after we launched the site, after a fan submitted it to StumbleUpon. Keep in mind, however, that such random visitors generally check out the link in question and then leave. It takes a lot to get them to stick around at your site rather than head to the next random link.

However, when you generate these types of numbers, at least some will end up sticking, happy to have discovered your band.

We recommend creating an account on all of these sites so you can post links to your songs, sites or videos. They are easy to use to drive new visitors to your site. Here are a few methods to encourage people to vote on your links:

- **Salt and compel:** Make the subject of your submission compelling, intriguing, risqué, outrageous. Ideally, it should pose a question. The subject line of the links are clickable, so if the subject doesn't pique their curiosity, no one will click on the link, let alone vote for it.
- **Keep it short:** Make sure your description is short and to the point. Long descriptions are often ignored.
- **Get support:** Have a few friends vote on the link when it first appears. This will give it some initial momentum. Most of these sites will drive any recently voted link to the top of the 'new links' pages.

Actually, posting links at these sites works best if they appear not to be from your band. Of course, it's great when your fan network spontaneously promotes links on your behalf but sometimes it helps to plant the seed and see if it grows. In this case, you will want to create an anonymous, unbranded account for yourself so you look like a regular user.

SOCIAL-BOOKMARKING SITES AND WEB STATISTICS
Once you start posting your links on these sites, monitor your Web statistics daily to keep track of how your campaigns are doing. Social-bookmarking sites should appear as 'referrers' in your stats. You'll be able to tell how many people each particular site sent. Using your clickpath tracking program, you'll see when these people arrived and how many ventured on and explored your site. (See the previous chapter for more information on Web statistics.) This information will help you tailor your efforts in future campaigns for maximum effect.

WIKIPEDIA
Wikipedia is a massive, collaborative encyclopaedia that anyone can edit. Surprisingly, even though anyone can change it, the site has developed a large and dedicated community of editors who make it their business to uphold standards of quality and consistency.

Since Wikipedia is an electronic encyclopaedia created by the masses, it covers far more topics than any traditional encyclopaedia could. One such area is popular culture. Wikipedia has entries on many bands. Since Wikipedia entries tend to get a very high page rank in search engines, these entries are valuable. In fact, our Wikipedia entry is a nice contributor to traffic for our websites.

Some things many people don't realise about Wikipedia include:

1. It's an encyclopaedia, not a promotional tool. The Wikipedia community frowns on autobiographical entries and especially on blatant self-promotion.
2. The Wikipedia community will question any entry that seems insignificant or doesn't live up to its encyclopaedic standards: fact-based, no opinions, plenty of citations. Many entries about indie bands are routinely removed if they fail these tests.
3. If a Wikipedia entry is created about your band, you don't own it. In fact, your own input about your entry, either in edits you make or on the discussion page that accompanies your entry, will tend to work *against* you. We advise you to not take part or to at least avoid advertising that you're with the band.

Given this, your best bet in getting an entry on Wikipedia is to wait until you have a proven following or until you've done something significant and newsworthy. Wikipedia depends on outside sources for verifying the material, so press and media coverage of your band will help a great deal.

Ideally, a member of your fan network will spontaneously create your band's entry for you. Once you get an entry, you will want to check it periodically to make sure facts and links are correct. Since it's an encyclopaedia, keep in mind that anything you add should be factual. Don't insert opinions or, worse, upcoming plans and events. This is not a Web presence site to brand or use as a promotional tool.

▸▸CONVERSING

Now that we've covered the technologies which will allow you to broadcast to.your fans, it's time to move on to those that allow two-way communication and how to use them effectively. As with broadcast technologies, many of these should be integrated into your website as well.

SOCIAL-NETWORKING SITES

Few new technologies have affected bands more than social-networking sites. Tens of thousands of bands have signed up for them to showcase their music and many bands use them in place of an actual website (which, as we've said, isn't a good idea).

Although we always recommend a website of your own, these sites should still be a part of your Web presence. Most are free and some are the most visited websites on the Internet. Some are designed around individuals, while others allow groups and bands to create profiles, as MySpace and Facebook do. Like all Web presence sites, if you register your band, your profile should be properly branded.

Also, the possibilities of these social-networking sites to help you find and connect with other people who might enjoy your music are nearly endless. Members are organised in a variety of ways including interests, personal traits, geographic location, etc., with most of the information made public. Targeting the right people or groups can help create awareness of your band, promote word of mouth and ultimately, lead to new fans. For example, becoming an active member of a group based on a band that sounds similar to yours can expose your music to possible new listeners. In other words, go to where people who might like your music are and bring your music to them. Groups tend to have a common message board – such as the Facebook 'wall' – which encourage members to broadcast and share information, links and recommendations to the entire group. Of course, this is also true for groups centred around a particular interest that your music touches on or even your band's geographic location.

Social-networking sites have evolved to include applications that allow members to interact in interesting ways. For example, some sites allow the sharing of music playlists or jukeboxes. Encouraging your fan network to post your music in their playlists can lead to exposure of your band to their friends. In fact, some applications, such as Nimbit's Online Merchandise Table (nimbit. com), are set up to sell songs as well. Fans can embed these applications and essentially act as storefronts for your music.

But it goes beyond using these sites to broadcast your music or message. As we mentioned in Chapter 2: Your Network, you should interact with your fans and potential new fans using these tools. There are countless applications that allow you to interact with your network and new ones are being created all of the time (you can even create your own social-networking site – with many of the bells and whistles that MySpace and Facebook have – based around your band by creating a free account and site at Ning.com which we discuss below). Listing all the useful applications goes beyond the scope of this book but you can find the latest at our website DIYMusicManual.com.

MYSPACE.COM

In Chapter 4: Your Website we went into depth about why your MySpace page shouldn't be your only site. However, the attraction of MySpace is simple to understand. Within ten minutes, a band can have a blog, photo album, music player, show calendar, dedicated email address and more. Like most social-networking sites, MySpace also connects bands directly with fans via its 'Friends' feature.

The most effective way to use MySpace is to make your page a multi-media extravaganza. Like many social-networking sites, your content has to compete with all the advertising surrounding it. To stand out, your content needs to be more eye-catching than the ads. Your MySpace front page is essentially the only page; visitors are unlikely to visit your blog and photos unless they know you.

Although we don't recommend having your music play automatically when visitors arrive at your band website, at MySpace autoplay is expected. Since MySpace visitors may not hang around for long, set your page to play your strongest song first. This is a setting in your profile and we'll talk about this and other recommended profile settings below.

In addition to the music, you should embed any videos you've made, as well as any arresting images you've created to advertise your latest projects, albums or shows. Have these link to your website where possible. If there's something you want your MySpace visitors to know, make sure it's in big letters and link it to your own site.

SETTING UP A MYSPACE ACCOUNT

When you sign up for MySpace, make sure to create a 'music artist' account. The music artist account will get you the music player and a few other music features that you'll want.

You might wonder how other users have changed the look of their profile, the background and the colours of text and links. The secret lies in MySpace's bio page. It's here that they allow you to embed HTML code, which is extremely useful for branding purposes. Doing so is not as difficult as it seems, thanks to tools that help you create the profile look you want. There are also numerous solutions to allow you to format your MySpace page. We have a list of where you can find the latest MySpace tools at DIYMusicManual.com if you're looking for some.

We don't recommend putting your actual band bio under 'The Bio'. Instead, you should fill this space with embedded videos, pictures, digital posters and links to your other sites. Again, you don't have much time to get a visitor interested and your best bet is to give them lots of multimedia to look at and click on. The Bio is one of the only places where you have some flexibility to make the page look the way you want it to in order to engage visitors.

Note that the bio field will allow embed tags (such as for placing YouTube videos) but not script tags, which can limit what you can do with your MySpace page.

RECOMMENDED SETTINGS FOR MYSPACE PROFILES & SONGS

Thanks to spam, we recommend that you use the following settings in your MySpace profile in order to block people from posting spam to your comments area on your page. If you don't do this, your band's MySpace page might become even more of an ad space.

Privacy Settings (Under Account Settings, Change Account Settings)

- Check the box for **Comments – approve before posting** so that no one can can post anything on your own MySpace page without your approval.
- Block event invites from **Users (who are not added to my friends), Bands (who are not added to my friends), Filmmakers (who are not added to my friends)** and **Comedians (who are not added to my friends)**.

WHAT FRIENDS ARE FOR (ON MYSPACE)

The 'Friends' feature allows fans to be listed on your friends' list and comment publicly on your page. Typically bands wantonly accept any friend request that comes their way, since the common assumption is, the more friends, the more popular you are. While we don't go out of our way to do friend campaigns, some bands do. Keep in mind that your friends can post comments on your main page, blog and photos, so if someone is causing problems, you might need to remove them later. Just as your friends can post to your MySpace page, you can broadcast announcements to them individually or as a group.

MUSIC ON MYSPACE

MySpace limits the number of songs you can load in their player, so we suggest doing the following to make the best of what they offer:

- **Upload your best songs:** Put your strongest one first. And don't set the player to random. You don't get a second chance to make a first impression.
- **Auto-play:** Set the first song to play automatically, since that is customary at MySpace.
- **Allow embedding:** We highly recommend allowing users to add your songs to their profiles. If they want to highlight your music, you should let them. If you do this, be advised that, if you later take these songs down, you will break these links.
- **Use album art:** Make sure to upload album images for all songs that you upload so that they will display in the MySpace player.

Although MySpace allows you to block users from downloading your music, know that it is still possible to get around this. There are websites and techniques that will allow users to download and save any MP3 on MySpace.

REVERBNATION

Reverbnation is a social-networking site that focuses on connecting musicians to music fans. But it's also a one-stop-shop for many musician needs. With a focus on music promotion, Reverbnation offers musicians a variety of features and tools – some free, others at a cost – such as digital distribution, multimedia press kit creation, fan email and street team organisation software, and more. Additionally, they offer an ad-revenue sharing program with their users.

Creating an account gives you a profile page similar to MySpace but lets you decide which features – widgets – to embed in your page. These widgets give you the ability to syndicate your profile information (your Reverbnation blog, your uploaded music, etc.) to other Web presences through the use of embeddable widgets. That way when you update at Reverbnation, the embedded widgets update your other sites automatically through RSS.

As we discussed earlier, the area of Web statistics is often neglected, however within Reverbnation, they offer robust, real-time stats that track how music uploaded to their system is heard, who is listening, and which fans are actually sharing it with their friends and posting it on their pages.

MESSAGE BOARDS

Also known as forums, bulletin boards or discussion boards, message boards allow users to discuss certain topics in an organised and, usually, open way. Most message boards require users to register before they are able to post. Registration generally includes an avatar but may require more branding features as well. We'll discuss message boards you will create for your own site and external message boards you will frequent.

BRANDING SUGGESTIONS

As with all Web presence sites your band registers with, you should brand your identity accordingly. If you have multiple band members registering at the same board, you should decide whether to do so individually or pool your exposure. If necessary, go back to your Brand Toolbox and create individually branded profiles that associate each member with your band. Use signature lines that include your website and tagline, since each post you make is an opportunity to promote yourself.

MESSAGE BOARD FOR YOUR BAND

One of the best ways to interact with your fan network is to provide a message board where they can discuss your band. But there's nothing lonelier than a message board with no posts. People tend to assume that low message board turnout means you don't have many fans, even if that's not the case. As a general rule: most read, very few post. It takes a very large registered base to get any significant amount of traffic and postings. Therefore, you should create a bulletin board if you are really popular and want to use it as another method of keeping fans on your site. So a message board is only a good idea once you've cultivated a large enough fan network to sustain it. For example, while Jonathan Coulton and Brad Sucks have active message boards, they've spent time building the necessary fan networks first.

Although having a message board provides a forum to converse with your fans, that's only one side of it. A message board also gives your fans an opportunity to network with one another. They're there to talk to you but also to interact with others that share their taste in music. Your band is the common denominator. Interaction between your fans only strengthens the network and ties them closer to you. This works best when it evolves naturally, when the creation of a message board is driven by your fan network rather than created by you in the hope of it sustaining itself. We recommend PHPBB (PHPBB.org) or BBPress (BBpress.org).

EXTERNAL MESSAGE BOARDS

Message boards dedicated to musicians are great places to seek advice, solve problems or keep up on the latest trends within the music industry. We belong to a few of these message boards and have learned a great deal over the years, been warned about certain scams and services and shared some of our own insight with others.

As we noted previously in Chapter 2: Your Network, great things can happen when musicians work together. One of the most fascinating and positive uses of message boards we've seen is musicians booking gigs for and with one another. Often bands will play in cities they're touring by simply asking other bands to let them open and create a double bill. This type of cooperation between musicians has only been possible since the advent of the Internet and we suspect there will be more. And there should be.

Know your audience. The musicians who frequent musician message boards will probably not be your fans. Our recommendation is to avoid promoting your music to other musicians in these venues.

We normally frequent DIYMusicManual.com, Just Plain Folks (jpfolks.com) and CD Baby (cdbaby.org).

VIRTUAL WORLDS

As virtual environments improve, the representation of a person in these systems has evolved from crude bitmaps into detailed, lifelike figures or avatars. Functionality for building, exploring and communicating within these worlds has grown increasingly complex and powerful.

There are two types of virtual worlds: game-based systems and social-interaction systems. While game-based systems such as World of Warcraft have millions of users, they are usually not a good place to promote your band (although you can certainly promote in the many message boards and on the many websites discussing the game). On the other hand, social-interaction systems such as Second Life (secondlife.com) and There.com have created many opportunities for musicians to meet and interact with their fans and make new ones. Since you're a global musician now, meeting, connecting and conversing with your entire worldwide fan network is difficult. Virtual worlds offer a solution to this problem.

We are on the cusp of fascinating new possibilities – an entirely new way for people to meet and interact using the Internet. These virtual worlds are still evolving but because of the large numbers of people involved, developments have been occurring quickly and in surprising ways. While we're going to briefly cover what has been done with these worlds to date, if you are computer-savvy, you should consider keeping updated about these environments and the possibilities that they represent by following some of the blogs devoted to the subject.

SECOND LIFE

Second Life is one of the more popular virtual worlds. One of the engines spurring its growth is the fact that Linden Lab, its creator, decided to allow users to own the intellectual property rights to anything they created within the world. This means that anything a user creates can be sold by that user for profit. This simple idea has given birth to a vibrant economy. Second Life has its own currency, the Linden Dollar, which can be exchanged into real-world currency. Some people have made large sums of real money selling virtual objects, providing virtual services or selling virtual real estate in Second Life.

Second Life users, or 'residents' as they are called, are represented as three-dimensional animated avatars that can be completely customised. It takes time and technical artistry to create a realistic avatar and other objects in this virtual world but thanks to Linden Lab's decision to give users the right to sell their creations, there are many residents who are happy to sell their creations to you for the right price.

Second Life mirrors real life. There is no game, per se. Rather, living your virtual life is about interaction, creation and site-seeing. Business and entertainment. As a result, it should come as no surprise that there's a space here for music and musicians. Musicians have created avatars of themselves, set up stores to sell their music and promoted themselves within this world by putting up virtual posters on virtual walls of virtual buildings. Events such as virtual CD releases and signings are frequent.

Some bands even perform music 'live' in this virtual environment – inviting their Second Life fans to meet them at a certain time and place and putting on a show. Hundreds of concerts have occurred there, including performances by Suzanne Vega and Jay-Z. Even virtual festivals such as 'Woodstock Second Life' have taken place.

There are two ways to perform in Second Life. You can either stream your music (live or pre-recorded) while your avatars 'play' their virtual instruments according to pre-scripted motions or stream video and audio feeds of your band onto 'television screens' that other avatars can watch in-game. Both of these methods use streaming media servers to feed audio or video from your computer into the virtual world.

As technology and functionality improves in Second Life and other virtual world platforms, other methods of in-game performance are likely to be developed. Linden Lab suggests that anyone interested in running a Second Life concert should join the Live Music Enthusiasts Group that exists in-game. The two streaming services that work in-game in Second Life are ShoutCast (shoutcast.com) and IceCast (icecast.org).

MICRO-BLOGGING

While blogging is primarily a broadcast method of communication, its little brother, micro-blogging, encourages conversation. Micro-blog sites allow you to post very short messages about what's on your mind or what you're doing at that particular moment. In general, these posts are public and shared with all users on a timeline (though these services usually allow you to keep posts private as well). Micro-blogs also have 'friend' functionality that allows you to specifically follow the posts of others and, conversely, allows them to follow you.

This public and friend functionality makes this a great way for bands to keep in touch with others, promote themselves and their projects, share ideas and links with friends and otherwise personalise their band and stay connected to their fan network. But it shouldn't be reserved just for your fans. We often follow the micro-blogs of all our friends and acquaintances within our skill and opportunity networks as well, just to see what they're up to and what they think is important. In our case, we've used this to find new opportunities for our music, because some of our friends are podcasters, artists, musicians or other bright and creative people.

To ensure short posts, micro-blogging tools restrict the number of characters you can write. For example, one of the more popular micro-blogging sites, Twitter.com, restricts its users to posts of 140 characters, which happens to be the maximum length of a mobile text message. This encourages users to post from their phones wherever they go.

As an example, if you're interested in knowing what *we're* doing at this very moment, it's as simple as checking out twitter.com/beatnikturtle. We've also embedded our latest Twitter posts or 'tweets', on the front page of BeatnikTurtle.com. We found that having this tool to help our networks stay up-to-date on what we're doing (recording, writing songs, working on the website, heading to gigs) humanises us and reminds everyone that we're real people. The more your fans see you working on your band and music, the more likely they are to assist, advise and support you (through sales or donations), since they know how hard you're working and how seriously you take the endeavour.

Beyond personalising our band, we've used Twitter to reach out for assistance. For example, we once wanted to get in touch with the music planning committee for a particular convention at which we wanted to perform. We knew that some of the people who followed our posts were associated with that convention, so we posted our query on Twitter. Within minutes, they put us directly in touch.

We've also found a creative way of using Twitter beyond its networking capabilities. Reading our friends' posts, it occurred to us that a lot of the more witty tweets might make great lyrics. We soon started writing a few 'TwitterSongs', all appropriately shorter than 140 seconds and posting them to TheSongOfTheDay.com.

For example, we wrote a song called, 'I Am My Mom And Dad's Tech Support' based on a posted lament by one of our friends. Naturally, once a TwitterSong song was posted, we'd tweet about it and include a link to the file. Many times the micro-bloggers who'd inspired the songs would get a kick out of them and further promote the song by telling their network and blogging about it at their personal websites. The next thing we knew, we'd get more friend requests and many people hoping their own tweets would inspire the next TwitterSong.

As with all your Web presence tools, you'll need to properly brand your account. The advantage to micro-blogging is that it keeps you and your music in front of people on a daily, even hourly basis. In many ways we find this constant, bite-sized way of keeping everyone updated on our band is less time-consuming and more useful than newsletters. Of course, not everyone cares for micro-blogs, so it's simply one more way to present your band to the world.

MICRO-BLOG SITES

There are a few micro-blogging sites that you should consider. None of them is mutually exclusive and all vary in functionality. We encourage you to check these popular ones out:

- **Twitter** (twitter.com)
- **Jaiku** (jaiku.com)
- **Tumblr** (tumblr.com)
- **Pownce** (pownce.com)
- **Utterz** (utterz.com) Note: while the others above are text-based, Utterz is audio-based.

SURVEY SITES

Occasionally, you may want to survey your fan network. This can provide insight into who's listening, help assess how you're doing so far and suggest future goals for your band.

Questions you may want to ask include:

- Demographic information.
- How did you hear about us?
- What other bands and musicians do you enjoy?
- Where are you located?
- What's one thing you would change about our website?
- If we came to your town, would you attend a show?
- Do you have any ideas to help us spread the word?
- Do you have any other suggestions for us?

Some blogs offer built-in polling functionality. Additionally, there are sites that allow you to create surveys, embed them on your site and interpret the data. To encourage people to take the poll, we suggest offering something in return for participating such as a free song, remix or live recording.

If you don't mind your fans being advertised to then some free survey sites include Free Online Surveys (freeonlinesurveys.com), SurveyMethods (surveymethods.com) and MisterPoll (misterpoll.com). If you want to tailor the look and feel of the survey for your fans, then you may wish to use these pay sites: SurveyMonkey (surveymonkey.com) or Zoomerang (zoomerrang.com).

▶▶COLLABORATING

The Web provides some wonderful and exciting tools to collaborate not only with your skill, opportunity and fan networks but also with the other members of your band.

EMAIL

If you're anything like us, whenever you're not rehearsing, meeting, recording or touring, you take the conversation online. Discussing the band and its business over email helps keep your band in sync. While band meetings are where you might decide on larger goals, email is where you will divide up the tasks, discuss strategies or plan out the details of the next gig, rehearsal or recording session. If you do a lot of talking with your band over email, we recommend using a listserv. A listserv is a single email address that will send copies of each email to all members on the list.

The benefits of a listserv include:

- **It's convenient:** If you want to write everyone in your band, you no longer have to add them to the **To:** field manually.
- **It's inclusive:** Emailing the listserv address automatically emails everyone on the list once you hit 'Send'. No band members are accidentally left out.
- **It keeps a history:** All the conversations and threads on the listserv are archived. If a great idea is sent to the list, it's always retrievable.
- **It's easy to add and remove members:** Most listserv programs are simple to administrate.

We've relied on an open source listserv called Mailman (gnu.org/software/mailman/) for years since we're a large band with members living and working at different locations of the city. This became even more important as we worked on TheSongOfTheDay.com, allowing us to add other musicians around the country that we wanted to create and record with. To keep things simple, we created a new list for that purpose.

Ideally, your Web host should provide such functionality. If not, you can use free solutions such as Yahoo! Groups, Google Groups or others. These provide an email solution that works essentially like a listserv, as well as providing file-sharing and calendar-sharing features that can come in handy as well.

GOOGLE APPLICATIONS

Google offers many free Web-based services including word processing, spreadsheet functionality, calendars and more. And they're all designed for collaboration. Unlike software installed on a band member's computer, they're available 24/7, any time any member has access to the Internet. When we were busy creating, mixing, mastering, tagging and uploading songs for TheSong-OfTheDay.com, we relied on Google's spreadsheets to help our band collectively organise and manage the project. We created drafts of press releases in their word processor and shared with other members to review and edit. Using these tools helped us manage projects that would have been much more troublesome over phone and email.

SKYPE

Skype.com is a free program and service that basically transforms your computer into a phone. But unlike a regular telephone, Skype is a robust communication tool with digital clarity that can be used to collaborate in surprising ways. We've used it for most of the interviews we've done with podcasters. It's easy to record Skype audio and import it directly into their episodes. We've also used it to demo music to one another, talk through songs or projects with the band and even – when the songs call for it – record vocals (giving a new definition to 'phoning it in').

Skype goes beyond just audio. Skype's chat- and file-transfer features have been helpful as well. Often, we'll Skype each other from our respective homes to collaborate on the band's websites, press materials or even this book, for hours on end. Being able to share files, cut and paste text, throw hyperlinks to one another and set up a quick video chat as we're talking things out is extremely helpful.

BOOKING TOOLS

Web services such as Eventful (eventful.com) have helped revolutionise the way to tour. Touring can be expensive and time-consuming. However, rather than touring in concentric circles (or on a whim) based on your physical location and growing your fan network that way, Eventful provides the tools for you to find out exactly where your fans on the Internet are and whether they'll come to a show if you travel to where they're located. If you're a gigging musician, the Eventful Demand widget is a tool to incorporate into your Web sites and Web presences so fans can tell you where they're located. In other words, your fans can help you book and target your tours. We'll talk more about Eventful and the free tools they provide in Chapter 9: Get Booked and Play Live.

SOCIAL-NETWORKING TOOLS

The Long Tail predicts an infinite number of social networks. So, while there are a few big players in this space (MySpace, Facebook, Bebo), there's nothing stopping you from creating one with all the same features for your band or your fans. Ning allows you to create your own free social-networking site and Web presence at Ning.com. You can choose to keep it private (for instance, if you want to reserve it as a collaboration tool for members of the band or as a platform to mobilise your fan street team) or public. Ning allows you flexibility in the design of your social-network site – allowing you to add photos, music, a forum, etc., as well as import or embed other Web services such as photos from your Flickr account. And, like all social-networking sites, it fosters communication between the members and keeps track of the activity within the network.

INVITATION SOFTWARE

Any band that plays live knows that there are always some people who promise to come to a gig only to be a no-show. When you absolutely need a minimum number of people to show up at an important performance, use invitation software to gauge the numbers. Formally requesting people's presence this way often raises the stakes and encourages those who commit to actually come to the show.

The most popular invitation site is Evite (evite.com). It's easy to set up an event, design the invite and send out invitations to a large list of people. Don't settle on the invite templates they suggest; brand your Evite accordingly. Evite is ubiquitous, so most spam filters don't usually block it. Keep in mind, however, that Evite makes the email addresses of your invitees visible to all. This means that, if you're using your mailing list (rather than making a list of people you know personally), you may be in violation of your privacy policy. The way around this is to either restrict your Evites to people you know personally or to revise your privacy policy to include the use of Evite and similar services.

We've never used Evite to announce shows to our mailing list. Instead, we've found it useful for planning some of the smaller events we've done, including band events such as video shoots. Other bands we know have used it as a way to spark interest in a particular show. Naturally, this technique should be reserved only for your most important events. If you abuse this method, it will probably stop working for you.

MUSIC COLLABORATION SITES

Some musicians – even some who have never met in person – use the Web to collaborate and create music by trading WAV files with one another to build songs. For instance, one might record a bass line and allow others to layer in the drums or vocals. We'll talk more about music collaboration sites in Chapter 6: Your Albums and Merchandise.

DIYMUSICMANUAL.COM

Our personal favourite of course is DIYMusicManual.com. Think of it as the musician's back office. While this book can explain the hows, whys and what-to-dos, DIYMusicManual.com can show you where to go and who to talk to. Not only does it contain all the links mentioned in this book, it's here where you can keep up to date with all the useful resources, services and tools that can help you get your music out there and win fans. Most importantly, it's where you'll find other motivated musicians like yourself to network with.

▶▶CHAPTER SIX

YOUR ALBUMS AND MERCHANDISE

Before you need to worry about getting heard, getting publicity and getting distributed, you'll need to record some music, possibly press an album and create merchandise so that you can take advantage of all the attention you have drummed up. In this chapter, we'll cover how to record music, how to replicate CDs and how to create and sell merchandise.

▶▶RECORDING AND MASTERING

In this day and age, it's extremely likely you'll be recording music at some point. Recording is, of course, a broad topic that fills many books. It's also one where the technology is mutating rapidly, with new tools and techniques appearing all the time. The *Manual* will cover the recording issues you'll have to deal with no matter what techniques you're using. For example, we'll cover whether you should record yourself or hire others to record you in a studio. We'll tell you how to minimise recording time and keep costs down. We'll also talk about the recording process in general, because most detailed recording books gloss over this topic. Finally, we're going to talk about mastering, which is perhaps the most misunderstood part of the recording process.

If you want to learn more about recording, we suggest checking out DIYMusicManual.com as well as *The S.M.A.R.T. Manual to Mixing and Mastering Audio Recordings* by Bill Gibson or *The Mixing Engineer's Handbook* by Bobby Owsinski.

IT'S THE SOURCE THAT MATTERS

John Lisiecki, a recording engineer for Chicago's Millennium Park with years of experience recording everything from rock bands to symphony orchestras, says that what most musicians forget is 'it's the source that matters'. This may seem obvious but we can't stress it enough: no amount of recording technology will help you if the source isn't good. This includes the following:

- **The songs:** Ever hear a great song recorded by a punk band using a tape recorder in their garage? The music is king and the sound quality is just a detail. Our advice is to write and record a lot of songs to give your creative process momentum. Your quality will rise with the quantity.
- **The musicians:** Your band members' sense of rhythm, style and musicianship will show through instantly when you record. If you're having trouble, just remember this rule of thumb: 'in time and in tune'. Anything that at least meets this standard will help make a decent song. That isn't to say that an out-of-tune song with bad timing won't be charming sometimes but it certainly doesn't help.
- **The instruments:** The quality of your musical instruments doesn't tend to matter as much for live performances as it does on a recording. Pay special attention to the maintenance of your instruments before recording: replace strings, reeds and the like as necessary, use top-quality wires and make sure to lock down anything on your instruments which might make extraneous noise. For drums, pay attention to the tuning of the drums and consider using fresh heads at the start of a big session.

HOME STUDIO RECORDING VS PROFESSIONAL STUDIO RECORDING

The first decision regarding recording is whether to do it yourself or hire a professional studio and engineer. Quality sound-recording equipment and software has become inexpensive enough that a home studio is in the reach of almost every single band. In fact, by the time you've paid the average professional studio to record just one album, you've probably spent the equivalent of a very capable studio set-up for your house, one where you could have recorded as many songs as you'd ever want. We will go over the pros and cons of each option below.

HOME STUDIO RECORDING VS PROFESSIONAL STUDIO RECORDING

	Home Studio	Professional Studio
Cost	More expensive initial outlay but very cheap to maintain thereafter.	Can pay by the hour to avoid an initial outlay but you must pay each time you want to record.
Time	No time pressure for recording sessions, so you have time to write music on the fly and be creative. But you must spend time learning the software and recording techniques.	Time pressure for each session because you are 'on the meter', but professional engineers usually do it right the first time and you can leverage their expertise.
Convenience & creativity	You can make recording part of your creative process for the ultimate flexibility. You can also work on projects whenever you want.	You can focus on the music, rather than worry about the recording process.

HOME RECORDING

Setting up a home studio can be quite inexpensive if you just want to try recording yourself. You can get a decent quality microphone for under £150. Headphones are very cheap and the recording software Audacity (audacity.sourceforge.net) is free and available for all operating systems. On Apple systems, GarageBand is a capable recording solution, perfect for getting your feet wet. You can also get a standalone digital recording device if you don't have a computer or if your existing computer doesn't have the necessary horsepower for multi-track recording.

Bands that have their own studios tend to be more prolific because they can do it all 'in-house'. This can be an advantage for bands, because coming out with new music regularly keeps your fans engaged with you. There are other advantages as well. You can:

- Produce and release new music whenever you feel a creative spark
- Easily create remixes of your music
- Produce different versions of your songs including instrumentals, loops and samples that can be used for other purposes such as podcasts, promos and ringtones

- Record and edit professional-quality podcasts
- Work on audio tracks for film and video projects
- If you have a portable recording solution, you can record live versions of your music to provide new content for your website

We have four different band members with studios of their own. We trade source files between members so we can work on our music in more than one location, dividing up the workload and speeding up our output.

If you decide to record music yourself but don't have experience, we recommend reading some books on the subject so you can get the best sound. At the very least, you'll want to learn basic recording concepts such as microphone placement, compression, EQ and using other audio effects.

BUILDING A HOME STUDIO

When it comes to setting up a home studio, Lisiecki advises, 'It's the ends that matter. Everything else is a religious question.' His advice is to spend your money on the best microphones you can buy and the best monitors so you can hear exactly what you captured. The middle part (mixer, cables, recorder and so on) can be whatever you'd like it to be and the particulars are often debated. If you build a studio from scratch or you want to improve your studio, remember that the ends are what you need to spend money on first.

Other details to build a successful home studio:

- The room and how it affects the sound will likely be caught in the microphone along with the song, so make sure that the room is either dead (carpeted or otherwise insulated) or that it has a sound that you can live with.
- Have a variety of instruments and inexpensive musical toys handy, because you never know when you'll want to add a tambourine, harmonica, rain stick or some other unusual sound to add texture to a track. These little touches can make a big difference.
- Remove everything from the room that might cause extraneous noise (mobiles, telephones, snare drums that aren't locked down, dogs, etc.).

The rest of your home studio needs to be chosen based on the technologies that will meet your needs best. Fortunately, you can do this piecemeal. We recommend building a home studio slowly by just getting the pieces that you need and learning each new one as you go forward. Professional recording equipment can be overwhelming at first, so it's worth your time to learn it one piece at a time. You can replace parts of your studio that you want to upgrade as you go forward.

Most recording books will have other specific pieces of advice as it relates to recording particular instruments and we suggest that you read up on the latest when you go to build your studio. DIYMusicManual.com has information to help get you started as well should you decide to build your own.

PROFESSIONAL RECORDING

A professional recording studio has some nice advantages. They usually have a broad selection of microphones, sound processors, amps, instruments and rooms to get the best recording possible.

When you rent studio time, some of them won't let you even touch the knobs (or studio computer), so you'll be depending on your engineer to record your tracks. Many bands are happy to have a professional handle the engineering. Others may want to be more hands-on, in which case they may want to consider a home studio instead.

At a professional studio, you should always stay involved during the mixdown process. Quite a few decisions get made during mixdown, including which effects will get added to the tracks. Also, sometimes tracks are left out of the final mixdown and you'll want to be on hand to make these creative decisions.

The studio will probably have a contract that specifies the hourly fee you'll have to pay for your time. Make sure that the contract doesn't give them any rights to your music. You should own the copyrights and the master recordings for all your songs. If they try putting something like that in the contract, you'll want to go somewhere else.

SAVING MONEY AT PROFESSIONAL RECORDING SESSIONS

At a recording session, time literally equals money. Here are some simple methods for saving both:

- **Rehearse for your session:** The best way to minimise your recording time is to practise for your session the same way that you'd practise for a live show.
- **Bring extras of everything:** You get charged for the time it takes to go to the store for a battery for your pedal. Take care of logistics ahead of time to save money. Bring extra strings, batteries, cables, tuners, AC plugs, power strips, reeds, tools and anything else that you may need for your performance.

- **Prepare your instruments for recording:** Get new drum heads, break in strings and make sure all of your instruments are ready to go for your session.
- **Tune your drums:** Or find someone that knows how to do it for you.
- **Use *one* tuner:** All of the instruments in the band should use the same tuner, for accuracy.

PRODUCERS

Producers fill a somewhat misunderstood role in the recording process. You don't have to get a producer and in fact many bands make do without one. But there are some advantages.

If you hire a professional producer, sometimes they'll work for a cut of the album sales. In the somewhat standard industry contracts, their cut comes out of the royalties before the band sees its own. If you decide to work with one, make sure that your financial arrangement is both clear and acceptable to you. And be especially careful if they want a copyright interest in your songs or sound recordings.

Of course, in today's world, you might be able to get a producer willing to work for a flat fee. And we'd recommend this if possible.

THE ROLE OF A PRODUCER

A music producer is not the same as a film producer, which is where the confusion often comes in. If an album were a film, a producer would be a director. The producers are usually in the control room during a recording and will help manage the recording session. A good producer will help realise the full creative potential of the music.

Producer Michael Freeman, who has been in the recording business for decades, explains that the while a live performance is something that is only played and heard once, a studio album is meant to be heard over and over again. Pitch, metre, tuning, energy and feeling all matter a great deal during the sessions and bands need to be aware that it's a different process.

Freeman's advice to bands is to 'find a producer that understands your music. Ask yourself, does he or she "get it".' In fact, Freeman says that he spends a month or more working with the band in rehearsals on the songs to prepare for the recording before even setting foot in the studio. It's during this preparation period where producer and band decide how they are going to play the songs for the recording and agree on what their vision for the album is, so that everyone involved can make the best decisions about instruments, arrangements and recording decisions.

Some other examples of what a producer does for your band include:

- Help decide what kind of sound to aim for, as well as suggest which kind of microphones and recording styles.
- Arrange the songs to be more effective. For example, a producer might suggest that the song start with a chorus, rather than the first verse.
- Come up with ideas for extra parts or different sounds to give a song direction. For example, you might hear: 'That's good – but what if you played it *this* way...' Freeman's advice on this is to at least try out suggestions that producers make, even if you don't initially like the idea.
- Supervise the mixdown and mastering process.
- Help manage the entire process so you can stay focused on creating and performing the music.

Naturally, many bands do this for themselves in a recording situation, especially when they have their own studios. But even if you do, you should be aware of all of the work that a producer puts in to make a quality recording. You should be prepared to do the same work if you want the same, high-quality result.

You must feel comfortable working with your producer, since you'll be including them in every step of the creative process. In fact, they may take your recording in directions that you don't want to go. John Lisiecki says, 'The best producers will help you realise your creative vision. Not theirs.' If it starts becoming a question of your sound versus their sound, you may decide to find another producer.

RECORDING RESOURCES WITHIN YOUR ARM'S REACH

Thanks to technological advances, there are a dazzling array of new resources for making recordings.

SAMPLES AND LOOPS

With the right combination of samples and loops, you can create the illusion of a full band backing you or just enhance tracks with that little something extra that they need. While these tools have been around for a long time, there are many new sources that will sell them royalty-free. These sources, all over the Internet, can add new dimensions to your music.

The key to using these tools is to make sure that that the licence is pre-cleared and royalty-free. If it isn't, you can end up with a legal nightmare later on. Be sure to read the agreements carefully before buying or using them.

Some for-pay sample sources include Drums On Demand (drumsonde-mand.com), East West Samples (eastwestsamples.com) and Acid Planet (acid-planet.com). And for free material licensed under Creative Commons check out ccMixter (ccmixter.org). Additionally, the Creative Commons site (creative-commons.org) allows you to search multiple sites for pre-licensed material that can be incorporated into your music. Keep in mind that while much of the samples and loops may be free for non-profit use, you might have to contact the musicians if you want to sell tracks with their material. See Chapter 7: Your Rights for more information about Creative Commons licences.

For a current list of sample and loop resources, head to DIYMusicManual.com.

COLLABORATIONS WITH OTHER MUSICIANS ONLINE

Some musicians have taken to recording on each other's songs by sharing source tracks with one other over the Web. This is as simple as posting indi-vidual tracks to a forum online for others to add to or adding to other people's tracks. Sometimes, entire songs are written one track at a time. One might record a bass part. Another might record drums. And before long, there's a song with vocals and even background vocals by entirely different singers. All of this done by musicians that have usually never met each other.

Additionally, some musicians (with good bandwidth) meet online and jam in real time or write songs together. You are no longer limited to finding musi-cians in your area to jam with. Some collaboration sites include eJamming (ejamming.com) and JamGlue (jamglue.com). However, for a current listing of collaboration sites, visit DIYMusicManual.com.

VIRTUAL RECORDING SESSIONS

Thanks to the Internet, a musician can record a part for you anywhere in the world. The files are simply transferred over the Internet and merged into the song on your end.

The process usually works like this:

1. Send the musician a rough mixdown of the song in MP3 format, with an explanation of what you're looking for.
2. The musician records a track in sync with the mixdown and sends you an MP3 so you can hear how it sounds.
3. You offer notes on any necessary changes.
4. The musician records a final version and sends you a WAV file with their track.

You can also do this 'live' in the following manner:

1. Send the musician a rough mixdown WAV of the song.
2. Contact them using Skype.com or over the phone.
3. Direct the musician as he or she performs through the part.
4. Have the musician send you a WAV file of his or her recording.

The good news is that you can use these techniques with any musician in the world, if they're willing. You could even start a band where none of the band members live in the same city.

VIRTUAL MUSICIANS FOR HIRE
Using the methods that we just discussed above, professional studios and session players have gone virtual. This can be done for a fraction of the cost of an in-person session player. This goes beyond just getting a bass player or a drummer for a song. You can hire brass sections, wind ensembles, vocalists or people who play rare ethnic instruments. The possibilities are endless – for a fee. And the service goes beyond musicians. You can even hire engineers to mix or master your songs.

Don't forget that if you're a skilled instrumentalist, you too can be a session player. These websites and services always need different types of musicians handy and some virtual session players make some decent money on the side.

Note that you can get some *very* well-known studio musicians to record a track for you at a reasonable rate. There's a world of talent out there that you can tap into at services like ESession (esession.com), Session Players (session-players.com) and DrumsForYou (drumsforyou.com). A complete list can be found at DIYMusicManual.com.

⏩MASTERING

Mastering is a frequently misunderstood process, perhaps because it's much easier to hear its effects than to describe them. In fact, the difference between a mastered track and one that hasn't been mastered can be dramatic. We've had mastering houses offer to master one track for free, just so that we could hear the difference. They would only charge us if we liked it and decided to use it. If you can find a mastering house that makes the same kind of offer, we'd recommend it so that you can at least hear what the mastering process does. You'll probably be surprised.

MASTERING DEFINED

Mastering is best described as the finishing process for music recording. It normally happens after an album has been mixed down but before it is sent to a CD printing house or sold online.

Mastering involves the following processes:

- **Powerful and targeted EQ:** The mastering house will apply EQ (boost or reduce certain sound frequencies) to the entire recording rather than just the individual tracks, which happens during mixdown. They also EQ the songs in relation to each other, so that they share a common sound. A mastering house can bring out qualities in your recording you didn't even know were there.
- **Compression/limiting:** Mastering houses usually apply some compression (normalise levels) and limiting (prevent clipping) to the whole album, rather than on individual tracks. This again helps the entire album develop a consistent sound, rather than having some tracks stand out.
- **Volume normalisation:** Well-mastered albums don't have huge volume differences between tracks. During mixdown, each song is simply mixed at volume levels appropriate for itself, not in comparison to other tracks. Mastering makes the album into a coherent whole and puts all of the songs into the same dynamic range.
- **Track arrangement:** Details such as the ordering of tracks, as well as the connections and spacing between the tracks, are done during mastering. Mastering houses will often put a final volume drop-off at the end of a track to control how the album flows from one song to another.
- **Sound smoothing:** Mastering houses usually have a few vacuum-tube-based systems that can 'warm up' a digital recording, which might sound harsh and cold without some analogue equipment to smooth it out.
- **Crowd noise:** Because live albums are often put together in a way that eliminates waiting and silences in between tracks, the crowd noise might be added or inserted between tracks during mastering.

Most indie bands master their own work and you can do too if you want to learn the process. But as Michael Freeman suggests, you should never use the same person for mixdown and mastering. This guarantees a fresh perspective. The thinking is akin to book writing – while the author (band) writes the words and the editor (producer) shapes the overall tone and structure, they both let a copy-editor (mastering engineer) come in to do the detailed work to make the language flow. So a professional mastering house is often worth the money.

Surprisingly, mastering is a speciality and many mastering engineers don't do recording or mixdown work but focus on mastering alone. They can make a good album sound great. And when your recording sounds professional, you've raised the odds of getting it noticed by fans and licensed. Mastering is useful whether you record in your home studio or use a professional one, so although many indie musicians consider this process is unnecessary and skip it, they aren't doing themselves any favours.

In this day of the single, it's still worth mentioning that mastering plays a significant role in making a collection of songs into an album. Creating a group of songs adds an entirely new dimension to the process.

SAVING MONEY WITH PROFESSIONAL MASTERING STUDIOS

Hiring a mastering engineer is not a cheap process. In fact, it can easily cost over £100 an hour. Therefore, you want to get the most out of every minute of your mastering session. Use these techniques to save yourself time and money:

FINISH MIXDOWN FIRST

Listen to your mixdown over and over again at different sessions and in different environments. Play it for different people, especially other musicians, and ask for feedback. Freeman suggests that you make a instrumental mix, a vocals mix and a mix with both and try it out in different environments to make sure that mixdown goes well.

A mastering engineer usually can't fix a track that's mixed too loudly in relation to the others – that's only possible during mixdown. Although they can draw on a surprising variety of tricks, do not depend on them to fix any mixdown mistakes such as a vocal set too low. Some mastering houses will ask you to mixdown your songs with the vocals on a separate track so that they can combine these tracks and ensure that the vocals are heard above the mix. Also, you should leave yourself 'headroom'. If you mixdown a track close to 0db (the highest limit of a digital track) you'll handcuff your mastering engineer. As any mastering engineer would say: let me worry about making your songs and album as loud as other recordings.

BRING THE RIGHT FORMATS

Confirm with the mastering house which formats they require. Make sure you bring them what they can use, whether it's WAV files, CDs or something else. It's very expensive to schedule a session and then have the music arrive in the wrong format. (Note: The right answer is *never* MP3 files. MP3 is a lossy, low-quality version of your recording. A mastering house can't do anything with an MP3 file.)

PLAN THE TRACK ORDER AHEAD OF TIME

Decide on the track order before going to the mastering house and bring a written list. Debating the order among your members while the engineer is on the clock is a waste of money.

DON'T CLIP THE TRACK

Mastering houses like the space and noise found before and after a track, because it gives them a sound floor to analyse before the music starts. They will clip the tracks to the exact length and get rid of the junk during the process.

▶▶MANUFACTURING A CD

THE CD IS DYING

Musicians don't make money selling CDs.

You may be thinking, 'Excuse me, but I just bought a CD the other day.' Or, 'I just sold a CD to a fan at a show, so you're way off.'

But what you bought at the store and what you sold to your fan wasn't a CD. It was music. It just happened to be stored on a shiny piece of plastic, usually in a plastic case.

Why should you care about this distinction? Well, this section discusses how to duplicate or replicate (there's a difference!) hundreds or thousands of discs for yourself. What you have to decide is whether it's worth the money and effort. Although there's always a need for more music in this world, there's already plenty of plastic.

The truth is, the CD is dying, if not already dead. It's just a floppy disk full of music, a convenient way to hand someone your songs. It will certainly always exist, just like 8-tracks and records still exist. And there are currently a tremendous number of CD players in the world, so the infrastructure will be around for a while. But in the end people are just not going to the store to buy larger and fancier CD display racks any more; they're buying larger and more capable

MP3 players. And while there are certainly plenty of CDs still sold every day, the irony is that young people, the ones most likely to be interested in new music, are the ones least interested in buying CDs. They'd rather just have the songs in digital form. CD sales are headed down over the long term.

Once music is pure data, released from a physical object, it becomes vastly easier to store, organise and share, allowing people to make as many perfect copies as they want. If you live in Chicago, as we do, selling a CD to someone in the UK involves trucks, planes and middlemen. But we make sales to the UK all the time thanks to digital music services, with no vehicles involved and a minimum number of middlemen. We can sell a million songs from just one original.

From the phonograph to the cassette tape to the CD, when music is stored on a physical object, a few songs have to be chosen to be grouped together into 'an album'. This concept isn't necessary any more and while it certainly isn't obsolete, the definition of an album is going to become increasingly fuzzy. This will profoundly affect how you release your music in the future.

So if the CD is dying, how do you decide whether to make any or how many to print if you do?

CD OR NOT CD, THAT IS THE QUESTION

The decision comes down to money and PR and the PR reason needs to go first because it's a perception issue that may be worth the money. Today, some media outlets want an MP3 and some still want a CD. Others will ask for the MP3 first and then ask for a CD if they like what they hear. They don't want those pieces of plastic unless it's necessary.

Once you get past that initial gatekeeper with an amazing MP3, imagine them holding a CD in their hand. Do you want them holding a CD-R purchased at your local office supply store with marker written on the face? And do you want the CD cover to come from your home printer? Or do you want a professionally labelled and packaged disc?

Unfortunately, PR is exclusively about how things look. And while some in the press don't care if they're given a CD-R, many do. A professionally made CD shows that you take your music seriously because you've put money behind it. This will help them take it seriously too.

The alternative is to do it yourself. You should consider this before going to a CD printing house. Print-on-CD printers are getting very good and you can always have the covers printed at a copy store to get that glossy, professional look. But here's where the money comes in: figure out how much it costs you per CD when you do this. Printers, ink, glossy copying costs and empty CD jewel cases cost money and the per-disc cost may not be low. It's also a time-consuming process.

Once you have that per-disc cost, you should figure out how many you think you can sell at what price to your fans. Your CD sales will most likely be at shows and person to person. This is where the floppy-disk full of music comes in; it's where you need to have a way to hand people the music, losing a sale otherwise.

Now decide how many promotional CDs you'll need. Based on this, you need to determine whether it's worth the printing costs.

For example, we had one disc where we wanted to send 200 promos and even if we'd had no sales at all, we would have saved money by doing a 1000-copy run as opposed to making 200 handmade promotional copies. We'll have more information about the costs of using a CD printing house below so that you will be able to make an informed decision on costs.

Finally, it is worth noting that if you want to get a song played on the radio, especially commercial radio, a professionally printed CD is mandatory. Please read the section in Chapter 11: Get Played and Heard on getting played on the radio before making this decision because a radio campaign is not for everyone. Just because you'd *like* to get played on commercial radio – we all would! – doesn't mean you want to go through the enormous expense. If you are willing to spend enough to do a commercial radio campaign, a CD printing is the least of your costs and you should just go ahead and do a print run.

THE ALL-IMPORTANT CASE

Whether you make CDs on your own or have a CD printing house do it, the CD case that you use is actually very important. The CD libraries used by journalists, reviewers and radio stations are based around the size of a standard CD jewel case. Although there are slim cases, folders and other interesting choices, none of those work well in a standard library. You need to make it as simple as possible for these people to handle your music, so the best choice is a standard case.

Of course, every rule is made to be broken. George Hrab, an indie musician whom we've mentioned previously, has done a fantastic job packaging his CDs, making each album unique. For example, one of them comes in a tin box, another in an embossed paper sleeve and another in a large DVD-style box. Each one stands out as a piece of art, giving his fans a genuine reason to buy the physical disc as merchandise, not just a music-holder. His covers also tend to pique reviewers' curiosity enough to get them to pick it up simply because it's different. His sales have benefited from this unique approach.

AN ALTERNATIVE WAY TO MAKE CDS: PRINT ON DEMAND

One of the latest developments affecting the book publishing industry is print on demand, offered by companies like Lulu.com. Authors can upload a PDF of their book at no cost to themselves and when someone orders a copy, one is professionally printed, bound and sent on its way. While each book costs more than one that is made in a mass printing, any book done this way is profitable from the very first unit sold because there's no initial outlay.

A similar service is available for music CDs. In our estimates, the cost per CD is higher than doing it yourself by hand, which is why this method hasn't caught on very well. But these companies handle ordering, shipping and other services and at the very least can be used for rather expensive demo CDs or very short runs of physical-sale CDs. Mainly, though, they're used for profit-only online CD sales. Since online CD sales include the cost of shipping to stock the CDs at sales outlets, these costs can become comparable to printing your own and might make the CD-on-demand option worthwhile in certain circumstances.

STEPS FOR YOUR CD PRINT RUN

A CD print run is a laborious process, so it helps to plan out what you need to do ahead of time. The most time-intensive parts of making a CD are art related, so if you can't handle it yourself, get help from a graphic artist from your skill network if at all possible.

Before your print run:

1. Clear the legal status of all the music and art. (This can take the longest, so we list it first! We'll talk about this process in Chapter 7: Your Rights.)
2. Choose a CD printing house.
3. Decide whether to replicate or duplicate your disc.
4. Make a CD master.
5. Obtain a barcode.
6. Create the album art.
7. Write the liner notes.
8. Get a proof (optional).

CLEAR THE LEGAL STATUS OF ALL THE MUSIC AND ART

The copyrights on all songs, loops, samples and art on a CD being manufactured must be cleared before going to the CD printing house. They will require you to sign a form affirming that you've cleared them. (See Chapter 7: Your Rights.)

CHOOSE A CD PRINTING HOUSE

There are numerous CD printing houses, large and small. Most houses offer different deals with a variety of features related to printing, barcodes, mastering and other details. These deals change often, so carefully consider the latest ones.

Small differences in money and services aside, a printing house's reputation is the most important thing to consider. To evaluate this, just check their reputation on the Web. Fortunately, musicians are not shy about complaining when they feel that they've been ripped off.

Note that, as you compare these houses, the listed costs don't represent the whole story. Here are other hidden costs to look out for:

- **Shipping:** You usually have to pay for shipping. When you print 1000 CDs or more, this can be a significant amount – CDs are heavy.
- **Glass master charges:** Some houses will charge you to create the glass master if you decide to get your disc replicated. Fortunately, once this is created, it can be used in future runs. (We discuss glass masters below.)
- **Film and preparation charges** Depending on how the house handles printing the folder panels and on-disc print, they may charge you film preparation charges.

There are many options for these services. For our own band, we've used manufacturers such as NWMedia (nwmedia.com), DiscMakers (discmakers.com) and DiskFaktory (diskfaktory.com) as they're based in the US. Due to shipping costs, however, your best bet is to find those in your area. For instance, in the UK, there's DiscWizards (discwizards.com), A1Duplication (a1duplication.co.uk) and DiscusGroup (discusgroup.co.uk). Additionally, some digital distributors offer CD manufactoring in the UK and European Union such as Tunecore (tunecore.com). Given the multitude of options available depending on your location, we have a complete list of manufacturers at DIYMusicManual.com.

REPLICATION OR DUPLICATION

Most people call the process of making a lot of CDs *duplication* but be careful once you decide to make a CD of your own because this term has a specific meaning to CD printing houses and you may want *replication* instead.

CD duplication is the mass printing of CD-Rs or Recordable CDs. The art in the jewel case and the on-disc print are usually the same but the disc itself is of a lower quality and doesn't last as long as a true replicated disc. The other disadvantage is that they may be unreadable in some CD players. The main advantage is that it's cheaper to make CD-Rs in short runs, usually 300 or less.

The CD replication process uses a glass master, which allows the CD house to create a much higher-quality product. This is the type of CD that you buy at the store from major label bands. There's no downside to going with CD replication other than the fact that most houses won't consider doing a run of less than 1000 discs and that sets the price point quite a bit higher than a duplication run.

The decision comes down to the number of discs you want to print. At this time, it generally makes sense to do a duplication run if you're doing just a few hundred but beyond that it makes monetary sense to jump to 1000, even though that might be far more than you need. Since they can be used in PR campaigns as well as giveaways, the extra discs will usually come in handy at some point.

MAKE A CD MASTER

If you use a professional mastering house, they will hand you everything you need to give a printing house. If you do the mastering yourself, note that there are varying standards for delivering a master to a CD printing house, so confirm beforehand what yours will need from you.

These standards were created by Koninklijke Philips Electronics N.V. (Royal Philips Electronics N.V.), usually known as Philips. They are coded according to the colours of the standards book that is being used while creating the CD. The one most often used is the Red Book standard, for normal audio CDs. The Orange Book, on the other hand, is for combined audio and data CDs.

If you use a Red Book standard, note that it can introduce errors. There are tracks of information that can be included on a master disc that some mastering programs will perform that can help the error-checking process.

If you have any questions about this, your CD printing house will be happy to answer them, because getting this right makes both your jobs easier.

OBTAIN A BARCODE

You will need a barcode for your CD, especially if you intend to sell it through the digital music services. Also, with a barcode, the CD can be tracked by the charting authorities. For more on sales tracking, see Chapter 10: Get Distributed and Sold. If you wish to add a barcode, you need the barcode during *this step*, before you do the artwork, because it needs to be incorporated into the art itself. Getting a barcode is fairly inexpensive and most houses will include one for free with the cost of the discs.

You can also get a barcode from an online store like CD Baby (which is where we get ours).

There is another rare alternative that you may wish to may consider, which is to sign up and get a vendor UPC code. Although this is more expensive, it allows you to have multiple product codes underneath it. You can then create product codes for each disc or product that you want to sell. Unfortunately, this comes at the cost of an annual fee. Information about this can be found at the official site for UPC codes: gs1.org/productssolutions/barcodes/.

CREATE THE ALBUM ART

The album art that you have to prepare depends on your choice of CD packaging. This can be a standard plastic case with a four-panel booklet or just a sleeve. You also need to decide whether to use colour or black-and-white. The CD printing house will give you the necessary templates.

Note that the album cover is the most important part of your album art, since this is the only image retained by online retailers and MP3 programs such as iTunes.

To get ideas for the art, pick up a few CDs from your own collection and look them over closely to see what elements appear on each panel. You'll be able to make better decisions about what goes where. A lot of musicians get creative during this process. You don't even have to write your band's name on the album if you don't want to, but we wouldn't recommend going that far. Only a few bands can manage a *White Album* (or a *Black Album*, for that matter).

What we do recommend is the following:

- Use a graphic artist from your skill network if you can't do it yourself.
- Use a palette of colours that go well together, using CMYK values in your art program. Remember that *printed* colours are sometimes different from *on-screen* colours. This is where Pantone numbers come in handy.
- Get permissions for any copyrighted materials that you use in your artwork. Remember that all photographs, including ones made of your own band by other photographers, are owned by the photographer and you will have to work out the rights if you want to use them on your album.
- Put a barcode on the back cover, usually in the lower right corner. When you obtain your barcode, it should be given to you as an EPS file.
- If you wish, you can use the Compact Disc logo on your CD if it follows the appropriate rules for usage of that logo. Those standards are owned by Philips. You can use the logo if your CD conforms to the one of the

standards, usually Red Book. Your CD printing house can tell you which standard has been met and should have the image available for you (it's also easy to find on the Internet). Using the Compact Disc logo image tends to make your CD look more official but there's no other good reason to use it if you don't want to go to the trouble.

■ Make a printed proof. We suggest actually putting it in a jewel case and showing it to as many people as you can. There's nothing more embarrassing than a mistake that has been reproduced 1000 times.

■ Check and then double-check the spelling and grammar of all the text on the CD art. We have a compilation CD in our personal collection from a Reggae label that says *Masteqrs of Reggae* on the side. Use a spell checker (and have your friends look at it as they'll have fresh eyes).

■ Make sure to account for bleeds. Usually, most templates suggest a bleed area of 30mm past the trim lines so that your image will look normal in case of small paper-cutting discrepancies. The templates will have a clearly marked bleed region that you should fill with your images or at least a solid colour.

Once this art is complete, you should carefully save the finished layered art files (not just the output file) in multiple locations and probably back it up in a safe location. You may need it again for a reprinting of your disc.

There are a few final items to consider when doing the art, depending on the printing package. You can use silkscreen with a few discrete colours, three-colour and even full-colour printing. You need to prepare the art accordingly, so follow the guidelines of the printing house carefully. The template requirements for these different options can be very specific. In particular, layering may make a big difference when discrete colours are used in the silkscreen process, because the layers tend to cover each other up.

Also, each panel may have different characteristics and it's not uncommon to do a full-colour front panel with a black-and-white inside panel. You or your graphic artist needs to take this into account. Keep in mind that not all images convert well to black-and-white from colour, so making a proof is an especially good idea if you need to do so.

WRITE THE LINER NOTES

When we made our first CD, we rooted through the liner notes of all the discs in our personal collections for ideas. We provide a list here of the various items that we ended up using to give you a place to start when writing your own liner notes. If you're a meticulous writer, these notes may take you a while. Do it in a word processor first, rather than directly into the art, because you'll want to revise it, share it with others for feedback, use the spell and grammar checker and print out copies for you and others to proof it, before turning it into tiny type for the CD.

There are no formal rules for this part, of course, and you don't need to include liner notes at all if you don't want to but most musicians have fun with them. Keep in mind that all of this information can also be re-purposed for your website.

Here's a small list of things you may want to include in the liner notes and in some cases various other places on the album art:

- Name of the band/artist
- Name of the album
- Lyrics
- Song titles and listing
- Song lengths/total playing times
- Copyright information for:
    - The author/publisher of each song
    - The affiliated performing rights organisation for each song
    - The sound recording
    - The art and photos
    - Cover songs, audio loops, samples, reprinted lyrics, artwork, photos, etc.
- Musicians for each track
- Instruments on each track
- Credits for producers, engineers, artwork design and photographers
- Thank you messages
- Mastering and recording studios used
- Band website and contact information
- Other albums and merchandise available
- Dates recorded
- And don't forget jokes…

We suggest repeating the copyright, credits and especially contact information on the back cover as well as in the liner notes. Also, your disc itself should repeat this information as well.

GET A PROOF (OPTIONAL)

Many houses charge extra for a full production proof but they are usually worth the money. As we said above, the last thing that you want to do is repeat a mistake 1000 times.

⏩MERCHANDISING

T-shirts, stickers, posters and other merchandise can be a major part of an artist's income. In fact, merchandise has only gained in importance thanks to recorded music becoming so easy to copy. Generally, people prefer buying merchandise from the band itself rather than seeking out fakes or pirated versions.

Fortunately, it's also never been easier to make, distribute and sell merchandise. There are numerous options available, including print-on-demand services that don't require you to spend money or house inventory. In fact, you can make money from the very first unit you sell.

YOUR BRAND AND MERCHANDISE

If you've managed to reach this point in the book without going through all of the preparation that we mentioned in Chapter 3: Your Brand, we're afraid that you can't put it off any longer. You will need your logo, colours, font and the rest of your Brand Toolbox to start making merchandise. We'll also be using the terminology that we introduced in that chapter, such as RGB and CMYK colours, rasterised and vectorised images and flattened and layered formats. Please go back to that chapter if you need a refresher, even if you use a graphic artist, because then you will have enough knowledge to at least discuss the issues with them, as well as with your manufacturer.

Many merchandise manufacturers will offer to convert layered vectorised files into the appropriate formats for their processes. If they want the flattened rasterised formats instead, carefully size the vector image to the exact dimensions first and use CMYK colouration, which is appropriate for colour printing. Resizing a rasterised image can cause serious distortions, so sizing first is particularly important. Also, this is where your use of Pantone colours for your Brand Toolbox images will come in handy and save you time, since most manufacturers work directly with such colours in their printing processes. If you haven't used Pantone colours, you may find yourself trying to find the closest Pantone matches for your colour scheme.

PRINT ON DEMAND VS KEEPING AN INVENTORY

Previously, to make T-shirts and other merchandise, you would have to print a certain minimum number to qualify for a volume discount at a manufacturer. Then you would have to keep that inventory on hand or pay for storage. Meanwhile, you would need to sell enough items in order to make back your original investment. Only after you'd sold enough to pay for the print run would you start actually making a profit. And if there's one thing that's difficult for indie bands, it's predicting how many people will want to buy their merchandise.

One positive trend for indie bands in recent years has been the rise of print-on-demand services. Typically, there is no initial cost. You upload images and they appear in a virtual storefront where your customers can select the one they want as well as the type of merchandise they'd like the image to appear on. The best print-on-demand services will show your customers what the item will look like with the image printed on it. Once your fans buy the item, the print-on-demand manufacturers make a single one and ship it directly to them.

Your profit depends on the price that you set. The print-on-demand store will charge a certain base price that builds in their profit and whatever you charge above this rate will be your net profit. Shipping is paid by the customer, so your profit per item is set.

There are a lot of benefits to print-on-demand services:

- No (or very low) up-front costs
- No inventory required
- You will profit from the very first sale
- The service will handle ordering and fulfilment
- You can try as many designs as you want and sell only the successful ones
- Many print-on-demand services have a range of products that can use the same image, so you can generate a storefront with clothing, coffee mugs, lunchboxes, calendars and other merchandise in just a few clicks

There are also a few downsides:

- The profit margin is far lower, so if you can sell a lot of units, volume manufacturing makes more sense
- If you want to sell the merchandise at your shows, you'll need to buy in advance and at cost, which is higher than had you created it at a volume discount
- Some of their financial arrangements are unusual, such as having a minimum required amount of profit before they pay you

Your volume manufacturers will give you a more consistent-looking product than the print-on-demand services. Fortunately, it's simple to buy a single item from the print-on-demand services to see how it will look. So, it might be worth your money to order one of your items to see how it looks.

YOUR MERCHANDISE
T-SHIRTS

A T-shirt with your logo on it not only makes for something unique to sell, it's also great advertising. Of course, to sell a lot of T-shirts, you should have a design that people will think is 'cool' to wear. So getting input from a lot of people can help you decide whether the design looks good and might sell. You can make T-shirt designs based on songs or your brand. Many musicians include or incorporate their website address on the T-shirt as well.

Once you have a design, you have a choice: go with a volume T-shirt printing store or use a print-on-demand service such as Cafepress (Cafepress.com), Zazzle (zazzle.com) or Spreadshirt (spreadshirt.com). If you decide to go with a volume T-shirt printing store, then you can go with a national chain or use a local one in your area. We highly recommend going local in that many of these stores have knowledgeable graphic artists on hand that can help you through the process. Best of all, though, you can actually see a physical proof and make revisions on the spot. As we've said above, you don't want to replicate the same mistake hundreds or thousands of times. Also, with a local store, they're more likely to hold your hand through the process. Plus, we discovered that the people who work at T-shirt stores tend to be in or know other bands. They are useful contacts to have.

One of the downsides to going with a volume T-shirt printing store is that you will need to print a range of sizes, colours and styles and you might guess wrong about which might sell the most. Plus, once you've made a design decision, it's set in stone or, rather, cotton. Obviously, this is where print-on-demand services excel since they offer flexibility. With them, you can offer your fans a variety of different designs, sizes, styles and colours of shirts to choose from.

STICKERS

Stickers are more effective than they have ever been in the past because you can put your website address on them. That website address can lead users to everything that your band has to offer. Of course, those stickers also reinforce your brand.

The best thing about stickers is that they are cheap enough to give away. They work well as incentives if you want something extra to give someone for buying an album or signing up to your mailing list. Stickers are a great way to keep your brand in front of people and can advertise your band to others. There are many services that make stickers, such as Stickerguy (stickerguy. com) and BandWear (bandwear.com) but a full listing of the current ones can be found at DIYMusicManual.com.

OTHER MERCHANDISE

Printing shops no longer limit you to the standard items that bands have sold in the past. Today, you can add your images to almost any item. To get an idea, you can see the variety of products available at a print-on-demand merchandise service such as Cafepress (cafepress.com) or a volume manufacturing solution such as BandWear (bandwear.com) or other services aimed at corporate clients such as PRstore (prstore.com) and Branders (branders.com).

We know of one musician, Frankendread, who used this branding technique well. Frankendread is a Caribbean musician from Chicago who tours across the country and plays many outdoor festivals. He decided that one way to make some extra money would be to sell bottled water at his performances, since most festivals occur in the summer and audience members get hot. However, selling bottled water wasn't enough for him. Being creative and understanding the importance of branding, he found a vendor that would allow him to brand their bottles of water with his logo. The Brobdingnagian Bards did something similar and branded bottles of bubbles. Although they did this on a whim, they discovered that many of their fans saved the bottles for years as prized mementos. So, keep in mind that you can brand a surprising amount of items that go beyond T-shirts and stickers. Offering such merchandise can help you stand out from the crowd.

BE INVENTIVE

Not every fan wants a coffee cup with your logo on it. Creating merchandise sometimes goes beyond simply branding what stores have available. Being creative, which musicians already are, can open up possibilities. For instance, you could write a book. Jonathan Coulton worked with one of his fans, Lee Peralta, to create a colouring and activity book based on Coulton's 'Thing a Week' songs. The very literate George Hrab self-published a 168-page collection of essays, stories, observations and illustrations in his *Non-Colouring Book*. By using print-on-demand services such as Lulu (lulu.com) and

CreateSpace (createspace.com), you can create a unique work based off your music. These services offer all the tools you need to create whatever type of book you envision through their site. For instance, you could create a photo book of your next big show such as a memento for those who attended. By taking photos of your attending fans as well as your performance on stage, you've got a great start on the material needed for a book. By adding in the set list, lyrics, fan shoutouts and thank yous and stories of the performance, you can create a unique book to memorialise your performance and sell. And, because sites like Lulu and CreateSpace give you all the tools you need to create and sell the book, it can be available to the public instantly. You could create a photo book about your show, make it for sale and announce it to your fans through your mailing list the very next day after the gig. Creating such a memento that close to a show can capitalise on the momentum you created at the show as well as helping you archive your performances for the years to come. Of course, if you recorded your performance, the book can be sold in conjunction with the recording. A little bit of inventiveness can go a long way.

SELLING YOUR MERCHANDISE
SELLING ONLINE

If you go with a volume manufacturer for your merchandise, you may want to sell it to your fans from your website, rather than just at shows. If so, you can always sell it yourself: take orders, ship the items and handle the entire transaction from your home. If you do this, you can use Web storefronts to take the orders such as Yahoo.com stores (smallbusiness.yahoo.com/ecommerce) or ProStores (prostores.com).

A second option is to use a fulfilment service. These services stock your merchandise, take the orders, ship the items and handle the transactions – for a fee, such as Fulfilment by Amazon (http://amazon.co.uk/gp/seller/fba/fulfillment-by-amazon.html). An interesting trend for these fulfilment services is to create embedded storefronts or widgets that can help sell these items on the Web. Nimbit.com – which you can use outside the US – is one that offers these applications and allow you flexibility on how to integrate its 'online merchandise table' into your website and on your Web presence sites. The only question is whether the money you pay for the services is worth the time that you'll save.

SELLING MERCHANDISE AT SHOWS

We talk about selling merchandise at shows in Chapter 9: Get Booked and Play

Live. It's usually simple to just haul your T-shirts and merchandise to a table and handle sales on the spot. Be aware that the larger venues will take a cut of your merchandise sales, sometimes as much as 40 per cent.

▸▸SPONSORSHIPS

While it may seem that sponsorships are out of your arm's reach, that isn't so. Sponsorships can come from smaller businesses as much as larger ones.

For example, Frankendread managed to get some beach clothing manufacturers to sponsor him. He had all his band members dress in the manufacturer's clothes and pitched their products from the stage. If you can think of connections that make sense for your own brand, you might be able to make the same kind of deals.

LEARNING MORE

To stay up to date on all the resources, tools, services and sites that can help you create and sell your albums and merchandise, head to DIYMusicManual.com.

▸▸CHAPTER SEVEN
YOUR RIGHTS

Musicians, more than almost any other type of artist, have their rights defined by some of the most convoluted laws ever created. Copyright laws come into play when you write a song, when you cover a song on stage, when you record a song of your own and even if you hand your song to a filmmaker to use for free. Each of these activities has entirely different legal issues associated with them. Worse, these issues only become more confusing since the laws behind them were originally intended to protect record labels, music publishers and other middlemen – not necessarily indie musicians making music today or using the Web. We're going to give you a step-by-step overview of using the laws to both protect and *promote* your music. You'll soon understand why it's generally safe to play cover songs in bars but why you owe money if you cover someone else's song on your album. You'll learn what copyright is, how music licensing works and how to trade mark your band name. And we'll do our best to eliminate the legalese and explain it in plain English.

Our goal with this chapter is to introduce you to these topics and give you a basic understanding of the law and the terminology. But many of these topics will spiral beyond the scope of this book. In fact, there are entire books and law school classes dedicated to them. But you don't need to be an expert, you simply need to know enough to know *when* to go to an expert and to be able to understand some of their lingo. Of course, if you have any specific questions, we recommend contacting a solicitor.

Note that while the focus and specific references to the law in this section will be on UK and EU law, know that much of the general principles apply to other nations within the Commonwealth such as Australia and New Zealand. Any significant differences between the countries will be highlighted.

▸▸YOUR INDIE BAND IS A BUSINESS

Before we start, we should make it clear that any musician or band making money from music is running a business. And whenever business and money are involved, legal issues tend to follow. This becomes more complicated when multiple people are involved in the band. So, to avoid any disputes it's best to agree in advance as to what everyone's individual rights and responsibilities will be in the band.

That said, many bands do well without any formal legal agreement between themselves, handling issues, business deals and money on a case-by-case basis. However, an informal approach does nothing to protect you from yourselves (e.g., a band member suing the band or leaving the group) or others (e.g., one of your songs infringes the copyright of another songwriter). If you take what you're doing seriously, set up a legal structure such as a partnership LLP or corporation for your band. This step will solve many of the issues that we'll be talking about throughout this chapter. Such agreements typically solve thorny issues such as:

- Band name, brand ownership and trade mark ownership
- How band decisions are made and who's authorised to enter into agreements on behalf of the band
- How profits, losses and expenses are handled
- Band equipment ownership
- Ownership of sound recordings
- How publishing revenue is administered and distributed
- How merchandise and merchandising rights are handled
- What happens when additional band members join
- What happens when band members leave
- How disputes are handled

This is by no means a complete list.

Creating a legal entity for your specific needs goes beyond the scope of the *Manual*. Links to governmental, legal and business resources are posted at DIYMusicManual as well as a list of business books and information to get you started. If you're in the UK, you should visit businesslink.gov.uk to find your local Business Link office. Then, when you're ready to take this step for your own band, get a lawyer and accountant to assist you.

YOUR RIGHTS • 151

▸▸COPYRIGHT

In the UK, as with other members of the European Union (the EU), copyright law is legislated by the member country. However, the EU has passed certain standards to help harmonise the various copyright laws across Europe and the UK has adopted these. In general, copyright protects the authors of original works of music, text, graphics, videos or other art forms. As an indie band, you will probably be creating all these types of works. While some think of copyright as a single right, it isn't. It's better understood as a collection of many more specific rights – all of which can be divided, sold, retained or amended as you see fit.

When musicians have copyright questions, they often want clear, black-and-white answers. The truth is, the law is still evolving and it's often at odds with technology. The law doesn't map well to the needs of a post-net indie band for a variety of reasons:

- **The law is about getting permission; the Web is about copying and sharing:** The purpose of copyright is to help you control your work but the purpose of the Web is to easily copy data from one computer to another.
- **The Web is global; the law is not:** While the *Manual* will focus on the laws of the UK and Europe, the instant you put your music and other intellectual property on the Web, it's available to a global audience – with different laws and attitudes towards intellectual property.
- **The law is old and changes slowly; technology changes rapidly:** The law usually evolves by force-fitting old rules onto new situations. It's because of this retrofitting that most terms that lawyers use to describe music are out of date. For instance, the law calls any recording a 'phonorecord' although most music never makes its way onto a phonograph of any kind.

That said, because copyright affects just about everything a musician does, it's best to understand the basics. A full treatise on copyright law goes beyond the scope of the *Manual* but we'll cover the basics any musician should know.

COPYRIGHT LAW BASICS

The underlying principle behind copyright law is that creative works benefit society. Therefore, creators should be rewarded and given protection so that what they create – and any value that comes from it – can be theirs for at least as long as they live. As a result, copyright protects 'original works of authorship' whether they be literary, artistic or musical. The Intellectual Property Office, which is the governmental body responsible for overseeing copyrights, designs, trade marks and patents in the UK (ipo.gov.uk), does not ask creators to send in their works so they can keep track of who wrote what and when. Copyright occurs automatically from the time you:

- **Create and express something original:** Only an original work can be granted copyright protection. Additionally, copyright doesn't protect the ideas underlying your work, just the unique way you express it. For instance, with music, the subject of the lyrics, the title of the song and the chord progressions would not be granted copyright protection. Ultimately, in the case of disputes, it's the court that decides what's original.
- **Capture it in a fixed, tangible format:** With text, this is as easy as writing down your words, but with music, you have more options. You could write it down in notation form or record it in some way such as on your computer, a video camera or even your phone's voicemail. Playing a song live, however, would not be copyrightable unless you record it.

Once those two requirements are met, you instantly hold the copyright in that original work that you've captured and it's your property. There are no formalities to obtain protection nor any reason to 'register' the work with a governmental body. You need only have your name be associated with the original work.

Like any property, you can sell your copyright, rent it, divvy it up or give it away for free. As the sole owner, you alone have the right to copy your work. In general, the law grants you two types of rights – one economic and one moral. The economic rights are those rights associated with generating income from the work. These are rights that can be contracted and negotiated. For instance, the law grants you the power to use, sell, perform or display your work. It also gives you the right to make modifications, translations or other such derivative works from the original you've created. It allows you to do this or to sell or rent – known as licensing – these rights to others. If anyone exercises any of the above without your permission, you can enforce your rights and sue for infringement. Most of the time, however, you'll be looking for ways to let others use your work in exchange for money, licensing it to them for specific purposes.

The moral rights, however, are rights that cannot be contracted away – they're born out of the fact you created the work. Moral rights include the right to be identified as the author of your work, the right to object to your work being used in a manner that you don't approve of (derogatory use) and the right to object to someone erroneously claiming they created the work. These rights are automatic, although in order to get the right to be identified with a work, you must make it known that you are in fact the author. Although moral rights cannot be contracted away or assigned to others, they can be waived and ignored if you so choose to.

The law grants you these broad powers for as long as you own the copyright. With songs, this is currently your entire life plus 70 years after your death. With sound recordings, this is 50 years after the recording date or date when it was first published – such as you uploading your recording to your website. Why the distinction? We're glad you asked…

TWO FOR ONE: THE SOUND RECORDING COPYRIGHT AND THE SONG COPYRIGHT

If you write music the old-fashioned way – on sheet music – then your song is copyrighted the moment you write the words and music on paper. Writing down your original song in this way gives you a copyright to the *song*. Most likely though, you'll create your music by recording it onto your computer or some other sound recording device. If you do, you actually create two copyrights in one: one for the musical performance that was captured (the *sound recording*) and one for the words and music (the *song*). While it's hard to think of the recording as separate from the song, under the law, it is. The Beatles' record company owns the rights to the recording of the Beatles' version of 'Yesterday' but it's John Lennon and Paul McCartney who own the song copyright (well, until they sold their rights to others, that is). As owners of the song copyright, they're the ones who benefit when others record cover versions of their song – not the record company.

THE SOUND RECORDING COPYRIGHT

The sound recording owner can be a person, a group of people or even a legal entity such as your band. For signed bands, the owner is usually the record label since it needs to have the exclusive rights to these recordings in order to make and sell albums or license it to other media use the recording. As an indie band, you have the benefit of making money off the sound recording, just like a label would. We'll talk more about this about later.

THE SONG COPYRIGHT

The song copyright owner is split in two:

- **Author:** This is the songwriter or songwriters who write the words and music to the song and grant permission as to how the song can be used.
- **Publisher:** The publisher works for the author and handles all the business work the song generates, such as copyrighting the song, convincing others to perform it, licensing the song for use in film and television and collecting the royalties.

The law sees the author and publisher as a team – two sides of a single coin working together on behalf of the song. Indie musicians usually keep track of who wrote what percentage of each song but they rarely define who the publisher is. This is a problem since customarily the two roles split any income a song makes 50/50. So if an author wants to earn all the royalties a song may generate, someone has to fill the publishing role. For an indie band, the publisher is usually the author, through an individually owned publishing entity, or the band, through a joint venture created with all of its members.

You can also sell your publishing rights in a song or song catalogue to an established music publisher that specialises in promoting the use of songs and collecting royalties. Another option is to hire an established music administrator. Just like music publishers, administrators handle all the business issues of licensing and collecting royalties but won't help actively exploit the songs. We'll talk more about this in a later section.

DIVIDING THE ROLES

For an indie band, when it comes to dividing up the roles of author and publisher, some of the more common options are:

- **Songwriter as author, songwriter as publisher:** Each songwriter creates his or her own publishing company in order to receive 100 per cent of the royalties for a song – 50 per cent for being the author and 50 per cent for being the publisher. If there's more than one songwriter on a song, each songwriter has his or her own publishing company and so the author share of 50 per cent is divided equally between the songwriters and the publishing share of 50 per cent is divided equally between the publishers.
- **Songwriter as author, band as publisher:** Rather than have the songwriters in the band earn all the licensing royalties, some indie bands have opted to share the publishing rights. The songwriters split this share according to their author ownership percentage while the band's publishing entity receives the full amount of the publishing share. For this method,

the band needs to form a publishing entity. This publishing share is then divided between the band members based on their agreement.

- **Band as author, band as publisher:** Some indie bands decide to give the band both the author and publisher shares. To do this, the band needs to form a publishing entity and have an agreement between themselves in place stating that, no matter who writes the songs, the band gets the income from both the author share and the publisher share. This is then split according to the band agreement.

The list above is not exhaustive. You can negotiate any other arrangement you choose. Some indie bands split based on who performed on the song. Whichever method you choose, the point is to get your agreement down in writing. If you want to create your own publishing company, you can find steps and tools to ease the process at DIYMusicManual.com.

KEEPING TRACK OF COPYRIGHT OWNERSHIP

For each and every sound recording you make – whether it's a studio, acoustic, live or demo – you will need to keep track of who the author, publisher and sound recording owner is since each have legal rights. This is especially challenging when defining the sound recording owner since recordings may be created over time on multiple band member computers or at different recording studios. Typically, a band agreement helps define some of these roles. Still, to avoid disputes, we recommend using the Song and Sound Recording Agreement to help record who's filling these roles for any particular sound recording you make.

SONG AND SOUND RECORDING SPLIT AGREEMENT

The best way to define the three legal roles for each song you record is to put it down in writing. Doing so may help avoid issues in the future. To get you started, we created a fully editable Song and Sound Recording Split Agreement form which you can download for free at DIYMusicManual.com.

DEALING WITH MULTIPLE AUTHORS ON A SONG COPYRIGHT

Typically, bands and songwriters choose one of two methods when it comes to figuring out songwriting percentages: they either divide authorship equally between all those in the room at the time of creation or they work out percentages based on who contributed what part and how much of the song. Of course, you can negotiate anything as long as you have an agreement in place. Having more than one author is known in legal speak as joint ownership, although this term is often misunderstood to mean something entirely different when talking to musicians.

Given the moral rights all authors have in their work, one author cannot necessarily grant permission to license a song without the permission of the other co-author. For example, if three people write a song called 'Sick of Sandwiches' and one of them wanted to license it to a fast food burger chain to cover in a commercial, that person would need to work out arrangements with the others. This may be difficult if the other two were vegetarians and objected. If one co-author doesn't want to license his or her song in that way, it could stop the deal. But, if the two vegetarians didn't mind licensing the song to the company (there is money in it after all), then all the authors would get paid for this use according to their ownership percentages or whatever they negotiated between themselves to make the deal happen. Interestingly, this negotiation would not occur in the United States: one author can license a song over the objections of another. This is because US copyright law doesn't recognise an author's moral rights. Of course, the objecting co-author would get his or her fair share of the licence money. It's just the co-author cannot stop its use.

GETTING PAID TO WRITE SONGS FOR OTHERS

When someone, such as a company, pays you to create a song for them, they may have you sign an agreement with a 'work-for-hire' provision. This provision makes them the copyright owner in exchange for paying you to create it. As owner, they can publish, record or license their song in any way that they'd like. For example, if you were hired to write and record 'Sick of Sandwiches' by a fast food burger chain for their commercial campaign, the song would be theirs to do with as they please. If you're ever hired to write a theme for a podcast, commercial, film or TV show, you'll want to be aware of this provision since it'll affect all the rights you have that we discussed above. Know that whether to sign a 'work-for-hire' agreement is your choice. It's negotiable.

▶▶ HOW SONGS AND SOUND RECORDINGS CAN BE USED BY OTHERS

When you have the rights to your songs and sound recordings, you can license them for various uses. You can do this for free or charge a royalty (a licence fee).

Working out whose permission is needed and who gets paid – the author/publisher team and/or the sound recording owner – depends on what is being used. We'll go over the most popular uses below.

THE SONG

Any time a song is licensed, it's the author/publisher team that grants it and receives the royalties. The sound-recording owner only comes into play if the user licensing the song also wants to use that specific sound recording. If so, then a separate licence will be negotiated with the sound recording owner (which we'll talk about in the next section). The table 'Rights in the song' outlines in brief the many uses and rights that we'll discuss below.

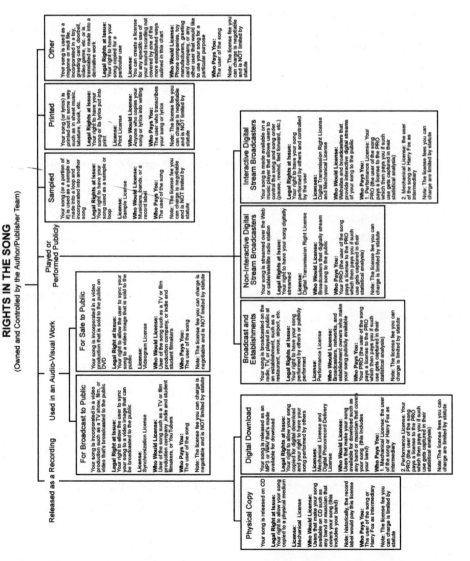

RIGHTS IN THE SONG
(Owned and Controlled by the Author/Publisher Team)

THE SONG IS RELEASED AS A RECORDING

The author/publisher must grant permission whenever their song is released as a recording for the first time. After your song's been published and thus made publicly available, the law allows anyone to record a version. However, you're still entitled to a royalty for each recording copy made, whether physical or digital. This is known as your 'mechanical right'.

In the UK, the Mechanical Copyright Protection Society (the 'MCPS') (mcps-prs-alliance.co.uk) administers, sets royalty rates and collects money for author/publisher when their music is copied in this way. In Australia and New Zealand, this is handled by the Australasian Mechanical Copyright Owners' Society (the 'AMCOS') (apra.com.au). At the time of the printing of this *Manual*, the MCPS and AMCOS charges a small fee per copy for songs depending on the length. These rates are adjusted every few years, so to get the most up-to-date rates see the MCPS and AMCOS websites. You can always charge less than this rate (including nothing at all) but you can never negotiate anything higher. These royalties are owed to you whether or not the copies are intended to be sold or given away for free. It doesn't matter if it's for promotional purposes, a charitable cause or handed out as a gift. As long as a copy is made, you are technically owed these royalties, unless you waive them.

Most songwriters don't realise that when their band duplicates 1000 CDs of the songs they wrote, the author/publisher are entitled to a royalty for each copy made – to be paid by your band. The law sees your band as covering the songwriter's songs. In fact, when you sign an agreement with a CD printing house, that agreement typically has you vouch for the fact that you have all the necessary permissions for all the songs on the album they are copying – including permissions from the author/publisher within your band!

Of course, paying the band's songwriters for the right to use the songs on your band's album (on top of all the money spent to make the CDs in the first place!) may not only break your band's bank, it may even break up the band. But it goes beyond CDs: releasing songs digitally also results in mechanical royalties being owed. This includes uploading MP3 and WAV files to your band's website and each subsequent download (whether free or paid). The author/publisher should get a royalty for the upload and download.

Indie bands often skirt this issue by having the author/publisher waive their rights to these royalties or by working out a deal with them to get paid after the album has recouped the initial outlay of funds. This is yet another reason why a band agreement can help solve these issues at the outset.

WHY YOU CAN RECORD COVER SONGS (FOR A FEE)

The law allows anyone to record a song previously made available to the public. In other words, no one can stop you from recording a cover version of a well-known song for your album. This is called obtaining a 'compulsory licence'. Just as we said above, you need to pay a statutory royalty for each copy of the cover song you make. To do so, you need to contact the publisher of the song although many publishers align themselves with the MCPS (or AMCOS in Australia and New Zealand) which collects mechanical royalties on behalf of its members. We'll talk in detail about the role the MCPS and AMCOS play in helping indie bands track down publishers and pay the requisite fees online in a later section.

DEALING WITH DIGITAL DOWNLOADS

Allowing your songs to be downloaded as an MP3 at your website triggers an additional songwriter right – the 'performance right'. This is in addition to the mechanical right. Although your band's songwriters may waive these rights for your website, you will have to obtain this license for cover songs. We'll talk about this additional licence in the 'Performed Publicly' section below.

SONGS USED IN AN AUDIO-VISUAL WORK

The author/publisher can grant permission for their song to be tied to a visual image. The author/publisher can license the use for a royalty. Examples include songs used in:

- Films and film trailers
- Television shows
- Television commercial campaigns
- Documentaries
- Music videos

Using a song in such a way is known as a 'synchronisation right' since the user of the music is syncing the song to the visual image. If the user wants to also sell the audio-visual work to the public in the form of a DVD or digital download, the author/publisher can grant a second licence, called a videogram license. Unlike a mechanical right, your synchronisation and videogram rights are not limited by the law. You can negotiate any price or deny the use of your song altogether. It's completely up to you.

SONGS PLAYED PUBLICLY

Once an author/publisher publishes a song, the law allows anyone to play it. There are no royalties for private performances of the song such as when you listen to an artist's album in your car but when it's publicly performed, that's a different story. A song can be performed publicly at or through:

- Airplay such as broadcast media, for example, TV, film and satellite, cable and terrestrial radio
- Public establishments such as restaurants, bars, shopping centres, hotels, theme parks, airports, etc.
- Online uses such as digital stream broadcasters, webcasts, websites or web-simulcasted radio stations

Each time the song is played publicly, the author/publisher is entitled to a royalty. This is paid by the broadcast media performing the song and the establishment that allows it to be performed. Performance royalties share the same rates as mechanical royalties. So, once again, the statutory rate is paid to the author/publisher team.

Obviously, knowing when your song was played is one challenge. Trying to get paid for it is another. This is where Performance Rights Organisations (PROs) come in. PROs include organisations such as PRS in the UK and MPRA in Australia and New Zealand. (In the US, these roles are handled by ASCAP, BMI and SESAC.) Since copyrighted music is being played all the time, it takes large organisations such as PROs to figure out what's been performed and then collect and distribute the royalties.

In general, users of music enter into music reporting and subscription arrangements with PROs to cover themselves for the copyrighted music that they publicly broadcast and perform. For establishments, like a bar, paying a general licence fee to a PRO covers whatever bands perform live on stage as well as songs publicly broadcasted throughout the place – including the jukebox, the televisions, whatever the sound guy plays before and after the band, and even the music you hear when you call the bar and you're put on hold.

But just because your song's played doesn't mean you'll get paid. There's too much music for even these organisations to keep track of. Where economically sensible, PROs conduct census surveys for a complete count of what exactly has been played, for instance by gathering playlists from radio stations. Otherwise, they conduct sample surveys to give an approximation of what songs have been played and how frequently.

Unfortunately, such methodology does not bode well for indie bands. The more plays, the greater the chance of being represented in these statistics. However, as we will discuss in Chapter 11: Get Played and Heard, most of the media that PROs monitor are gated off or extremely difficult for indie bands to get played on. It comes down to luck as to whether any of your performances get caught in one of their surveys. If you're lucky enough to have that occur, however, the cheque can be quite sizeable – anywhere from hundreds of dollars to thousands. More likely, however, you'll only get a letter at the end of the year stating that their sampling showed that none of your songs were performed during the last twelve months. So, for us indies, receiving performance royalties is rare – even if you can point to exact instances where your music was performed in public (although some PROs have set aside royalties for members that get played in media and venues that are not included in their surveys).

In the UK, you can self-generate performance royalties for your songwriters by playing your music live. Often venues ask for your setlist once you've completed your show. To the extent you register the songs you played with the PRO, the PRO could match your performance with your song. In this case, it's the venues that are paying you since they pay a blanket licence to the PRS to cover music played in their establishment. By the way, such method of generating income isn't possible in the US where its PROs don't recognise or keep track of these self-performances.

Of course, this also means music uploaded to your website generates public performances as well. This time, however, it's your website that needs to pay. Technically, your website should purchase a licence from PRS. If this doesn't seem to sit well, then you'll need to have your songwriters waive these royalties. The cost of joining these PROs as authors and publishers may be worth it. If you perform regularly or expect to have your songs performed by others beyond your own band, then it's worth joining and registering your published songs with one of them. While it's possible you won't receive any royalties, not registering guarantees that you won't. We'll discuss registering as an author and a publisher in a later section.

DIGITAL DOWNLOADS AND WEBSITES

Two digital distribution methods that generate public performances of music include websites that offer digital downloads and Web-based music players that allow the user to control the music delivery, such as by allowing the listener to pick the next song in a playlist, which is the case with MySpace's music player.

PROs generally offer websites like this blanket licences. Just as your band's author/publisher is owed mechanical royalties for any CDs you press, so too is the author/publisher owed performance royalties for any digital downloads made from your website or songs played from your website. The same advice we gave above in dealing with this situation applies here as well: you will need to handle or have the songwriters waive the performance royalties that are technically owed.

SAMPLED

The sampling right to a song is not as straightforward as the other rights we've discussed above. In general, when a sample of a song is incorporated into another's work, it's the sound recording owner that gives permission and gets a royalty, since it's the recording that's being used as an instrument.

However, depending on the length and use of the sample, the author/ publisher may be asked for permission as well. Typically, to avoid any legal issues, artists and labels that use samples in their music tend to err on the side of caution and get a licence from both the author/publisher and sound recording owner. If you license some of your music to be used as a sample, you'll want to check with your PRO to see if they track samples. Some, such as the Performance Rights Society ('PLS') in the UK, allow you to register your samples with them. Doing so increases the likelihood of you receiving performance royalties from your original sample being incorporated into another's song.

PRINTED

The author/publisher must be asked permission whenever the music or lyrics of their song are printed. The author/publisher can license such use for a royalty. The music and lyrics can appear in magazines, books, on websites and even in greeting cards.

Although you may get a licence to perform or record a published song, the printing rights are not related to these rights and are subject to a separate royalty. If you print the lyrics of your songs in the CD booklet or on your website, your band's author/publisher are owed a royalty. The same is true for cover songs. Even if you've received a mechanical licence to record the song, you'll still need to negotiate a separate licence for the right to print the lyrics.

THE SOUND RECORDING

Any time someone wants to use the sound recording they must ask the sound recording owner for permission. The author/publisher team is always excluded in sound recording licence analyses (to the extent they aren't the sound recording owner!). However, as outlined in the above section, any licensed use of the sound recording usually results in a separate licence being needed for the song since, by definition, using the sound recording is using the song. The table 'Rights in the sound recording' outlines in brief the many uses and rights that we'll discuss below.

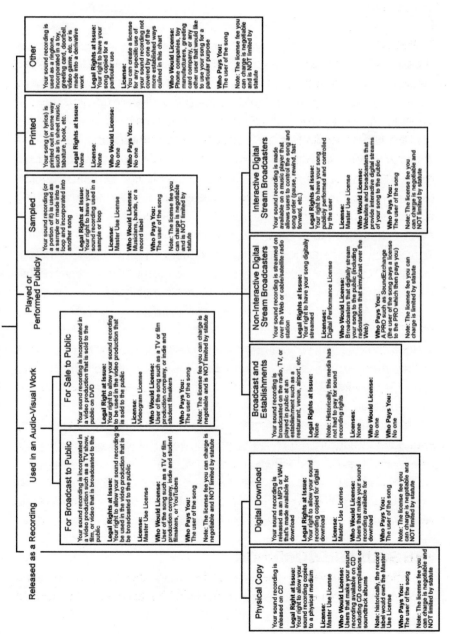

SOUND RECORDING IS RELEASED

The sound recording owner must approve any release of the sound recording and is entitled to a royalty for each copy made. This includes the use of the sound recording by others such as on compilation CDs or soundtracks. It also includes any digital downloads whether at your website or in someone else's podcast. This is commonly known as the 'master use right'.

The master use right is similar to a mechanical right with one important exception: there is no compulsory licence option available to force the use of the sound recording. Unlike a song which can be performed by other musicians, the use of a sound recording depends solely on the permission of the sound recording owner. And, unlike a mechanical royalty, there is no statutory rate imposed on how much the owner can charge.

SOUND RECORDINGS USED IN AN AUDIO-VISUAL WORK

The sound recording owner can license their master to be used with a visual image such as in a film, documentary, music video, television show or commercial. Similar to the above, this licensing is not compulsory and the rate is negotiable.

SOUND RECORDINGS PLAYED PUBLICLY

Performance and airplay rights in the sound recording date back to 1934 in a UK and 1969 in Australia. Once again, however, knowing where and when your sound recording was played is a challenge. Therefore, separate PROs were created to help sound recording owners collect and distribute royalties. In the UK, the sound recording PRO is the Phonographic Performance Limited ('PPL') and in Australia it's the Phonographic Performance of Australia LTD ('PPCA'). We'll discuss how to register your sound recordings with the PPL or PPCA in a later section below.

SAMPLED SOUND RECORDINGS

The sound recording owner must be asked permission whenever their sound recording is sampled or otherwise used as a loop, groove or instrument. Once again, the sound recording owner can deny its use or license the master use rights for a royalty. As with all sound-recording owner rights, there is no standard fee or process to obtain permission.

OTHER USES AND RIGHTS

The rights we listed above for the song and sound recording are the more common ones you'll run into. But those aren't the only ways your song might be licensed. Other uses for music include musical greeting cards, musical toys or even the creation of those kitsch singing plastic fish that were briefly popular a few years ago. You can license your song or sound recording for any of these uses and new uses for music seem to be invented every day.

Your licences for novel uses of your music or any that are not limited by a negotiation ceiling as imposed on mechanical licence (such as sync and videogram licences) should be:

- **Non-exclusive:** This way you can continue to license the song to others at any time. Exclusivity should come at a higher royalty rate.
- **Limited for a specific use:** Don't grant more rights or uses than the user wants at that moment. That way, they have to come back for additional licences should they ever need to use the song in different ways in the future.
- **Limited by territory:** Worldwide rights should earn higher royalty rates than in one territory.
- **Limited in duration:** Never grant rights 'in perpetuity', which would allow the licencee to use your song for ever.

Taking these factors into account can help you reserve the rights you have in your song so that, if a new technology comes along, the licencee will need to come back to you to make a new deal.

USING YOUR RIGHTS TO GET YOUR MUSIC OUT THERE

As an indie band, you need to do anything you can to get your music out there. This includes creative licensing, which we'll talk about below.

LICENSE YOUR SONGS AND SOUND RECORDINGS UNDER CREATIVE COMMONS

To paraphrase Tim O'Reilly, a publisher and Internet luminary, 'obscurity is a far greater threat to authors and creative artists than piracy'. Uploading music to your website and shackling its use does not encourage people to discover it. That's why we strongly encourage everyone to 'download, play and share' our songs at TheSongOfTheDay.com. The best way for people to discover what we're all about is to hear our songs.

Unfortunately, the default setting of copyright is: 'you can't copy without permission'. So unless you state otherwise on your albums or at your website, fans who share your music with friends are infringing on your rights. One way to encourage people to share your music is to issue it under a Creative Commons licence. That way they can share it freely.

Creative Commons (creativecommons.org) is a non-profit organisation that provides free tools to help authors, musicians and other artists create simple licences that change their copyright terms from 'All Rights Reserved' to 'Some Rights Reserved'. The organisation has drafted a number of pre-made and linkable licences that are free to use and customise depending on your needs. These Creative Commons licences tell the world which rights you're willing to grant and which rights you wish to retain – whether for your music, website, photos, artwork, etc. If a user wants to use your music for a purpose not expressly given by your Creative Commons licence, then they need to contact the author/publisher and sound recording owner as outlined above.

The licence we recommend using is their music sharing licence, also known as the 'Attribution-NonCommercial-NoDerivativeWorks'. Licensing your music this way allows anyone to use and copy your songs as long as they attribute your band, don't modify them and don't use them for commercial purposes. Any person who wants to use your song or sound recording for a commercial reason (i.e. TV show, film, website with advertising) must license it from you as outlined in the previous section. There are other licences, including one that allows users to sample, mashup, remix, loop or otherwise transform your songs. We use this licence for our music to encourage our fans to get creative with our songs.

Note that when you issue such a licence, you need the permission of both the author/publisher and the sound recording owner. They all have to be on board with this decision, otherwise you don't have the necessary rights to issue the licence. And they should be aware of the fact that the licence is granted in perpetuity – you can't revoke it once you've released your songs under this licence. We suggest that you read it carefully and are comfortable with the terms before using it. However, if you license your music this way, it helps to promote your music and could lead to opportunities.

For instance, Jonathan Coulton released 'Code Monkey' during his 'Thing a Week' project under a Creative Commons licence that restricted commercial use. When a television production company wanted to use the song for their television show of the same name, they still had to obtain the necessary rights from Coulton. In fact, the company will need additional licences if the show makes it to DVD. Also, since the show airs on the G4 network in the States, its airplay is monitored by Coulton's PRO. If the song is detected in its survey, Coulton will have a sizeable cheque coming to him.

SUB-LICENSE YOUR PUBLISHING RIGHTS WITH EXTERNAL MUSIC PUBLISHERS

Another way to get your music out there is to negotiate a deal with a professional music publisher who will actively lobby television production companies and other commercial music users to license your music. These publishers are essentially agents for your songs. They spend their entire day promoting, marketing and pitching the songs in their catalogue to others in the hopes of getting someone to license them.

Music publishers get a cut of your publisher share in order to earn royalties on the songs they promote. Although, sometimes, they will pay you an advance against the royalties they expect the song or catalogue to earn. Music publishers include major companies such as BMG, Sony and Warner/Chappell, as well as mid-size and independent publishing houses. Typically, music publishers work on a song-by-song basis, although some may want to publish your entire music catalogue. Whether you can get an external music publisher interested in your music depends on whether they believe they can get your music licensed. Since their job is to match existing music to the needs of their customers – the music users – a lot depends on your style, genre, lyrics, the quality of the sound recording and, of course, luck.

Alternatively, you can negotiate a deal with a music administrator. Unlike a music publisher, music administrators do not actively try to get a song licensed. They simply handle the business side of things should you make a licensing deal happen on your own. In exchange for handling this work, you pay them a recurring fee.

Along these lines, other music services are stepping into the music publishing arena. For instance, although they do not actively promote your songs like a music publisher would, CD Baby offers its musician clients the option of giving them a percentage of any synchronisation licence royalties in exchange for providing television and filmmakers a list of those songs in their catalogue that are available for licensing. The virtual record label Magnatune (magnatune.com) does something similar with the artists on their books. Since synchronisation fees are not limited by statute, these licensing deals can be substantial. To the extent you make the deal happen (or it comes to you), you're now obligated to pay these third parties a share of the revenue. When it comes to your rights, you always want to weigh the pros and cons.

ACTING AS YOUR OWN PUBLISHER

Of course, you don't need a publisher to license your music. Given your well-branded website, if a music user wants to license your music, they can come directly to you. For instance, ABC Family/Disney contacted us at our website to license our song 'Get Out!' from *The Cheapass Album*. They decided that the song, about 'living life in my parents' basement', was perfect for a television commercial campaign promoting their new reality TV series about twenty-somethings who were forced to leave their parents' house to get an apartment, job and life.

Given that they specifically wanted to use the sound recording from our album, we negotiated both a non-exclusive synchronisation licence (for the song) and a master use licence (for the sound recording). Disney didn't license the performance rights because they weren't performing anything. Because they needed the song for 30-second spots, both licences gave them the right to make a derivative work so they could chop up the song and have a narrator talk over it. Lastly, although both licences gave them the right to use the song and sound recording worldwide (since they're a cable network), we limited their use to the length of the commercial campaign (a period of nine weeks). Because we had all the rights in the song and sound recording, we negotiated and finalised the deal within a week and they were able to use the song in their commercials. Best of all, the author/publisher and sound recording owner received all the money negotiated.

We predict there will be more direct licensing deals with indie bands in the future now that many production companies simply surf iTunes looking for a song title or style that fits their needs. Brad Turcotte of Brad Sucks believes this is exactly what happened when VH-1 licensed his song 'Sick As A Dog' for a scene in a television show that showed someone puking. Often, companies don't care if you're a 'known artist'. They just want a song that fits their needs. It's only an added bonus for them that indie songs are less expensive than those encumbered by middlemen.

If you're interested in music publishing and want to know more about what publishers do, we recommend *Making Music Make Money: An Insider's Guide to Becoming Your Own Music Publisher* by Eric Beall.

REQUESTS FOR MUSIC: LICENSE YOUR SONGS THROUGH MUSIC AGGREGATORS

Sometimes production and advertising companies rely on music aggregators to find music. There are two types: a 'go-between' music aggregator that connects musicians with production and advertising companies and music production libraries.

A go-between music aggregator gathers music requests from production companies and publishes these requests on its website. Musicians who subscribe to the aggregator's website can upload their music (or even create new material) for consideration, usually for a fee. The aggregator then filters the submissions, passing along the closest matches to the production company for consideration.

This is how Taxi (taxi.com) works. They make 'wanted' listings available to their members for a yearly fee of approximately US$300. Submitting a song for consideration costs a small fee (to encourage musicians to discriminate rather than upload their entire catalogue for each listing). Taxi's staff reviews each submitted song and decides which ones to send on. They'll even critique the song and the recording for the musician. If the music user chooses your song, Taxi puts them in touch with you to work out a licensing deal.

Sonicbids (sonicbids.com) also connects musicians to licensing opportunities. Sonicbids started as a way to connect musicians to bookers and venues but they have expanded their service into other outlets such as TV, film and other music users that look to license music. As with Taxi, you have to pay a fee to submit your music to a particular opportunity. Unlike Taxi, this fee is not fixed and is set by the music users offering the opportunity (which they get a cut of). Note also that Sonicbids has a monthly fee. We'll discuss Sonicbids' other services in greater detail in later chapters.

Production companies can also license music from companies that create music libraries. These music aggregators hire songwriters and musicians to create original music in a variety of styles, which they in turn sell or license to music users for use in their productions. Because their clients are often in radio, television and film, they create a variety of versions of each song, chopping them into fifteen- and thirty-second clips and making instrumental versions. Depending on the music aggregator, the music is either licensed per use, covered by a yearly subscription arrangement, or sold royalty-free.

These music aggregators often negotiate a work-for-hire arrangement with musicians, paying in advance in exchange for the song and sound recording. Others work out deals that allow the songwriter to retain some of the rights and receive additional royalties when a song is licensed. Typically, performance rights for the author/publisher are not affected but the music aggregator may want part of the publishing rights. Songs are licensed to these catalogues exclusively. Naturally, the music aggregators need to ensure that the song and sound recording are only available through their library.

Musician Brett Ratner, of the indie band Socialite Fiasco, writes and records music for the music aggregator WildWhirled (wildwhirled.com). WildWhirled has paid agreements with nearly a hundred songwriters like Ratner, who specialise in writing and recording different genres of music. The company's music has been used in countless television shows, films and advertising campaigns. For instance, many of Brett's original alternative-country songs have been used on the popular US television show *My Name Is Earl*.

Some music aggregators such as WildWhirled do not take unsolicited submissions of recordings. Instead, they assign musicians on their books to write songs to match what they're looking for. Others, such as NOMA Music (nomamusic.com) do accept submissions. If you wish to use a music aggregator, you should carefully look at their licensing options and requirements.

GET COMMISSIONED AND WRITE SONGS FOR OTHERS

Rather than exploit your existing songs, you can always exploit your talent at writing songs. Music made to order for television shows, films, commercials, the theatre and video games is big business. Professional songwriters usually create under work-for-hire agreements. While writing themes for television shows and films may seem out of your arm's reach, you can still write music for podcasters, YouTubers, indie and student filmmakers or other website owners. Often, these music users just use whatever music is handy, infringing on copyrights simply because they don't know where to find the right music to fit their needs. As an indie band, you can help not only improve their production values but also keep them out of legal trouble. At the same time, you'll be getting your music heard while promoting your band.

We've been writing songs, themes and other incidental music for years under Beatnik Turtle's 'Songs-On-Demand' service, offering to write themes, beds and bumpers for anyone for money, barter or sometimes for free. We generally keep the rights to the music and grant a non-exclusive licence solely for the intended purpose, making that clear in an email to the requester. We also ask for attribution (and a link back) and allow derivative works so users can cut, speed up, talk over and otherwise incorporate the song into their work. Then we expressly state that all other rights not discussed are reserved. That way, if they have a new use, such as putting their work on a CD or DVD to sell, they need to come back to us for permission.

When we write music for a fee, we enter into a more detailed agreement to clarify which rights the music user is getting and which we retain. This, too, typically occurs over email. However, if we're hired to write music for a commercial endeavour, such as a theme for a television show, a contract is always drafted and, if it's not a work-for-hire relationship, we typically license many of the rights to the song and sound recording (including derivative rights) so the music user has some flexibility.

Get every commissioned work arrangement – whether free, for barter or for pay – in writing. For the purpose of expediency, we usually rely on email to work out the licence details but that's not without its risks. Any good lawyer would tell you that, given that you can never know exactly how a song or sound recording might be exploited and used in the future, it's always best to be as explicit as possible. If you decide to travel down this road, know what you're risking or, better still, mitigate this risk by enlisting a lawyer to help draft the licence.

▸▸COPYRIGHT PRACTICALITIES

Now that you have the basics down about copyright and licensing, let's address some practical issues that indies face.

REGISTERING YOUR SONGS AND SOUND RECORDINGS
REGISTERING YOUR SONGS AND SOUND RECORDINGS WITH A PRIVATE SERVICE

You do not need to register your copyright with any governmental body in the UK. This is true for the EU, Australia and New Zealand as well. You may, however, register your works with a private copyright registration service. Registering your songs and sound recordings with a private company does not 'prove' you wrote the work you're submitting to them, only you can create that proof. Keeping copies of your date-stamped sound recordings, demos, notes and other items that can help show you wrote the work is the best evidence for this if a dispute ever arises.

What these services can do is help to independently establish a date when you claim you created the work. Of course, you can do that as well. The UK Intellectual Property Office recommends one inexpensive way to handle establishing a date of creation: send yourself a copy of your work by special delivery post – and then don't open it. The date and time of the postmarks on the envelope can be used as a valid way to help prove when you wrote what you did.

In a sense, copyright registration services such as the UK Copyright Service (copyrightservice.co.uk) perform a more elaborate method of cataloguing, archiving and dating your work than the post can do. Many offer additional services, such as egistering amounts to filling out the necessary information with the service and providing them with a copy of the work. It's important to note that these services don't listen to what you send in or compare it to other works in their system. All they do is create a file in their database, store a copy of your song and sound recording and outline the details of your claim. It's only later, if you run into a copyright dispute, end up in court and need to prove when you wrote the song, that you'll need them to retrieve the file and verify when you submitted it. Given that these services are one step removed from the copyright holders that pay them to store their music, their records generally carry a lot of weight as to when something was created.

Each service charges its own fee and has its own submission methodology, so you'll need to see which one suits your needs. Keep in mind that some offer a one-time fee, while others charge a recurring fee to archive your work. Unless you're getting additional services beyond registration such as legal assistance in case your work is infringed, we recommend choosing services that charge a one-time fee.

A list of the available copyright registration services in the UK and other countries can be found at DIYMusicManual.com.

REGISTERING WITH A PRO FOR SONG PERFORMANCE ROYALTIES

As stated above, when your songs are performed or receive airplay performance royalties are generated. In the UK and EU, this includes when you perform your own original music. This is why live music venues request your setlist – the venue owes you or your band's songwriters money for the performance of the song. To ensure you actually see this money, you'll want to join a PRO. Becoming a member allows you to register information about your songs (usually online) so the PRO know who to pay when they receive song lists of what was played back from venues, radio and television stations, Internet radio stations and other places where music is heard publicly.

PROs are usually easy to join but each one has their own registration requirements and application fees. Typically, once you've made your music available to the public, such as by releasing an album for sale, you can register as an author and publisher with one of these PROs. But all PROs are different. The PRO that collects and distributes performance royalties in the UK is the Performance Rights Society ('PRS') while the one in Australia and New Zealand is the Australasian Performance Rights Association ('APRA'). These require documented proof that at least one of your songs has been played publicly. A setlist from a recent live performance or a reference to your song being broadcasted at a broadcaster's website usually suffices.

While some PROs are free to join (the APRA is, for instance), some cost money, such as the PRS, which charges £100. For the sake of simplicity, PROs encourage, and often require, membership in only one organisation. Each PRO calculates royalties differently. Some also offer perks such as discounts for music equipment at music chain stores, career assistance and health insurance benefits, so you'll want to choose the best one for your needs. There are of course other PROs in different countries as well as ones for specific genres of music such as Christian music. For a complete listing, see DIYMusicManual.com.

Once you've picked your PRO, remember that they only pay author royalties to authors and publisher royalties to publishers. As stated above, if you're both the author and publisher of a song and neglect to sign up as a publisher, you will lose out on the publisher royalties they collect.

REGISTERING WITH A PRO TO GET SOUND RECORDING PERFORMANCE ROYALTIES

You should also register your sound recordings with your local sound recording PRO. In the UK, the PRO that obtains performance and airplay royalties for sound recordings is the PPL (ppluk.com). In Australia and New Zealand, it's the PPCA (ppca.com.au). Since sound recording rights are different from the song rights, you can join your local sound recording PRO in addition to one of the song performance PROs. Plus, registration is free in both cases.

Since royalties are split and distributed between the sound recording copyright owner and the performers on the song, you should register as both if you play on your recordings. If you don't register both, it will result in lost royalties. Registration as a sound recording copyright owner and the performers who played on the songs is done at the PPL website (ppluk.com).

If you have had airplay but haven't registered, all is not lost. It's possible the PPL is looking for you. Orphaned airplay and performance plays of sound recordings that aren't matched to someone in their database are accessible once you register. You can check this list – and make a claim to any royalties you might be owed if yours is on it. Visit the PPL website for more detailed information about registration.

Also, both the PPL and PPCA don't stop with sound recordings – they'll also collect royalties on airplay of your music videos – videos made to support the song and sound recording you made. Note that the PPL does this under the name of Video Performance Limited. If you are the sound and, in this case, video recording owner, then you can register it at vpluk.com. Again, registration is free. Visit the VPL website for more detailed information about registration and their services.

GETTING PERMISSION TO RECORD AND PLAY OTHER PEOPLE'S MUSIC

PLAYING COVER SONGS LIVE

In general, when playing live, whether on stage or for a radio station in-studio, you can perform any published song you want – even something by Robbie Williams. Copyright law grants you the right to perform any published song and the author/publisher doesn't get a say in the matter. Robbie Williams can't stop you from playing one of his songs even though he and everyone else in the room may want to. Still, if you play one of his songs, Robbie's owed a royalty. Chances are, however, that you've never paid a cent to Robbie (hopefully). Are you in trouble?

Yes.

And no. Recall that PROs like PRS and APRA work out deals with establishments and venues for the right to have music performed publicly. This is likely to include the very place you're playing at since music no doubt makes up a lot of its business. It's the venue that's paying for your performance – not you.

Technically, however, if the venue doesn't have a licence with a PRO to cover your performance, you're actually liable and need to pay for the performance right. Now, being liable and actually being sued are entirely different things. It's most likely that the song owners won't come after you and all the other bands that have performed copyrighted music at the venue, since it's the venue itself that should have known better than to operate without a PRO licence. Most importantly, the PROs know exactly where the venue is. If you discover that a particular venue isn't paying a licensing fee, then PROs probably want to know. Be sure to leave the tip anonymously, though, since you'll still want to play the venue.

RECORDING COVER SONGS

When you record a cover song, you need to obtain a mechanical licence from the author/publisher and pay the requisite fee. As outlined above, it doesn't matter if the song is given away for free or used as a promo, a copy is a copy and, to avoid an infringement claim, you're supposed to obtain a licence. If you plan on having your recorded version on CD as well as making it available as a digital download, you need to obtain two mechanical licences.

Although a mechanical licence allows you to record a cover, it does not allow you to make a derivative version of the song. What constitutes a derivative version as opposed to a cover version is up in the air but, in general, it means you can change the style and genre to make it your own but can't change the basic melody or a substantial part of the lyrics. Also, obtaining a mechanical licence does not allow you to do anything with the original sound recording of the song. That's a different licence, obtained from the sound recording owner.

There are two ways to get a mechanical licence: by contacting the publisher directly to work out a deal or by using a PRO service as a licensing intermediary. Contacting the publisher of the cover song you want to record to ask for permission and negotiate a licence fee is likely your best bet. Figuring out who the publisher is and the right person's contact information can be a challenge. Sometimes the publisher's name and contact information is in the CD booklet or comes up in a simple Internet search. However, you can also look up the publisher's contact information by checking your local PRO's online database (discussed below) using other PROs' databases (such as ASCAP's or BMI's in the US), or, if the song happens to be one written by an American artist, by checking the US Copyright Office online database. (copyright.gov)

Once you know who to contact, you will need to send an email or letter asking for permission. It's not as simple as saying who you are and how many copies you want to make. Publishers often want to know the purpose behind covering the song, if you're going to sell it or not, what media you intend to make it available in and whether your use would disparage the original work or other moral rights the author has in it. All these concerns should be addressed in your initial enquiry to the publisher. For a suggested sample letter and downloadable template as a starting point, visit DIYMusicManual.com.

Another method is to use a PRO's online database to procure licences for songs, such as the one found at MCPS. In many cases a publisher has affiliated itself with the MCPS to administer the mechanical licensing process and collect royalties on its behalf. Simply type in the name of the song and, if they have the rights, they'll issue you a licence. Of course, you will need to answer a few questions about how many copies you intend to make, whether they will be available physically or digitally and your contact information.

Pricing for licensing varies depending on the length and number of copies you are making (limited to 2,500 copies or less – whether copied physically or digitally). Going through the MCPS rather than direct to a publisher also adds some administrative costs that are built into the licence as well. Presently, there are some curious constraints on the limited licensing service they offer, such as the fact the limited licence doesn't allow you to sell music through any third party (such as iTunes or other digital music stores) – you are restricted to selling on your own.

In the US, many publishers have turned to Harry Fox (harryfox.com) for the administration and collection of mechanical royalties. Harry Fox allows a similar limited licence (accessible at songfile.com) but allows American musicians the right to sell via third parties. We used SongFile when we recorded a version of 'Older' by They Might Be Giants for our live album, *Thanks For Coming Out: Beatnik Turtle Live!*. We only wanted to release the album digitally, so we purchased a mechanical licence for digital distribution. If at some point we decide to release the album on CD, we'll need to obtain a mechanical licence for pressing physical copies. And the CD printing house will require proof of this licence.

It's possible MCPS and AMCOS may eventually mirror their limited licence to include the right to sell the songs through third party music stores. You may want to check the MCPS website for future enhancements to their licensing procedures.

RECORDING WORKS IN THE PUBLIC DOMAIN

Of course, if the song you're recording is in the public domain, as is the case with traditional folk music, you don't need anyone's permission. We did this when we recorded an album of traditional Irish pub songs called *Sham Rock* which featured our band's take on songs that were in the public domain such as 'Tell Me Ma', 'Beer, Beer, Beer', 'The Holy Ground' and 'Finnegan's Wake'. Since these are old songs that have been passed down through the generations and have fallen out of copyright, we didn't need to license any rights from anyone. Of course, our versions of the song and the parts we added – our unique guitar, horn and lyrical arrangements – are copyrighted by us, as are the sound recordings. If another band wanted to do a cover of our cover using our arrangements and the parts we added, they would need our permission.

USING OTHER PEOPLE'S SAMPLES AND AUDIO LOOPS

Whenever you incorporate any samples and audio loops in your music, you need permission from the sound recording owner. Whether the owner allows you to use the sample in your song is entirely up to them and if permission isn't granted you're out of luck. If the owner does grant you permission, however, be prepared to pay large fees, since there's no limit to the amount the owner can charge for a sample clearance licence. The clearance may cost you anywhere from a few hundred to a few thousand dollars. Additionally, they may ask for a percentage of the income derived from your song and a bonus payment when a certain threshold of copies are sold. Additionally, depending on the type and extent of the sample or loop, you might need to get permission from the author/publisher as well. This, too, will result in fees.

Solutions to this financial nightmare include:

■ **Recording a cover version of the sample or audio loop:** You can always record a cover version of the sample or audio loop you wish to use. If you do so, you'll need permission from the author/publisher as outlined above.

■ **Using pre-cleared samples and audio loops**: Some companies produce royalty-free loops. These are available on CD, DVD and online. See Chapter 6: Your Albums and Merchandise for a list of such sites. Always verify the licence restrictions to confirm that they allow derivative works.

■ **Use samples and audio loops issued under creative commons licences:** A large number of musicians believe in sharing their loops royalty-free and release them under a Creative Commons licence. Of course, some of these samples and loops are not licensed for commercial purposes, so if you decide to sell a song incorporating such samples, you'll need to clear it with the sound recording owner.

■ **Record your own samples and audio loops:** You can always create your own loops and license them to yourself – if you're feeling generous that day.

COPYRIGHT BEYOND MUSIC: TEXT, PHOTOS, GRAPHICS AND VIDEO

So far we've focused on your rights as they apply to music. As an indie band, however, you're probably doing it all – creating text, photos, graphics and video for your brand, website, albums, merchandise and more. All these intellectual properties are copyrighted too. Often a band agreement will outline who owns the copyrighted works you'll be creating as a band.

It's on the flip side of this copyright issue that most indie bands get themselves in trouble. Often, they'll incorporate other people's copyrighted works into their own materials. Many indies use copyrighted images on their website, sync their music to copyrighted video footage on YouTube or use copyrighted band photos on their albums and posters. Just as you need to get proper permission to use and cover other people's music, so too do you need proper permission for the use of other non-original works. This goes for any original photo, text or video a fan makes and sends to you as well. If you're collaborating with someone in one of your networks, you need to get permission and work out any money matters – especially if you're incorporating a fan's original work into your own that you may sell. Although we suggest resources for royalty-free text, photos, graphics and video throughout the *Manual* and DIYMusicManual.com site, the intricacies of getting permission from copyright owners for this material is outside our scope. Instead, we recommend a detailed book on the subject, *Getting Permission: How To License and Clear Copyrighted Materials Online and Off* by Richard W. Stim.

WORKING WITH PHOTOGRAPHERS

If you get a photographer to take pictures of your band, know that the photographer owns the copyright to the photos of your band – not you. This is the case even if you pay them to take the photos. Each use you want to make of the photos must be cleared and licensed with the photographer. So, just because your photographer gives you permission to use one of their photos on your website, that doesn't mean you can necessarily use it for promotional materials or an album cover.

Make sure that you are clear what rights you are getting from the photographer. And, of course, get it in writing. If you can, you want a photographer that will work for hire so that you own the photos. Some might charge you more for this option.

CROWN AND GOVERNMENTAL COPYRIGHT

In the UK, Australia and New Zealand, it's the government that holds copyright in any work it creates during its normal course of business. Incorporating it into your work requires a licence. This is generally known as the Crown Copyright. The duration of the governmental copyrights vary depending on which country produced it, so if you are thinking of incorporating such a work into your music you will want to check with your appropriate governmental authority such as the Office of Public Sector Information in the UK (opsi.gov.uk).

Interestingly, in the US, governmental works fall instantly into the public domain. As a result, works by NASA or other US governmental bodies are there for your taking. And while you have the luxury to freely use these works created by the US government, note that your American musician counterparts can't 'take' from your respective countries as its government enforces the copyrights of other countries within its borders.

MORE ABOUT COPYRIGHT

If you are interested in learning more about copyright we recommend *Free Culture: How Big Media Uses Technology and the Law to Lock Down Culture and*

Control Creativity, by Lawrence Lessig, Professor of Law at Stanford Law School and a founder of the Creative Commons organisation. While the book deals primarily with US copyright law, it goes into depth on how the Internet is challenging the concept of copyright and affecting the law. The book is freely available under a Creative Commons licence at free-culture.cc.

▸▸MERCHANDISING RIGHTS

As mentioned in Chapter 6: Your Albums and Merchandise, merchandising – the business of using your brand iconography to sell products – can be a major part of your income. Merchandising involves:

- The owner of your copyrighted brand images and text
- The merchandising rights owner who has the contractual right to sell products with your copyrighted brand images and text

Your band agreement should outline who or what owns your band name, brand and merchandising rights although, to the extent that your products have lyrics from your songs printed on them, such use actually falls under the author/publisher's printing rights. Permission must be obtained or worked out beforehand before using any lyrics. Song titles, on the other hand, can't be copyrighted and are fair game.

Record labels would often try to take a cut of the merchandising rights. Bands that hold on to these rights would typically sell them for an advance (and possible royalties) to a merchandise company that would handle everything from design to order fulfilment. However, these one-stop shops only purchase the merchandising rights from national or major label acts.

As an indie band, these rights are yours. And doing the merchandise yourselves means that all the profits will be yours as well. One notable exception: often, venues want a cut of any merchandising revenues earned in their establishment. Any such cut should be negotiated ahead of time, with an agreement in writing.

▸▸TRADE MARKS

Since indie bands now reach a global audience, the issue of protecting your band name and brand is more of an issue than ever. The law protecting your band name and brand is known as trade mark law. Trade mark law is an entirely different body of law from copyright law, with different principles and procedures to learn.

TRADE MARK LAW BASICS

A trade or service mark (for simplification, we'll stick with the word 'trade mark' since both are essentially the same) is a distinctive word, phrase or symbol that uniquely identifies your product or service to the world and separates you in the mind of the public from competing products or services. For an indie band, trade marks include your band name, logo, tagline or mascot. The value of these marks grow over time as you repeatedly and consistently use them to represent your band and music to the public. This value can be protected under trade mark law. In fact, the more you use your marks and the longer you use them, the stronger your trade mark rights become.

Under the law, the first person to publicly use a mark for a specific product or service in commerce automatically owns it. So, if you were the first indie band in the world to use your name, logo, tagline or mascot online in some public manner such as your website, a newspaper ad announcing a show or a poster, you are probably the trade mark owner. This doesn't mean a person or company can't use the same marks with a different product or service, however. In general, you only have the rights to those marks for music purposes.

Of course, to the extent your mark is at all similar to another famous mark outside of music, you are likely to be infringing and may be contacted in the future to stop using it. For instance, in Chapter 3: Your Brand, we said you would not want to name your band 'Google' regardless of the fact that no other band exists under that name. Given trade mark law, it's likely that Google would successfully prevent you from operating under this name regardless of the fact that you're a band, not a search engine.

Why? Unlike copyright law, which protects your song copyright for your life plus an additional 70 years before falling into the public domain, trade marks – even famous ones – can fall into the public domain if not diligently protected. After all, if you're taking a word or symbol out of the public domain but aren't actively using and protecting it to ensure that it identifies your product or service, then someone else should be able to use it. This is why famous brands such as Coca-Cola, Harrods and McDonald's have to aggressively protect their trade marks from any use that might confuse and 'dilute' the value they've built in their marks with the public. Only through active maintenance of their marks does the law allow companies to keep them.

Additionally, the law gives trade mark owners some common sense rights.

For instance, if you name your band a variation of the word Google such as 'The Google', 'G00gle', 'Gooooogle' or even 'Gue Gull', the company would have a strong case against your band as well. These are fact-based decisions for courts to decide and there are always exceptions for lawyers to argue over but our general advice is to avoid any name or mark similar to ones already in use. If you're still stumped about what name or mark would be considered fair game, consult your lawyer.

Once you are a trade mark owner, on the other hand, you will need to protect it from dilution and confusion in the marketplace just as aggressively. If another band starts using your name or any other marks of yours, you have the right and obligation to prevent them from doing so. This is true even if the other band plays different music from yours. The public – and your fans – may become confused about which band is which when it comes to shows, albums and merchandise and the longer you let the other band's use of the mark stand, the more strength they will have to defend it in a court of law.

Unfortunately, enforcing your rights costs money. You'll need to hire a solicitor to send a cease and desist letter to any infringing party and either negotiate a compromise such as allowing them to choose a different name retaining some element of their former name or prevent them from engaging as a band under that name.

You'll need to determine who the trade mark owner is in your band. Typically, band agreements turn the band name, brand and trade mark over to the band as an entity.

DO YOU NEED TO REGISTER YOUR NAME?

Like copyright, a trade mark is automatically generated as long as you meet the requirements outlined above. However, registration with an official governmental authority will give you additional rights, a public record that you spent the time and money to protect the rights you have in your band name and brand and act as a deterrent to other bands searching for a name of their own. Whether you choose to register your mark is typically a matter of cost and, unfortunately, registering a mark is expensive.

As an indie band you do it all: you sell products (which are covered under a trade mark) and perform music (which is covered under a service mark). Every product and service is designated into a particular class of goods and services. You should consider registering your marks under the following classes:

- **Class 9:** The sale of digital media (CDs, downloadable audio files, etc.) under your band name.
- **Class 16:** The use of your band name in posters, pamphlets, newsletters and other promotional materials.
- **Class 25:** The use of your marks on T-shirts and other merchandise.
- **Class 41:** Entertainment services including the use your name in conjunction with performing as a band.

Keep in mind that each trade mark you register (name, logo, tagline, mascot) and each class you register it in costs money. The fees vary depending on which country you are registering. For instance, in the UK at the time of writing, registering for a trade mark in one class is £200 with additional classes at £50 each. This is just the application and does not include the costs of hiring a solicitor. If you have to choose just one, we recommend trade marking your band name in class 41.

REGISTERING YOUR TRADE MARKS WITH A GOVERNMENTAL TRADE MARK OFFICE

You have a choice as to where to register your trade mark since each country has its own trade mark office and registration office. To register your marks within the UK, you can do so via the UK Intellectual Property Office (ipo.gov.uk). Another option that will protect your marks throughout Europe is to register instead with the EU's Office for Harmonisation in the Internal Market ('OHIM') (oami.europa.eu). Registering with the OHIM costs more money but expands your protection through the expanding EU. Better yet, as new Member States join the union, your mark is automatically protected within their borders as well. Registration in Australia is handled by IP Australia (ipaustralia.gov.au), while registration in New Zealand is handled by the Intellectual Property Office of New Zealand (iponz.govt.nz).

You can register on your own but we recommend using an solicitor. Trade mark registration is a complicated process, although all the governmental trade mark offices have detailed information explaining the process and their fees. The UK Intellectual Property Office even offers a confidential search and advice service to help you determine if your mark would be acceptable for registration before you submit it. Although this service costs around £80, this service is cheaper than the application fee – which is not refundable if your application is denied.

Although you may file and pay for a trade mark application online, the process of review and advertisement (that is, publishing to 'the world' the fact you are applying for a particular mark so others with similar marks can object through your respective governmental office's trade mark journal) can take many months. Assuming your application doesn't run into any issues once your registration is approved, you're the proud owner of a registered trade mark.

▸▸OTHER ISSUES: TAXES, INSURANCE, CONTRACTS AND MORE

There are many legal and business issues that go beyond the scope of the *Manual*. As a reminder, you can find links to governmental, legal and business resources at DIYMusicManual.com as well as a list of business books and information on this and other subjects.

▶▶PART TWO

GET FANS

▸▸CHAPTER EIGHT

GET NOTICED

Getting noticed is no longer about trying to get the attention of the 'music industry' and getting signed; it's about getting people interested in your music. Fortunately, this process doesn't have to cost you money. You simply need to be smart about making your music and your message stand out from the crowd.

In this chapter we will detail powerful strategies for winning over new fans.

▸▸THE LONG TAIL (REPRISE)

We examined the implications of Chris Anderson's book, *The Long Tail*, in the first chapter, but in this chapter we'll talk about how to apply the Long Tail to gain traction. We live in a world of niches. Each niche has its own unique interests and each niche can have its own soundtrack as well.

Getting played on television or commercial radio is daunting. But getting your song about the beauty of riding a chopper down the highway on a motorcycle website doesn't seem all that difficult. If you've written a song about motorcycles, motorcycle enthusiasts will listen to it whether or not they know who you are.

The top-down approach made sense in the old days, when most media were mainstream media. Now, the world is filled with what we like to call 'niche media'. The Internet isn't just a broadcast medium, it's a two- (or more) way street with an endless number of channels. Because of this, you can find a forum on most any topic imaginable and participate through your music or just about anything else you can create.

Once you can see the world as a universe of niches, each one seems a lot easier to break into. There are seven effective strategies for getting your band and music noticed. But before you reach out to them, you need to know who your audience is.

▶▶KNOW YOUR AUDIENCE

In the pre-net era, you focused on getting noticed locally. Today, focus on getting noticed globally. The Internet allows you to win over more fans than you can imagine. But that wonderful planetary reach makes it much harder to know who's actually listening. Instead of seeing the faces of your fans, many of them will look like nothing more than cold, hard Web statistics. Still, you need to get to know them so you can put your music where they'll find it. Who are your fans and what do they like?

Our band straddled both the pre-net and post-net era and we found the process of transitioning from one to the other enlightening. Our pre-net fans loved our live show. They had a good time listening to our music and they loved our horn-powered energy. As the post-net era arrived, the most popular elements of our live show didn't translate to the Internet. We had to rely on different strategies to win over global fans. These included projects targeting niches beyond our locale such as creating *The Cheapass Album*, which we'll discuss below.

If your music means something to you, then it will probably resonate with the people that share your interests, no matter where in the world they are. So who are your fans? Are they teenagers? Baby boomers? Kids? Thirty-somethings? Geeks? Truckers? Knitting fanatics? The more you know about your own fans, the easier it will be to target them in new and compelling ways.

▶▶SEVEN EFFECTIVE STRATEGIES FOR GETTING NOTICED

THE STANDING-OUT STRATEGY

There are over 225,000 indie artists at CD Baby. The best sellers all have stories to tell but one of the most surprising ones is about an artist who wrote an entire album about sailing. While that topic alone isn't enough to get an album to the top sellers list, the musician managed to get her album reviewed in a popular sailing magazine, which generated tons of sales. A review of a sailing album in a *music* magazine would probably have received little notice. But because the review appeared in a *sailing* magazine, people read the article and bought the CD.

Dedicated music publications and sites review stacks of CDs and songs. Even if your band gets its album reviewed – and even if it's a good one – it just doesn't stand out. It's just one of many in a sea of other music reviews. Sailing magazines, on the other hand, don't get many albums to review as they're focused on sailing. So when a review of one actually is published, it stands out. This goes for *any* non-music speciality magazine, blog or website. By targeting her niche, the woman's CD sales skyrocketed.

We call this the Standing-Out Strategy. The great thing about it is there's room for everyone. While your music probably occupies a musical niche depending on the type of music you play, this represents only one, highly competitive channel for your music. By using non-music channels where your music will be the only music to choose from, you'll get noticed.

This is a major shift in thinking that takes some getting used to. It's no longer necessary to stick to places where people listen to music. Forget radio – music can be played on any website. There are forums, podcasts, webzines, publications and sites dedicated to activities where an existing audience might appreciate your music.

Our example of this started out accidentally, after we found inspiration in an unusual place: an off-the-wall board game named Deadwood, designed by a company called Cheapass Games out of Seattle. A card in the game led us to write a song called, 'Were All These Beer Cans Here Last Night?'. It was only a few weeks later that we hit on the idea to email Cheapass Games and share the song that they had unwittingly inspired. We sent them the song and, surprisingly, they wrote back the next day and asked if they could put it up on their website. Within a few months of it being posted, the demo was downloaded well over 5000 times, since they had a large audience. Soon, it took on a life of its own, winding up on blogs, message boards and Internet radio stations, all without our help. Their website was so popular that when searching on 'Beer Cans' on Google at that point, our demo song was on the first page of links. This was great exposure but it didn't end there. We applied the Standing-Out Strategy and took this idea a step further. We teamed up with Cheapass Games to create an entire album of songs based on their games: *The Cheapass Album*. Best of all, they agreed to distribute and give it worldwide distribution along with their games.

Carla Ulbrich (carlaulbrich.com), who makes her living as a folk singer, summed it up best, 'Go to where you're a novelty.' Ulbrich did this by using her wit and off-centre perspective to turn an unfortunate series of medical problems into inspiration for new music. After releasing albums on these topics, she found new audiences and not only gets traditional shows, she also plays lucrative gigs at medical conventions, where any music stands out.

THE PIGGYBACKING STRATEGY

Piggybacking can broaden your exposure by taking something people already know well and leverage it for yourself. There are three different ways to apply this strategy.

RIDE COATTAILS

As we said in Chapter 3: Your Brand, one of the simplest ways to piggyback is to mention the bands that you sound like on your website. People who know those bands and search on them will find your site and are likely to give your music a chance. In fact, this is exactly how Web presence services such as Last.fm work. The ultimate way to piggyback is to cover a well-known song by a famous artist. In fact, it's usually these cover songs that are an indie artist's best initial sellers. They act as a great gateway for people to discover their original music.

But music is not the only thing that you should piggyback on. Consider all the niches that exist in the world and see if there's a place for your music inside one of them. And niches don't have to be small. In fact, we know of one band that wrote a song about the Indiana Colts American football team before they went to the Superbowl. While Colts fans are a niche, it's a very large one. The band got a ton of airplay, articles and a lot of fans bought its music because it successfully piggybacked on the Colts at a time when people were paying a lot of attention to them.

Also, there is more than one way to piggyback on a niche. For example, Pete Shukoff, of the group Nice Peter, wrote a song called '50 Cent is a Pussy'. The forums on his websites were buzzing after he released it and he got a lot of angry comments but an equal number of supporters and new fans. He successfully piggybacked on the same guy he was dissing in his song.

Even album art can provide you an opportunity for piggybacking. The art for Beatnik Turtle's *The Cheapass Album* was created by the renowned comic book and game illustrator Phil Foglio (studiofoglio.com). Foglio has millions of fans and when we released the album, some people bought it just because they collect his artwork. Our album got listed on a website that tracks everything that Phil Foglio illustrates and he even distributes the album for sale from his site.

Again, the place to start is not the traditional music mediums. Instead, brainstorm about concepts, ideas or even events that can take you further than you would be able to go on your own. For example, when the *Star Wars* thirtieth anniversary came up, we leveraged a song that we had written for the Song of the Day called '*Star Wars* (A Movie Like No Other)'. We managed to summarise the entire original Star Wars trilogy in a single song. Later we made a video using a video mashup feature at StarWars.com. It ended up getting played over 15,000 times thanks to the active community at that site.

RIDE A TRADITION

Another way to piggyback is to make an album or a song about a holiday, festival or other tradition that people know well. When people search on 'St Patrick's Day', for example, your band might come up if you do an album for it.

We did an album for Christmas called *Santa Doesn't Like You*, and, like clockwork, that album gets a slew of new sales every December. We come up in searches for terms like 'Santa', 'Christmas' and 'Holiday'. The titles of songs, such as 'Coed Naked Drunk Xmas Shopping' and 'Smokin' The Mistletoe' get people to sample our music online out of sheer curiosity.

RIDE TRENDS

Current events and popular culture provide opportunities for piggybacking as well. When a topic is hot, a large number of people are guaranteed to be searching for information about it.

The Brobdingnagian Bards are always looking for ways to ride trends, so when the Monty Python musical *Spamalot* got popular, they posted a blog entry with the subject about *Spamalot* and talked about the Monty Python music that they had covered previously. The post got a ton of hits, got them noticed by new fans and resulted in sales.

Piggybacking can also be a tool for good, not just good publicity. Grant Baciocco of Throwing Toasters put together two compilation charity albums called *Laughter Is a Powerful Weapon*, with music donated by himself and many other well-known comedy artists. The money from one went to the Twin Towers Orphans' fund and the other went to the Red Cross for Katrina victims.

THE AGENT STRATEGY

Most bands start out promoting and representing themselves because they start out small. But, when possible, it's a powerful advantage to have a person outside the band represent you. People tend to pay attention when someone who is not directly part of the band talks it up. There's an air of objectivity, even if it's promotional.

Agents are distant enough from the music that they can come up with promotional angles, strategies and ideas that you might never have thought of. They can claim that you're the best band ever. And if they do something that's a little too outrageous, well, they're just an agent, it doesn't reflect directly on the band. It's also why agents are most useful during negotiations, because they can be mercenary. If you negotiate for yourself and you give the other side a particularly hard time, they'll start to dislike *you*, rather than your agent.

Also, people tend to assume that you've reached a certain threshold of popularity simply because you can afford to have someone act on your behalf. Before she got an agent of her own, Ulbrich would often pretend to be her own agent over the phone, employing a thick New York accent. When someone asked to have lunch with the agent, she'd always be too busy but they were always in luck, because Ulbrich herself could make it.

THE MULTI-TASKING STRATEGY

None of the musicians we interviewed for the *Manual* rely on one project for their income. Most of them were working on *many* different projects beyond playing live, selling albums and selling merchandise. For instance, Jonathan Coulton participates in the *'PopSci.com' Popular Science* podcast and licenses his music. Brad Turcotte of Brad Sucks maintains multiple websites including StripCreator.com and also licenses his music. Grant Baciocco of Throwing Toasters writes and produces the multiple-award-winning podcast *The Radio Adventures of Dr Floyd*, does voice-over and acting work and produces a podcast for the Jim Henson Company, among other projects. George Hrab is a drummer in a popular cover band that plays at weddings and corporate events, writes and produces his *Geologic Podcast* and has written a book. The Brobdingnagian Bards produce a popular Celtic music podcast called *Celtic MP3s Music Magazine* (in addition to four other podcasts and multiple newsletters), maintain multiple Celtic music websites and even have a comic book.

The notable thing is not that these musicians do so many projects but that they use each one to promote the other. The Brobdingnagian Bards' Celtic podcasts originally featured their own music but eventually they got so many submissions from other Celtic bands that they began to highlight the music of others. This not only grew their Celtic musician network, it also drew in new Celtic music audiences, broadening their fan network. And once a fan discovered one of these projects, he or she would find the others because the Bards had co-branded everything.

THE LONG-HAUL STRATEGY (THE DEATH OF THE BIG SPLASH)

For some reason, indie musicians have internalised the big splash strategy that major labels were forced to use because of their business model. The major labels are rarely focused on long-term artist development, instead relying on the power of newness and huge initial sales. Their back catalogues are just gravy, more fuel to pay for new artists rather than developing established ones.

As an indie band, it's unlikely you'll have the money for a huge initial marketing push with billboards, paid-for radio play and expensive publicists. Instead, indies must allow development and word of mouth to occur naturally and gain audience and momentum over time. The good news is this strategy has never been more powerful than today – thanks to the Web. Word-of-mouth mentions you have online usually stick. Where in the past events faded in memory, online they're archived and can be rekindled. Future fans can come to search, link and stumble upon a past campaign and discover your music. The key is to build presence, be patient and settle into a 'long, slow burn' as Gavin Mikhail recommends. But with each success and connection, you grow your fanbase.

For instance, Brad Turcotte created his own development cycle to maximise his exposure for his band's music. In 2001, he released his album online in the form of MP3s, garnering some initial interest and some donations. This money allowed him to make a CD and when he released this he gained another surge of new fans. A little later, he released the source tracks to his music, this time making new fans among people who enjoy remixing songs. When he packaged the best remixes into another CD, there was yet another surge of new fans who loved both the remixes and the original material. Finally, when he released his second album, it generated interest in his previous albums. This album cycle should continue as he releases additional albums and new material. As you can see, Turcotte's original material has generated exposure and income for him over the years.

Just as the album cycle takes time to gather momentum, getting noticed within a niche also takes time. Carla Ulbrich noticed that live festivals and conventions also have a cycle. Effectively breaking into each live festival and convention took about three years. Ulbrich needed that time to make the necessary connections and establish her reputation so that she could consistently get booked at events.

Most of the artists we've interviewed have agreed that it takes time to get noticed, develop a following and acquire a steady income stream. As Gavin Mikhail said, there's a 'being the cool kid in class' mentality that needs to happen.

That is, as you work to get your music noticed, people will naturally want to know who else likes what you're doing and what else you've done. This is one of the reasons music reviews and testimonials are important. Being able to capitalise on smaller successes to grow them Jonathan Coulton noticed during his 'Thing a Week' project that, when there were bursts of traffic for a particular song release, visitors to his site showed up in huge groups and quickly left. But with each surge, some stuck around because they liked his music. Over time his regular visitors steadily increased. This will happen for you as well. So whatever you do to get noticed, keep your mind on long-haul strategies.

DRAW THEM A MAP

Your fans have the most power to spread the word about your music. But they don't necessarily know how to do it best or even know if they should. You will have to tell them. For instance, the Brobdingnagian Bards noticed that their mailing list had fewer entries than they had podcast listeners. So, they decided to ask people to sign up. When they announced it on their podcast, they got 300 new members. All their fans needed was a push. They decided to take this further and told their fans exactly how to promote and book them, which we discuss in Chapter 12: Get Publicised.

THE STAY-TUNED STRATEGY

When radio DJs are about to play commercials, they never go directly into the ads. Instead, they announce what they're going to play after the break, to keep people tuned in. You should adopt this same technique. Always talk about your next project when you talk about your band, whether you're talking to the press, your fans or other musicians. Here's why:

- Your fans will be motivated to keep tabs on you until that next project is released.
- It entices the press to ask questions about your upcoming projects and write future stories.
- It encourages people to get involved and help out. If you don't announce what you have planned, no one will know that they can help.
- It will also keep your own band members motivated and working towards the same goals.

So always have a soundbite on the tip of your tongue about what you're doing next. Movies have trailers and a band should have announcements of what's to come.

▸▸ THE ARM'S-REACH LESSON

The arm's-reach strategy, which we first introduced in Chapter 2: Your Network, should be a key part of everything you do. No one expects you to get your music into a major motion picture or play a stadium immediately. You have to focus on strategies within your reach. But once you succeed at a few projects here and there, you'll find that your reach has expanded. You'll have new people in your networks and new opportunities available. Once you become established, opportunities will come to you.

This isn't to say that you can't dream of playing a stadium but it doesn't pay to focus on things that are not currently within your reach. Don't aim low but focus on what you can imagine yourself doing right now. In fact, that's what this second section of the *Manual* is all about: getting you opportunities that are well within your reach today.

ALWAYS BE PREPARED

You might start out in smaller niches but you never know where those opportunities might lead, especially on the Internet. You have no idea who's listening. And, when things connect, you should prepare to take advantage of those opportunities when they come your way.

The Cheapass Album is a good example of this, which got us a licensing deal with ABC Family/Disney for a commercial campaign. It also created a fan in Mur Lafferty, a notable podcaster, author and fan of Cheapass Games. She discovered us through that niche, liked our music and asked us if she could play 'Were All These Beer Cans Here Last Night?' on her podcast, *Geek Fu Action Grip*. Little did we know that this chance acquaintance would eventually lead to creative collaborations and an introduction to her friends, fans and talented network of podcasters. This resulted in many podcasters using our music, tens of thousands of song plays and many new fans. She also ended up using our music videos in a business project for Lulu.tv that got our videos displayed around the clock in a convention with over 30,000 attendees.

Our online *Indie Band Survival Guide* that we wrote for musicians is another example, since always being prepared to recognise and take advantage of opportunities when they come knocking led to the book you're reading now.

SEE WHAT STICKS

As you can see, there are many different strategies available to help you get noticed. There are no rules to this new music business, so we suggest experimenting with many projects and ideas to see what works best for you. Just keep what sticks and move on from those that don't.

▸▸ CHAPTER NINE

GET BOOKED AND PLAY LIVE

We asked both Jim DeRogatis, music editor for the *Chicago Sun-Times* and co-host of NPR's *Sound Opinions*, and Todd Martens, a music writer who has written for *Billboard* magazine and the *Los Angeles Times*, how they find out about new bands. Their answer: live shows. And if they hear a buzz about a band, they look at the listings to see where and when they're playing. This makes sense. After all, since the larger clubs and venues need a minimum audience in order to make it worthwhile to book a band, they don't take chances. By the time a major venue books a band, it's safe to say that those bands have a following.

Getting to those larger venues takes time but we can summarise the essence of how to put on a great show in one sentence: **YOU ARE THERE FOR THE AUDIENCE**.

We've seen bands go on stage thinking that the audience is there for them. That's the wrong focus. Many musicians forget that music is entertainment. The audience is there to have a good time and you are there to make sure that they do. And with live shows accounting for more and more of the money a musician makes, a gig is more than just music; it's a show.

In this chapter, we'll cover all aspects of playing live: from practising to publicity to packing up afterwards.

▸▸ BOOKING

Booking gigs is another one of those art forms that could fill a book by itself. We can't cover everything here but like the rest of the *Manual* we will give you an overview and all the gotchas.

As George Hrab told us: 'Talent won't get you the gig but it will let you keep the ones you get.' So we'll make you a deal: you bring the talent and we'll tell you how to get the gigs.

DESIGNATE A BOOKER

We suggest designating a single person in the band to handle bookings. If you use an agency, you should still have just one contact. You don't want any embarrassing collisions when multiple gigs are booked for the same date. Nor do you want any confusion among the venue bookers over who they should talk to.

The person doing booking should be a 'people person'. Booking is about relationships. It's about having a beer with the people who book bands at the bars and also about having a thick skin to deal with rejection. Your booker should be persistent and have a mobile. It also helps if your booker researches the bands that are most similar to your own that book in your area. The phrase, 'I see you've booked so-and-so, we're very similar to them' can get you into a lot of doors by using bands that have already won their way into the venues.

SCHEDULING

Bookers struggle with scheduling more than any other obstacle. Most bands need every single member to be available to put on a gig. We recommend creating an online band calendar marked with all of the dates that band members *can't* make. Google and Yahoo both offer nice shareable online calendars for this purpose, although there are lots of other options. We prefer the Web-based ones, though, because they allow the band members to add dates to the calendar as they learn of activities or dead dates wherever they are and let the booker check the calendar from any Internet connection.

Of course, you'll also want to add all solid show dates to the calendar after they're booked, so the band members know not to book new events on those nights.

BOOKING KIT

Dealing with bookers is one of the few times as an indie musician that you'll still need printed materials. You're going to be handing them a CD, so you also need to hand them basic bios and contact information. You should have all the source documents for your booking kit online so that you can print them at a moment's notice and so that bookers can download them if they find your website.

A booking kit should have:

- **A CD:** Include a CD of your latest album and perhaps even more than one if you think it'll help you get booked. (And keep *all* of your contact information on the CD itself, in case it gets separated from the rest of it.)
- **A cover page:** Include your contact information, your website and some basic details about booking such as where to find your sound set-up and other show needs. You need a page on your website (see Chapter 4: Your Website) that has booking and show information. Note that you should have contact information and your website on every page that you give a booker, in case they lose one.
- **Your band bio:** See Chapter 12: Get Publicised for information on how to create a band bio. You will include this one-page document here.
- **Press clippings:** Nothing sells a band to a venue better than a press clippings page or a page of review quotes if you're fortunate enough to have them. Sometimes it helps to have a list of prior show dates to convince a new venue that you're an experienced band.
- **A 20x27cm photo:** The 27x27cm band photo is the size most often used by venues, so you should have one available on your website. Most venues don't ask for glossy photos any more because they have an easier time getting copies off your site, but some might. You need to find out ahead of time what their expectations are.
- **A live DVD:** Possibly the most effective part of your press kit would be a DVD of your band in action, especially if you're trying to book a wedding or corporate show. Video will prove better than anything else that your band can perform.
- **Testimonials:** Providing testimonials can take someone who is on the verge of buying an act to make the commitment. Include them if you can.

GETTING YOUR FIRST SHOW

Most venues hate taking a chance on new bands, so first shows are some of the most difficult ones to get. It's the famous saying: 'How do I get an audience if no one will give me a gig?'

You may have to do some footwork to get that first show. Ask around at local venues to see how they handle new bands. Many require you to perform at an open mic. Others will give you an off night, a Monday or Sunday, to prove yourself.

One of the easiest ways to get that first show is to open for an established band. As we explained earlier, it's a good idea to build relationships with other bands in your area because they can leverage you into venues where you haven't played before. But be ready to play for the exposure and the experience – i.e., for free – rather than for a cut of the door.

No matter how you get your first show, you need to impress the venue enough to get asked back, hopefully to headline at a weekend. And what impresses a venue isn't usually the music. They don't make money on that. The door funds also don't make them money, as that money usually goes to the bands and the sound guy. Smaller venues exist to do one thing: sell alcohol. That means they want you to pack the place with as many warm bodies as possible.

So how do you pack a place for your first show? Here's a simple recipe that has worked for many bands, including ourselves: free alcohol. Invite all of your friends and all of their friends to see your band debut and then to a party either right afterwards or right before. You want to pack the venue when you play and have them stick around for other bands (so as not to be rude).

This should get a lot of people to come and see your band (with, admittedly, a bribe of beer but if you split that between the band members, it's not that expensive). It also makes a big party out of your first show.

We did this when we debuted (after a few tentative open-mic nights in dive bars to get us used to playing) at the US Beer Company in Chicago. We jammed people into the place when we performed and played a great show musically. They not only asked us back, they had us headlining at our second show.

GETTING MORE VENUES AFTER STARTING OUT

Once you're an established player, it might still be difficult to book new venues. In Chicago, where we operate, until you become very well known, the fact that you've played in one venue doesn't help you get into any others. You need to prove yourselves anew for each one. This is why your press clippings and previous show calendar can be very helpful.

Your most important tools in booking venues are personal relationships and persistence. Every venue has an in-house booker, so the key is to know who they are, present your materials to them and then follow up. It takes a special knack to know the difference between being persistent and being annoying. Make sure your band's booker possesses that knack before setting him or her loose on the venues. Most bands that we've interviewed agree that persistence gets them their shows but you don't want any restraining orders either.

The simplest way to grow your bookings, besides using a professional booker, is research. Which bands are similar to yours and where do they play? It's much easier to convince a venue to book your band if they book similar ones. This is where your press kit can work for you, especially if you give them a good clippings page and a live DVD.

Another technique is to form a cartel of bands and alternate opening for each other. Often, venues want an entire night of entertainment. A group of bands can work together to provide this. And, as we've said, it's especially effective to network with bands elsewhere. If you can get in touch with a band in a town you're heading towards, you can share the bill with them to get access to their audience.

Another good way to get bookings at venues you've never played at is to use Eventful (eventful.com). They have a unique service they've created for musicians called Eventful Demand which you can sign up for as a musician and which is a free widget that can be incorporated into your website and Web presence sites. With a click of a mouse (and a free account at Eventful) your fans can go 'on the record' and state that if you come to their area, they will show up to see you. In other words, they're demanding that you come play in their town. When you get enough demands in a particular area, the Eventful Demand number can act as verifiable proof that you have a draw there. Note that Eventful Demand numbers are usually a little less than will actually show up at a gig, because not everyone signs up for the service. Also, your fans that do show up will be inclined to bring friends.

Venues have begun using Eventful Demand numbers as a better means of judging a band's draw instead of relying on the band's word and (supposed) size of its mailing list. The demand number can give them an idea of approximately how many people will be likely to show up if you played there. Therefore, we recommend signing up for a free account at Eventful to start building your demand numbers. These numbers should be included in your press kits when approaching a venue. (We talk more about Eventful and other touring solutions they provide in detail below.)

Once you do book a gig, do not *ever* cancel. Ever. Venues will often ban you if you cancel, especially if it's at short notice. Our drummer once cancelled on us a few weeks before a gig and we ended up playing the show without him! We billed it as Beatnik Turtle's 'acoustic night' and performed the gig as if it was one of our coffeehouse performances. Although it was a difficult gig, the bar was very grateful and we kept the relationship and have played there many times since. Another option is to find another band to play in your place. It's always useful to have subs available.

BOOKING AGENCIES

If your band gets really busy, it's often a good idea to use a booking agency which has established connections with bookers and venues. If they are a reputable company, they will audition you first to make sure you have a quality group. Venues will put more trust in bookers that are picky about which bands they represent.

There are generally two types of relationships that you might form with a booking agency. In an exclusive booking arrangement, all of your bookings go through the agency. The booker will be listed as your main contact and anyone looking to book your band will have to call them. In a non-exclusive agreement, you can still find bookings through others. Usually, a booker will book their exclusive clients for gigs before their non-exclusives.

No matter which way you go, make sure that your relationship with the booking agency is a good one and that you understand the business relationship before agreeing to it. Often, they will take a cut of the door and the venue will pay them, not you. Your cut then comes from the booking agency.

Booking agencies don't want to deal with multiple people in a band. They aren't there to drag the drummer off the couch before the gig if he's got a hangover. They prefer to deal with the band manager. If you're managing yourselves, designate a single responsible contact to deal with them.

HOUSE CONCERTS

Thanks to the Internet, house concerts – small shows hosted at people's residences – have continued to grow in popularity. Although these types of concerts are better known in the folk music community, where the intimate setting is appropriate, some bands have added these small shows to coincide and supplement a standard tour. If you do decide to perform house concerts, ask your hosts to guarantee a minimum payment. You might want to suggest the cover amount and the minimum number of people paying that cover – with the difference to be covered by the hosts, if necessary. This way they share in the risk and have an incentive to bring in enough people.

There may be some legal issues associated with house concerts due to local zoning laws prohibiting commercial practices (that is, charging money for a concert) in a residential zone (that is, where people are to reside and sleep). So ask your local council about any such restrictions, otherwise you run the risk of having your show shut down. For more information about house concerts, we recommend the book *Host Your Own Concerts* by Joe Taylor as well as HouseConcerts (houseconcerts.com).

TOURING

If you're serious about your live shows, playing on the road is a necessity. According to Fletcher Lee of Lee Productions, an agency that's been booking for decades, touring is a critical component in developing a live band. You need to play live often to grow your audience but there's only so much you can do in one area over a period of time. At some point, the local audience needs a break from your sound and it becomes necessary to spread your wings a bit. Shows on the road win over entirely new networks of fans and are worth the extra time developing the necessary out-of-town relationships.

The traditional wisdom of booking is that you start in your physical location and tour in ever-expanding concentric circles around your 'base'. But, as a global musician, it's likely that your fans will be spread across the country, if not the world. Understanding where they are and being able to play for them is quite a battle. However, as we've mentioned above, a Web service called Eventful (eventful.com) has created a useful solution. Eventful is the world's leading events website that allows users all over the world to discover, promote, share and create events from concerts to campaign speeches. As a subset to their service, they have created free tools for the performers at these events – the Eventful Demand Widget and the Performer Dashboard – to allow them to capture and understand where their fans are across the Web and make informed decisions about where to spend time and money on touring.

We've already discussed the Eventful's Demand service that allows your fans to influence where they want you to appear and to 'demand' you to come to their city. While the Eventful Demand widget allows fans to demand your band, it doesn't help if you can't interpret the data or communicate with those fans that did the demanding. The Performer Dashboard allows you to freely track your Demand campaigns, and provides demographic and geographic information of those demanding you. In addition it allows you to send messages directly to your demanding fans – in that particular city or area. That way, if you do book a gig at a particular city where you know you have fans in the surrounding area, you can reach out and invite all of them to see you. If you tour, we highly recommend using this service. It can help you plan targeted tours – saving you time and money.

Finally, note that you can sometimes get a string of shows – big and small – on a tour. Marc Gunn and Andrew McKee of the Brobdingnagian Bards spend much of their time touring and always perform along the way to each destination. For example, if they play a convention, they will plan house concerts going in both directions, often getting themselves a place to stay as well as travel money. If you are too loud or your band just won't work in a house setting, there are also always smaller venues in towns on the way to destinations. The Bards also recommend taking a break in between each tour to avoid burnout.

SETTING A PRICE AND GETTING PAID

When setting prices, consider how much you *need* to do the show, rather than how much you're *worth*. This will give you a solid basis for your price quote. You'll also have a better idea of how far you can bend on the prices that you set.

To do this, take stock of all of the expenses for doing the show, especially if you have to travel. Also factor in your time and the lost opportunity to do other shows or projects during those dates. Once you determine this number, you'll feel more confident when it is time to negotiate.

Make sure that you are clear on any cuts of your CD and merchandise sales that the venue demands. The larger venues will ask for as much as 20 per cent of your take. If there's a contract, read it carefully. Some venues, like colleges, won't let you sell merchandise at all. All of these factors need to be worked into your costs.

Carla Ulbrich warns that musicians often think they're making more than they actually do because they get paid in cash. If you've got a fat wad of cash in your wallet from the CD and T-shirt sales, it can feel like you've hit the jackpot, even though in reality a portion of this has to be shared with your silent partner in all things dealing with income – the government.

CONVENTIONS

Many successful independent bands have found that conventions can be a fantastic source of paid gigs that also expose their music to large numbers of new people.

The conventions that you can play depend on your style of music and the contacts you manage to make. While it might seem obvious to seek out music conventions, most bands actually do other kinds of conventions because there is less competition and more opportunities to stand out. For example, Ulbrich makes a good living playing medical conventions, because some of her music is based on her experiences as a patient. The Brobdingnagian Bards, being a Celtic band, are partial to Renaissance fairs and similar events.

As we've said, it usually takes a few years to really insinuate yourself with a convention and get regular bookings with them. Many will ask for your credentials, which need to be in great shape for you to be considered. The key to conventions is the convention committee. Find out who they are and focus your marketing efforts on them.

WORKING WITH FANS TO HELP YOU BOOK

Some bands have had luck letting their fans help them book gigs. The advantages are that your fans know the venues in their local area and can actually do the footwork for you. By the time you get a contact from the venue booker, a lot of the difficult initial contacts have been handled and then you can just deal with the details. There's another advantage with fan booking: they don't usually ask for a booking cut. They just want you to play in their area and are happy to convince you to come to their town.

As we mentioned before, Jonathan Coulton has had luck with fans helping him book. The Brobdingnagian Bards have gone a step beyond and requested that their fans make the arrangements for them. This worked out so well that they eventually put together a list of steps that their fans would have to do in order to help book them.

ONLINE TOURING AND GIG TOOLS

Playing live is a huge part of a musician's life, so it shouldn't be surprising that there are now online tools to help connect performers with venues.

MESSAGE BOARDS

There are many message boards for musicians to help each other get shows in different cities. You don't even need to know someone in a city to try to get gigs there. It can be as simple as posting that you'll be on tour in that area and asking for suggested venues to call. Some bands will offer to let you open for them, which is ideal because you don't need to arrange anything on the ground in that city, leaving logistics to the local band.

Naturally, you should also watch these boards to see if there's anyone you can help book in your own city. Some of the message boards we recommend are Just Plain Folks (jpfolks.com), Velvet Rope (velvetrope.com) and DIYMusicManual.com.

GIG DEMAND SITES

Gig demand sites such as Eventful, which we mentioned earlier, provides a widget for your website to let fans request a performance in their area. Each visitor that votes using the widget raises the count higher for that area, giving you a clear idea of how your fanbase is divided geographically. This is important information when assembling a live show schedule, particularly if you are gaining popularity through the Internet. Your fans could be all over the world and you need to know where they are so you can go and play for them.

Because the people on these gig demand sites are hoping that you'll come to their city to play live, all of the ones that asked become an instant resource that will do footwork for you and can help you book. And one thing to remember about those sites is that they often undercount the number of people that would come to your shows. Not everyone wants to sign up in order to be counted on the site. Jonathan Coulton said, 'I've found that if there were 40 people signed up that probably there'll be 80 people that will come to the show. They'll bring their friends, there are other people that will hear about it and fans who aren't signed up.'

ONLINE BOOKING AGENCIES

Naturally, the Web has also found its way into getting people in touch with bands so that they can handle bookings. We're going to cover just two examples of this, each with a different focus.

Sonicbids (sonicbids.com) allows you to create an electronic version of your booking kit (Electronic Press Kit – a term they've trade marked) so that you can make yourself available to book shows, connect with talent buyers and perform other show management tasks. Musicians can use Sonicbids to host their Electronic Press Kits for the general public to view as well as to use their services to submit their band for bookers and venues or their music to outlets such as TV, radio and film that look to use music. Setting up a presence on Sonicbids won't guarantee you gigs but it may help open up some opportunities. Some festivals and venues use it as their exclusive way to handle submissions. Note that Sonicbids has a monthly fee.

Gigmasters (gigmasters.com) has a front page that aims itself more directly at people booking events such as weddings, parties and corporate events. If you can imagine that you are on a social committee of an organisation and just want to 'book an act', Gigmasters is a site that can find you a band based on style, size or any other needs. Gigmasters also has a monthly fee but Carla Ulbrich told us that she's booked many gigs using this tool.

ONLINE VENUE LISTINGS

Search engines such as Yahoo have listings of venues in your area. DIYMusic-Manual.com takes this one step further by providing the venues in your area as rated and reviewed by other indie musicians. Musician-important details such as what the sound system is like, the size of the stage, who's played there before and how the management treats its musicians is also captured and shared by the indie community.

GIG OPPORTUNITIES

The average number of fans you bring to any particular show is called your 'draw'. It's your draw the venues are interested in, not you! You might have 300 people on your mailing list with only 30 coming out to see you on a show night. Only a fraction of your fans will ever attend any one of your shows. To get as large a draw as possible, you should always be trying to get new fans.

To do so, you need to play many different types of shows, not just at regular venues. If you get more established, of course, you can play larger shows. But by then, it's likely that you've already got a publicity machine large enough to advertise and bring people in.

These techniques will help a band get established and become large enough to be a draw on their own.

OPENING FOR OTHER BANDS

One of the easiest ways to get new fans is to open for another band. You generally should only open for bands that have a bigger fanbase than your own. While this might seem obvious, we've ended up playing for many 'headliners' that didn't have close to the draw that we did.

Many people show up quite late for shows because they know that there's an opening band, so remember that the other band's draw will probably only see the end of your set. Also, the opening band will often get less money than the headline or no money at all.

We suggest that you also be open to sharing your own audience with others by letting bands open for you. Some bands are possessive about their draw, which makes very little sense. Everyone's fans are people that like to see live music. The more people that go out to see music, the better it is for everyone.

Another common misconception is that one band's fans only like the kind of music that they play. People who enjoy live music tend to have broad musical tastes. Don't assume that people that like folk music won't like heavy metal. In the end, it's all live music and audiences often enjoy more diverse entertainments than they are given credit for.

PLAYING CHARITY EVENTS

Charity events deliver a lot of benefits to bands that play them. Usually, all proceeds are donated to the charity but the events usually have their own press releases, which often get mentioned by the press. The resulting articles invariably list the participating bands. You can also do a press release of your own about the show and the cause that you're supporting. Those press releases often get more attention because of the human interest element.

Playing a charity event is a great way to piggyback, as well as network with other bands and even other community artists – sometimes charity events are more than just music shows. It's a good value for fans, too, because they can sample a variety of bands for the price of admission.

PLAYING MUSIC FESTIVALS

Because festivals are such good opportunities to play for new audiences, getting booked can sometimes be a challenge. There can be a lot of competition. Your best bet is to get to know the organisers of the event or, if that isn't possible, at least connect with someone who knows them. The 'cold handoff' almost never works. Always try to forge a personal connection to the organisers in any way you can. Your booking kit needs to be especially good to book a festival and this is where your press clippings can really help you stand out.

If you manage to get in a festival, get the most out of it by doing the following:

- **Reinforce the brand:** Announce your band name often, as someone might have just walked in to the venue and might not know you. Ideally, bring a sign or banner on stage.
- **Build your list:** Make sure that you bring your mailing list and ask people to sign up.
- **Sell merchandise:** Get a friend to run a store with your CDs and merchandise. Keep your mailing list at the table, too.
- **Call to action:** Announce your next shows and upcoming projects to draw people in. If you have a poster for your next show, place it around the festival.

Some cities have an events committee to evaluate bands for city-sponsored festivals. Chicago, our home town, has a committee to book bands for the city's frequent street festivals. Getting into their list of bands is, of course, rather difficult but if you can manage it, you have access to a lot of shows.

There's a good listing of festivals at Festivals.com (festivals.com), and also check out DIYMusicManual.com. For a more UK-focused site, check efestivals. co.uk.

CONFERENCES AND SHOWCASING

Showcases give you an opportunity to play for a conference or event that is attended by people within the music industry. Examples are booking conferences, college conferences or a meeting for the Performance Rights Organisations such as ASCAP or BMI.

Some showcases let you just pay to get your chance to play for the people at the conference and others are juried, which means that you'll have to send in a demo and prove yourselves to a panel (although they may *still* charge you after asking you to come in and play). Either way, you'll have to decide if the showcase is worth the cost of attending.

US COLLEGE GIG BOOKINGS

If you want to travel overseas and break into the US college tour market, you can work with the Association for the Promotion of Campus Activities (APCA. com) or the National Association for Campus Activities (NACA.org). Both of these associations hold once a year conventions to showcase bands that draw in talent buyers from colleges across the country. Both of these conventions charge the bands to play. We've been told by other musicians that by the third college gig you book out of these conferences, you will probably have recouped your convention fee (although your travel fees, naturally, will take another gig or two to recover).

Also, there's an entire world of college gigs waiting for you in venues that are simply near or on campus. Venues near colleges are always looking for bands to play and their audiences are always looking for new music.

PLAYING WEDDINGS

Many bands play weddings to supplement their income. It's an area with its own pitfalls but those who can successfully navigate it can secure a dependable source of gigs. George Hrab buttresses his indie music income with steady work playing with a wedding band, the Philadelphia Funk Authority.

One of Chicago's top wedding bands is the High Society Orchestra (high-societyorch.com), run by Alan Heiman, who has been in the booking business for decades. His number one piece of advice is to treat a wedding band as a business. The professional expectations for a wedding are very different from those at regular venues. Your marketing materials need to be flawless, your band's presentation has to be polished and your dealings with customers need to be managed with extreme care.

Heiman started his band with a splash. He rented out a hotel ballroom at his own expense and catered an evening for wedding planners, hotel venue managers and others in the wedding industry to enjoy the band. That one event, along with an advertising campaign in bridal magazines and other publications, got him 52 bookings that first year. The point isn't that you need to spend a lot of money to start a wedding band, although that helps. Instead, remember that you need to win over the wedding planners and the hotel venue managers. These are the people who can refer new business to you.

The High Society Orchestra gets all their gigs through word of mouth. They don't bother advertising any more. In fact, they're completely booked for years ahead. Each wedding where they perform gets them multiple new bookings from people in attendance. This is a key lesson: the better your wedding show, the more likely your band will be hired for additional bookings by other guests.

When it comes to putting on a great wedding show, Heiman gives the following advice:

- **The MC is key:** The MC should interact with the audience throughout the evening.
- **Focus on talent:** Many of High Society's musicians are members of organisations like the Chicago Symphony Orchestra or the Lyric Opera. Your wedding band should feature the best musicians you can find.
- **The set list is critical:** Heiman is constantly tweaking his set lists to provide an enjoyable variety of songs for his audience.
- **Don't lose momentum between songs:** The music should always be going unless the band takes a full break. High energy is key.
- **Stick to tried-and-true favourites:** Dancing songs, medleys and sing-alongs are always sure bets with wedding audiences. Get everyone up on their feet and involved.

CORPORATE SHOWS, BAR MITZVAHS AND OTHER SPECIAL EVENTS

The High Society Orchestra also does corporate shows, bar mitzvahs and other gigs. But these are much more sporadic and difficult to get. Still, the secret to any of these other types of shows is again in the presentation of your materials and in knowing who handles hiring the bands.

In the case of corporate shows, the bookers can often be employees on a company events committee or someone in the human resources department. Because these positions often rotate frequently, it's hard to keep getting steady shows at each firm.

For other types of shows, your booking information on your website and the personal contacts that you make will be the best way to keep a steady stream of opportunities coming in.

STREET PERFORMANCES

The Brobdingnagian Bards started out playing in a park four days a week, for free. Eventually, after a year of playing, they had a hundred people showing up regularly to hear them. This group formed their initial fan network. When the Bards recorded their first album and played their first paid gigs, they already had an audience.

It's not always necessary to play formal shows – parks, streets and other public areas are perfectly good alternative 'venues'. But keep in mind that most cities impose restrictions on public performances of this type and you may require a permit. Make sure you check with your local council.

▸▸ SHOWMANSHIP

Musicians often argue the issue of 'staying true to the music' versus 'pandering to the audience'. This might make an interesting debate over beers but it's not useful when it comes to putting on a show. In the end, you're there to entertain the audience. Of course, you need to follow your aesthetic tastes – which might include a dark brooding look or a screaming spandex serenade – but don't forget: *You are there for them*.

Having the attitude that your audience is 'lucky to hear you' will *not* result in a good show. David Bloom, one of Chicago's jazz gurus, captured it best: 'Don't reduce music to the size of your ego. It's a lot bigger than you. It was here before you and it'll be here long after you're gone. Music is something to look up to.' If you look up to music, the audience will look up to you. But if you look down at the audience, they won't be there next time you play.

If you want to win fans, it doesn't matter the size of the audience you play to. Every show counts. As Brian Austin Whitney, the founder of the music community Just Plain Folks, says, 'Don't worry about playing to 20 people; play like you're playing to 20,000. If you make the best music you can and play the best you can play, you will grow your audience.'

Here's how to put on the best possible show for your fans and keep them coming back for more.

THE SECRET TO GREAT SHOWS

Think back and try to relive one of the most memorable live shows you've attended. Why exactly do you remember it? Did you feel involved? Connected? Energised? Were you transported to another place? In other words, did you feel something – not just hear it?

In the best shows, the band and the audience connect.

Fans want to connect with the music and musicians they love. Tom Jackson (tomjacksonproductions.com), a musician and one of the leading live music producers for tours, showcases and shows, has spent decades working out what makes audiences connect to musicians and what keeps fans coming back for more. He's boiled it down to three reasons: audiences come to be captured and engaged; to experience moments; and to experience change in their lives. While this might sound lofty, there's no question that music can do this for people. What Jackson does for a living is to teach musicians how to *create* this connection in their own shows. And, since much of an independent musician's income stems from the money made at a live show, converting the audience from listeners to fans through this emotional connection is more important than ever before.

A live music producer acts somewhat like a sports coach does with his athletes – teaching the skills, testing out the 'plays' and getting the individual parts to work together as a team. It's not about developing your musical chops (that you do on your own time); it's about developing your show for the stage. This may mean having the lead singer walk to the side of the stage at a certain point, having the lead guitarist come forward when it's his time to solo and rearranging the song in ways that you wouldn't have done in the recording but work well live to get an audience involved. If this sounds a bit confusing, it's only because these techniques are better seen to be understood – but these are the same techniques that bands like U2 and Prince use to pull off such spectacular shows.

As Jackson says, 'Just because you learned how to play music doesn't mean you automatically know how to perform in front of an audience.' If you want to win fans, your live performances must be more than just taking your recorded music and playing it really well on stage. Jackson says a live show is 15 per cent technical, 30 per cent emotional and 55 per cent visual. Most musicians spend their time practising the technical part but neglect the other 85 per cent. Since the visual part of a show is the most important, think about your own set. Even though it's likely that each of your songs *sound* different, be honest: do they *look* different on stage? As Jackson says, 'Audiences get bored and disconnect when all of your songs look the same.'

Here's a small sample of the advice that Jackson gives to help build that connection with the audience:

- **The performance should visually match the song:** You can't control the audience's eyes but you can control what you do on stage. Give the audience *visual* cues that match moments in the song. When one musician has a solo, she should be forward and the others should step back 'out of the picture'. If a song builds, bring musicians forward as they add their parts. The audience's view of the stage changes dramatically depending on where your band members stand, so always let the audience know where they should focus their attention.
- **What's good for a recording isn't necessarily good for the stage:** Abandon the idea of reproducing your radio-friendly, three-minute long track at the stage door. In a live show, three minutes goes by so fast that most audience members don't even know what happened. They didn't pick up on that cool riff. They didn't notice that harmony vocal. Jackson will often work with musicians to find the highlights of songs and then retool those parts for stage performance. Techniques that he uses include extending intros to songs, repeating the cool licks or hooks that sound great on the recording but go by too quickly on stage or breaking down a part and vamping on its underlying rhythms.
- **Less is more:** Most bands try to pack a set with as many songs as they can. After all, they're musicians and want to play. But the point is to make the songs you do play special and memorable for the audience. Applying the techniques above lengthens the songs you do play and this means you'll play less songs in a set.
- **Plan and rehearse:** Just as you practise your instrument and the songs you play, you must spend time practising your live performance and planning your set. As Jackson notes, all those live shows of your favourite big name bands looking like they're making it all up as they go along are really planned.

The techniques and skills a live music producer can apply to your own music go beyond this *Manual* but note that they work no matter what type of music you play or whether you're in a band or just on stage alone with a guitar. There are moments to be created in every performance and connections to be made. And it's this connection that's the secret to creating a great show.

START BIG AND END BIG

For ideas on how to put on a great show, learn from Hollywood. Take any successful action film. They often start with a bang, literally, an explosion or perhaps a gunfight or car chase. And no matter what happens in the middle, it always ends with what they call 'the ticking clock' featuring a chase scene and heart-pounding stunts and sequences as time runs out. The Hollywood action movie mantra is, 'start big and end big!'

This formula *works*. You should use it whenever you perform. Beatnik Turtle always kicks a show off with a rocking song – usually one that uses the entire horn section. And we always end with an up-tempo number that gets the crowd jumping up and down and yelling. Even if you must start subtle, always end with a lively closing song.

Think of a fireworks display. They always end on a big finale that fills the sky with lights and explosions. Your show should follow the same principle. People remember the ending best. They forgive problems in the middle of the set if you end on a strong note.

Our goal as performers is to have the crowd more red-faced and excited than we are when we finish. We usually succeed, because we close with wild, rocking songs that have choruses that get people jumping up and down as they sing along. The reactions we get from the audience after our shows are the reason we've kept playing all these years. That's when you hear fans say, 'You guys were AWESOME!' and you know they really mean it.

COVERS VS ORIGINALS

There's an ongoing debate over doing cover songs versus doing originals. What you choose depends on your band.

First of all, if you are concerned about the rights of playing cover songs, see Chapter 7: Your Rights for more on that issue.

There are some purists who wonder why anyone plays covers at all. With all that music easily available on CDs and as MP3s, you could play the songs by the original groups to your heart's content. The truth, however, is that people love live music (when it's played right). And if your band is creative, you can put your own spin on the covers. By performing a cover song, you also won't have to work as hard to prove yourself to your audience, because they'll already be familiar with the music.

If you do original songs and you're still establishing yourselves, throw in some covers as well. Doing so will give your audience something to hook on to in between the unfamiliar songs. You can do this until you get established and your own originals become familiar. At that point, you'll be playing your older favourites as anchors for your fans as you introduce your new originals.

SOUND CHECK

The sound guy (yes, we call them sound guys even if they're women) can never make a bad band sound good. But one can definitely make a good band sound bad. The sound at a show is the most important part of a show that you can't directly control. If you can't use or don't have your own sound guy, make friends with the one you're given. And, most importantly, *do not skip the sound check.*

Here's how to make the most of a sound check:

1. Get there in plenty of time.
2. Provide your microphone chart, so the sound guy can see where things go. For examples of stage plots, see DIYMusicManual.com.
3. Designate one member to answer the sound guy's questions and have them tag along with him or her throughout the check to make sure things get resolved quickly and correctly. Every band has some oddities with its microphone set-up, so it pays to have someone there to answer the sound guy's questions.
4. Be very particular about the sound. If you need more volume or a different mix, take care of this now. It's impossible to change the monitors besides yelling 'turn it up' or 'turn it down' during the actual show.
5. Let each vocalist try their mics. If there are a lot of harmonies, make sure that each vocalist can hear the others during the check.
6. Have the member with the best ears stand in the room to double-check the sound. This is exactly where you can catch the mistakes of a bad sound guy.
7. Tell the sound guy about any instrument changes to expect. For example, one member of Beatnik Turtle plays sax, sings and then plays flute (yet only gets one pay cheque). He often gets one mic for saxes and one for flute *and* vocals. When he switches between flute and vocals on that mic, he needs different levels.
8. Buy the sound guy a beer or give him a tip.

Make friends with your sound guy. Offer free CDs or other band merchandise. This gives him or her a personal incentive to make you sound good. Also, the sound guy is usually connected to other venues in your area and that connection might just get you more shows. Sound guys can put you in touch with other musicians and otherwise expand your skill and opportunity networks.

In our experience, sound guys tend to be an unusual breed and it's always interesting to get to know them. One of them would get drunk, hit on our female friends and do a lousy job with the sound to boot. Another did great work but posted a note facing the stage: 'Do not play "American Woman". ' Naturally, we announced that we were going to play it in the middle of a set. He made this hilarious hand-waving motion like he was trying to get a plane to stop landing on a runway that was mined to explode. Of course, our audience missed the entire joke and just wondered why we wanted to play *that* song.

BANTER

We recommend a little small talk between songs because it can get the audience more connected to the band. But you should practise your banter. In fact, if you can get some jokes or material ready ahead of time, it can make your banter much more effective. You should also have 'stalling banter' prepared. This comes in handy when one of your band members breaks a string and has to fix it, if you need to tune or something else happens that causes a delay. Have a story ready to go so you can keep the audience entertained during these inevitable breaks.

Other banter you should rehearse beforehand is your band introduction, an announcement about future shows and a plug for your CDs, merchandise and website. Some people are better at impromptu speaking than others but it always helps to practise some of this material prior to the show.

REHEARSALS

The most difficult thing about rehearsals for most bands seems to be finding a rehearsal space. You should definitely get a permanent one rather than wander from place to place. It gives you a home base, which can help keep the band together. That said, a lot of bands have trouble finding a place where their music won't cause issues.

If you can't find a basement or garage to play in, you might try renting a space. We knew one band, The Hillbillies From Space, that rehearsed at night in a warehouse during the off hours when no one was working. It worked out well for everyone. You might be able to do this too, if you know someone who owns a warehouse, perhaps giving them a little money.

Once you have a space, practise at least once a week. If you're just starting the band, you should try to practise even more often to make sure that everyone in the band is synchronised. Your goal is to get so good that you can recover from a train crash on stage. Then you can drop back on practising. We don't recommend practising less than once a week (unless you're performing all of the time) because you will start to get rusty and your band members will begin to drift into other activities. Cutting weekly rehearsals is a great formula for losing band members.

During your rehearsals, don't be shy about bringing up problems and tackling them. Rehearsals are not the time to dance around issues that might just fester for a long time. If anyone is too sensitive to handle working on their parts, you'll probably lose them eventually anyway.

Remember, the sound in the rehearsal room is nothing like the sound on stage. You can sound as great as you want in the practice room and never hit those same heights on stage. In fact, on a lot of stages, you can't even hear the other band members, so part of the reason for your rehearsals is to learn what the rest of the band will be playing when you can't hear them.

We recommend doing a full dress rehearsal before shows and to use a timer for each song to get an idea of how long your sets are. Include the banter in between changes as well as the songs themselves.

END OF THE SHOW

Don't forget to thank the sound guy and anyone else that helped you during the show. If appropriate, encourage your audience to buy more drinks. Take one last time to plug your store and your website and then thank your fans.

When you finish a wedding, definitely thank everyone. George Hrab always thanks the maître d' and the caterers. Some have told him that, in years of working in the business, they've never had any other wedding bands thank them. They were very grateful and you never know when one of them might direct new business to you in the future.

In a smaller venue, pack up quickly and go and talk to your fans. It's that personal relationship that will keep them coming back. This is also another opportunity for you to sell a disc, give out a flyer, get people to sign up for the mailing list and talk up your next show. Having felt-tip pens handy to sign albums is also a good idea.

Another idea to consider came from our friend Yvonne Doll from The Locals (localsrock.com), a Chicago band. They have a cute little doll named 'Danger Boy' and they take pictures of their fans with the doll for the website. They even have little cards to give out with the Web address explaining that the pictures would appear there. This connected the fans with the website *after the show*, ensuring that they would bring other people to see their picture at the site as well as visiting it themselves.

Finally, if people who hired you for the show are really happy with how you did, take the opportunity to get a testimonial from them on the spot that you can use for your press kit and website.

POST-SHOW GAME TAPES

If you're heading out the door to a party, chances are you'll check in the mirror to see how you look, straighten out your hair and clothes. If you're practising for a show, it makes sense to record your performance to accomplish the same thing.

It doesn't have to be a high-quality recording to be useful. You can literally dig out an old cassette deck. If you have a laptop or even a desktop computer that's in your practice space, you can buy a microphone online or at an electrical goods store and record directly to your computer, which would allow you to distribute the files more easily to the rest of your band.

For actual performances, ask someone you trust to watch the equipment and hit record when it begins so you don't have to worry about it. You can use audio recordings of your shows to find out how the sound guys did and give them more specific feedback in the future on how to handle your music.

The best option for shows is to get your hands on a camcorder. Watch how your band moves during songs and presents itself during a show. Look at it from the point of view of a music fan who's come to be entertained. Is the banter smooth? Did you remember to announce your CDs? Did you say your band name enough times? Remember, at every show there will be people who don't know who you are and some will walk in right after you finished that last song. Keep announcing who you are.

By studying recordings of your band in rehearsal and at gigs, you will learn a lot of surprising things and some fixes will be as simple as straightening your hair before a party.

⏩ SHOW PUBLICITY

Once you have a show scheduled, you come to the fun part: promoting your show. There are a lot of things you can do to boost your draw and get the most people in the room. We'll talk about many of your options below.

POSTERS

You've seen them at every venue: posters for every band with an upcoming performance. When you have a show coming up yourselves, you should join them and get a poster up at least a few weeks ahead of time.

When you're a newer band and not necessarily well known in your town, you may doubt that a passer-by would come to your show after seeing a poster. In truth, most won't. It's not a great way to get new people to come to hear you play. So why bother?

The answer is simple: posters are one of the best places to imprint your brand on people who love music. While they may not show up at your gig because of your poster, over time, passing by your poster as they come and go to see other acts, your own name and logo will sink in. Eventually, when asked, they'll even say they've heard of you. Get your name out there long enough and there's a good chance some new people will check your band out, eventually.

The better your posters look, the more effective they are. Get a graphic artist from your skill network to design one, assuming one of your own members can't do it for the band.

Brand every poster with your logo, your colour scheme, your fonts, and make sure that your band name, website and the *correct* date and time of your performance can be read clearly. If you use a Web service such as Myxer, you can include information on the poster to allow people to download, sample or purchase your music directly to their phone or PDA (see Chapter 5: Your Web Presence and Chapter 10: Get Distributed and Sold, for more information). You may want to get your posters professionally printed ahead of time, in bulk, with a blank space in the middle so that you can write in the show information for each gig.

Hang your posters in these locations:

- **The venue itself:** Place them in front, as well as throughout. And don't forget the toilets – those posters actually get looked at.
- **Music stores:** Find CD and record stores in the neighbourhood. At each store, give the employees free CDs and offer to leave one for the shop itself so they can play it on their PA system. These employees are your best advocates. If they allow it, sell your CDs on consignment at the stores, too.
- **Local shops:** Coffee shops are often good about supporting local music. It's easy to figure out if they're friendly, because you'll see posters for other shows in the window or on the walls. Also, offer any of the workers or the shop itself free CDs. They may recommend your band if they like your music.

■ **Colleges:** Any schools near the venue are a good target. Local universities are great places to get new fans.

Be careful about putting posters in your neighbourhood, as there may be local laws that prohibit you from postering public walls. Consult local regulations before you go nuts with that tape.

Janelle Rogers of Green Light Go publicity (greenlightgopublicity.com) recommends placing posters adjacent to posters for more well-known groups. This tends to give her posters more weight and a better chance of being seen.

Fly-posting – the display of advertising material on buildings and 'street furniture' without the owner's (often your local council's) consent is illegal in the UK. If you put up posters, they will be removed and you can be prosecuted. So be warned.

DIGITAL POSTERS

Create digital versions of your posters as well. These will be used primarily on your website as a banner or used as a comment in a social-networking site. Depending on whether you use a mobile service such as Broadtexter or Myxer, you can also message these to consenting fans' mobile phones and PDAs. You should also make it available for anyone else who wants to 'post it' so that you can get people to help you put it in places that it should go. For example, sometimes you can put it in a footer for postings that you write to message boards.

FLYERS

A flyer given out at a show can be used to promote future shows, your latest album, your website or all three. People often take flyers with them, which will remind them how much they enjoyed your band once they've sobered up.

If you want to boost your flyers' effectiveness, make them coupons for a special deal. Maybe a discount off a CD or admission to your next show or a special free MP3 off your website. Your audience will be less inclined to throw your flyer out if they can get something by hanging on to it.

The more compelling the design, the better. We've posted glossy flyers from other bands to our refrigerators or near our desks because we liked the images as well as the band and wanted to remember both.

Don't forget a 'call to action' when you're making your flyer. Tell people what to do, whether it's attending a show or visiting the website.

VENUE MARKETING

The problem with posters in bars is that no one gets a chance to hear your band. And it's hard to convince a bar to play your music, even if you give away your album to the bartenders. Beyond leveraging people's mobile phones and PDAs, there's a few other traditional routes. For instance, Yvonne Doll came up with a clever solution to this problem. About a week before her show, she put a little display up at the venues she was playing and stocked it with free demo discs of her music, each labelled with the show information. She coupled this with traditional flyers as well. This method brought in a lot of new audience members.

ANNOUNCING SHOWS TO MAILING LISTS AND SOCIAL-NETWORKING SITES

Announcing your upcoming shows to your mailing list is probably the most important and effective publicity that you can do. Naturally, your fans are the people most likely to attend your gigs but only if they know about them ahead of time. People make weekend plans weeks in advance, so give your fans plenty of lead time so they can schedule you in.

On social sites like MySpace.com, your latest posts will appear on your friends' pages, so you can post your digital poster there and effectively distribute it to your entire friends list. And, of course, mention upcoming gigs on your website and on any band blogs.

Depending on how often you play, you should also make an email announcement the day before a show to remind people of where and when the show is. If you play several times a week, a weekly or monthly announcement should work.

Finally, if your mailing list includes regular mail addresses as well as email addresses, it can be effective to send a postcard with your show calendar. The physical card can really help get more people in because, if you do a good enough job with the design, the recipients will want to put it up on the wall. This will keep them reminded about your band.

LOCAL RADIO

Local radio is usually a solid bet when it comes to promoting upcoming shows. Offer a ticket or album giveaway if they agree to mention the show. Most stations love free stuff to give to their listeners. Sometimes, you can incorporate a giveaway into an interview the day of the performance, reaping even more publicity for your event. We talk about this in detail in Chapter 11: Get Played and Heard.

NEWSPAPERS, MAGAZINES, WEBSITES AND BLOGS

An upcoming show is a great excuse to send out a press release to local publications. But keep in mind they will only publish something if you have an angle. This does not include the headline: 'Indie band plays show'.

So if you're going to send a press release, make sure there's something special about the show. Maybe you're playing for charity, throwing a CD-release party or doing your 500th performance. The easiest way to make your show special enough to warrant a press release is to play in another town. Ironically, it can be harder to get any publicity in your local area than it is when you travel, even to the next nearest city. Take advantage of this as much as possible if you're on the road.

Any show is also an excuse to write an email to any blogs or websites that cover music or entertainment in the area. Again, this is especially true if you're playing outside of your hometown.

You should always be thinking about new ways to publicise your band. This is especially true for shows, as your goal is to get as many new people to come to see your band as possible.

LOCAL MUSIC STORES

Aside from putting up posters in your local music store and giving out free CDs to win over the employees, you can use music stores to help publicise your band in other ways.

Our technique that worked quite well arose as a result of a happy accident at our CD manufacturer. We managed to get an extra 1000 CDs (discs only) for the cost of shipping due to a production error.

We packaged the discs in thin cases with a photocopied cover and little brochures about an upcoming concert. Then we went to record stores all over Chicago and offered to let them sell the discs. Before they could finish saying the word 'consignment', we added that they could sell the discs for a dollar and that they could keep the dollar. There isn't a local store in any town that will turn away free money.

We made a little display case for each store and those discs were usually placed right next to the cash register – a pure impulse buy. Few people could resist spending an extra buck to get another disc. We didn't give the discs away for two reasons. First, it gave the store a reason to push them and place the display by the cash register. Second, people don't value things that are free. You're better off charging something nominal so they will value it more.

That show was one of the best attended we've had. And even years later, we've had people write to tell us that they listened to the CD for years. If you have extra CDs, we highly recommend this technique.

This is just one of many possible ideas; you'll certainly come up with your own. Remember that local music stores have your perfect audience as their clientele. If you can think of other ways to get your band, your show information or your logo in front of those people, you should make use of it. There's a reason why you see band stickers all over those stores.

▶▶ SELLING AT SHOWS

Your shows are when it's most likely a fan will buy something from you. For one thing, there are no shipping costs. Also, you've just played live in front of them and people like to support bands they've seen in person.

Always get someone to run the store for you. It's a fairly easy job but it can be difficult to convince someone to do this for you. We once teamed up with other local bands and did an exchange programme where we ran the stores at each other's shows. (And we promoted the other bands' shows as well.) You should do everything you can to get people to help out the band in this way. Offer your friends incentives such as free CDs and T-shirts, free shows or anything else that would entice them to help you. The alternative is to sell from the stage, which is difficult and looks amateurish.

While on stage, remember one thing above all: *Don't forget to announce that you have music available for sale!*

And don't just do it once. Do it many times throughout a show. Some people just need a reminder, that extra push to get them to make the purchase. Effective marketing is based on repetition. Don't repeat it after every song but definitely remind people in the middle and at the end of each set. If you feel embarrassed repeating yourself like that, remember that some people will have just walked into the room and don't know where they can buy your music. Radio stations aren't bashful about reminding listeners what station they're listening to, even if most already know. You shouldn't feel bashful about announcing your CD a couple of times each set.

A display for your CDs and T-shirts will help quite a bit. It can make your store look more professional. A more formal store also makes people feel better about buying your music, because they will feel that they are getting something of value.

Make your mailing list available at your store as well and while the person running the store is getting change, they should ask the customer to sign up.

This is your most likely returning fan, so you definitely want them on your list. You should also have your flyers available to hand anyone who buys something.

CREDIT CARD SALES

Normally, sales at shows are cash only but there are ways for independent bands to perform credit card sales. If you'd like the ability to do this at shows, we recommend using CD Baby's credit card program. For a little money, they give you a credit card swiper and some receipts. They take a small cut of every sale for handling the credit card transaction but on the other hand these sales are tracked by Nielsen SoundScan in the US and if you register the sale right, you'll also get it into the Official Charts Company in the UK or ARIA in Australia.

People at bars often use all their cash to buy beer. We're all for that, of course! The problem is that leaves them with nothing to buy your CD. A credit card swiper is a good way around this problem.

DIGITAL MUSIC AT CONCERTS

If you have someone to run your store and can provide a laptop, you can sell digital music too. Tell your fans on your website and in your mailing to bring their iPods or MP3 players to the show. Then just rip your music to MP3 files and bring a USB cable and an iPod cable with your laptop.

You can afford to charge less than the price of a CD to sell your music this way because you don't actually have to duplicate any CDs. Doing something novel like this can also get even more people interested in buying your music. Some people take their MP3 players wherever they go, so you might even be able to make sales to some walk-ins. These are, of course, not tracked by SoundScan or the Official Charts Company.

POST-SHOW CDS

It's now possible to sell CDs of a show immediately after it's over. A dedicated engineer does a mixdown immediately after the show and then sends it to a fast CD duplicator. Usually only the larger venues have the resources to pull this off as of now but as the technology gets better, it will become more feasible for indie musicians. The Brobdignagian Bards sometimes do this with a notebook computer at some shows. While it ties one of them up after a show, they've been able to sell copies of a just-performed show.

And don't forget that even if you can't manage to make a CD immediately after your show, you can still sell the recording afterwards to fans from your website.

MAILING LISTS AT CONCERTS

As we discussed in Chapter 2: Your Network, you should have a mailing list at every show that you perform. If you can, you should have multiple mailing lists. These are the people most likely to come to your next show, so you will want to get their information while they are there. Most people are happy to sign up for mailing lists for bands that they like.

It's a good idea to ask for both their email and snail mail addresses, in case you want to contact them in different ways. You may mostly use their email addresses but later decide to do a postcard mailing.

You should make sure that your mailing list is available at the show store and you should also try to pass a sign-up form around the room in the middle of the show. Your best bet is to try to get some helpers to walk through the crowd and hand the punter a clipboard so that he or she feels compelled to sign up. It's the best way to get a good response. You can also have your floor people have a couple CDs on them, in case they can make a sale. And if you have a flyer, they should just hand them out to people, as people are more willing to take them. If you've ever walked down the street anywhere in Las Vegas, are over 18 and especially if you are male, you probably know how likely it is that someone will take a flyer if it's handed to them.

MORE ABOUT BOOKING AND PLAYING LIVE

If you wish for more in-depth information on booking and playing live, we recommend *How To Be Your Own Booking Agent: THE Musician's and Performing Artist's Guide to Successful Touring* by Jeri Goldstein. Also, don't forget that DIYMusicManual.com lists booking resources, tools and, most importantly, venues in your area as rated and reviewed by other indie musicians.

▸▸CHAPTER TEN

GET DISTRIBUTED AND SOLD

Most bands want to know: How do I get our music on iTunes? How can I get my CDs distributed worldwide?

In this chapter, we'll cover everything related to selling your music, whether online, in stores or in person. But, as always, there are some things you should be aware of and do, before you start selling. We'll begin with those preliminary issues and then move on to the nitty-gritty of distribution.

▸▸PREPARING TO SELL MUSIC

TRACKING SALES & CHARTING THE BEST-SELLERS

When you go to sell music on your own, you should be aware of how the charting authorities track music sales, and determine the best-selling songs. In the past only major labels could get onto the Top 40 charts, however, today, if you gain enough popularity and you register your songs properly, you might be able to get your own music on those charts. Of course, getting a song charted as a best-seller is still difficult for most independent musicians, but if you manage to chart, you're guaranteed to get some media attention. It's also a great excuse for a press release.

Each charting company has its own methodology for tracking sales. However, they all neglect the best method for selling that independent musicians have: selling albums at concerts. Depending on how much you care about charting, you may have to reevaluate which methods you use to sell your music.

THE OFFICIAL UK CHARTS COMPANY

The current charting authority is The Official UK Charts Company (theofficialcharts.com). The Official UK Charts Company has an elaborate system and methodology for tracking sales in the UK. Sales at over 6,200 retailers (including all the major high-street chains, approximately 600 independent stores and all major Internet retailers) are tracked using barcodes. To ensure that sales of your CDs are tracked in this system, you need to register your physical albums with a barcode from GS1 UK (gs1uk.org). To ensure your digital music sales are tracked, you need to obtain an International Standard Recording Code (ISRC) for each of your individual digital tracks and a digital barcode for each of your digital albums.

However, before you run out and get the necessary barcodes and ISRC numbers on your own, know that many of the digital aggregators that we'll talk about in this chapter and the CD replicators we discussed in Chapter 6: Your Albums and Merchandise incorporate these steps into their process and will sell or assist you in making sure you have the right barcodes and tracking numbers. To make sure the service you choose does this, be sure to ask.

AUSTRALIAN RECORDING INDUSTRY ASSOCIATION

In Australia, the primary charting authority is the Australian Recording Industry Association, (ariacharts.com.au). Like The Official UK Charts Company, the Australian Recording Industry Association gets sales retail data directly from retailers, including digital retailers.

Again, if you care about getting tracked in this region, you'll want to ask the digital aggregator or CD replicator service you're using if they will provide the necessary barcodes and ISRC numbers.

SOUNDSCAN (US)

If you plan on selling your music in the US, you will also need to be aware of SoundScan, the US music industry's primary method for tracking music sales. The Billboard Hot 100 charts are all based on the SoundScan numbers. SoundScan statistics are reported by online digital distribution stores like iTunes, Napster, and Rhapsody, as well as physical CD stores like Best Buy and Wal-Mart.

You need a UPC barcode for your album if you want your sales to register with SoundScan. Even if you're selling your music digitally, SoundScan requires the UPC in order to track the sales, because that's the unique code they use to identify each album. Again, if you care about getting tracked in this region, you'll want to ask the digital aggregator or CD replicator service you're using if they will provide the necessary barcodes and ISRC numbers.

Keep in mind that it's very difficult to make enough sales to register as more than a blip on SoundScan. So it's usually not worth it for an indie musician to bother, especially if he or she isn't interested in entering the traditional music industry. After all, music-buying customers don't really look at those numbers – they're more interested in the music you make.

PROMOTING MUSIC SALES THROUGH YOUR WEBSITE

We'll discuss every aspect of getting your music through the sales channels but if you don't promote your music on your own website, you're wasting your best opportunity to entice fans to purchase your music. Prepare this first, *before* putting the music into the sales channels, so that the material is ready to go when your album releases.

The best thing about having your own website is that you have full control over it. It looks pathetic when a band has to pitch its new album in between the ads on their MySpace.com page. When you have your own website, you can devote a page entirely to the album.

Your goal for an album page is simple: get people to buy the music. If you have any aversion to plugging your own music, it's time to get over it quickly. You'll be making your album pages to really pump it. The text and images should all work towards that objective. Sampling and then buying the album should be as convenient and fast as possible. We'll talk about techniques for this below.

SONG SAMPLES

Music is something that people want to try before they buy. That's why the radio has been such an important part of the music industry. People are willing to purchase a movie on DVD before seeing it. But they often aren't willing to buy music before hearing it. Perhaps this is because people spend more time listening to music and they also listen to music repeatedly. Movies are viewed far less often.

Demonstrate that your music is worthwhile by offering actual songs or clips of songs for download. On your website, stream every single song on the album for customers to preview. On an online store, make clips available of as many songs as they allow. Put your music where your mouth is. Perhaps one of those songs is just the one that a fan is looking for. On iTunes, customers can listen to a short clip of every song, especially useful because you can purchase music by the track.

The digital music stores do a great job of making samples easy to listen to on their storefronts. But it's also sometimes possible to embed their Flash player in your page directly to make this even easier. Otherwise, you can do this with your own player as we discussed in Chapter 4: Your Website.

We stream entire albums from our site. It may allow some technically savvy and unscrupulous people to copy the music but most just use it to get an idea of what the songs sound like. When it comes to music, 'try before you buy' is the way customers prefer to do it.

QUOTES

Feature favourable quotes about the band throughout your website but most importantly on your album pages. Getting reviews of your album before it's released is a very good idea if possible. Otherwise, use reviews of shows or of previous albums. We talk about how to get reviews in detail in Chapter 12: Get Publicised.

Think of the movie listings page in your local newspaper. It's filled almost entirely with quotes from reviews, because people trust quotes most when it comes to spending money on a movie. Albums work the same way.

OTHER TEXT

Include the liner notes and lyrics on your album page. Since many people don't even bother buying CDs any more, this might be the only place where they can find these. And if the notes and lyrics are particularly good, they may help make the sale.

Also, this text is useful in bringing more people to your site via search engines. The more text you have, the more often your site will pop up in searches for terms that appear within it.

EMBEDDING AN ONLINE STORE

The CD stores are there to help sell your albums but don't wait for your fans to go to them. Link to the stores throughout your website. The goal of your site is to make album sales; it should be simple for people already on your site to buy your music. We provide links to buy our albums on every page of the Beatnik Turtle site.

Some CD stores allow you to embed a 'shopping cart' on your own website, so that fans only leave your site when they're ready to purchase. We highly recommend doing this. Also, services such as Snocap.com, Hoooka.com and Nimbit.com have embeddable widgets to integrate the store into your site. The iTunes Music Store provide a link that opens iTunes and goes either directly to an album or directly to a song. The more seamless the experience for your fans, the better. Since the methods differ, you should design your site around the store that best suits your needs and embed that store's functionality as much as possible into the album pages. You should embed both digital and physical CD stores into your site.

GRACENOTE AND FREEDB

Ever wonder how the album name, band name and song names get filled in automatically in your MP3 player when you load a CD into your computer? The Gracenote Media Recognition Service (formerly CDDB) (gracenote.com) and freeDB (freedb.org) are the engines behind this. Both do exactly same thing but Gracenote's service costs money for the software developer to license.

The companies that run these databases get listeners to do the hard work for them. When a listener loads a CD that isn't already in the database, they often fill in the track info themselves so that they have it handy. Most music players have a simple submission button that allows you to upload this information to the database.

If you've released a CD, add your information to these databases yourself. Most fans, though they mean well, are not always the best spellers and they sometimes get the information wrong. If you do it yourself, you can make sure it gets done right. To do this, simply load your CD into a player that supports each service. When you do, you will have an opportunity to enter the names of each track and the other CD info such as band, album name, year, etc. Once you've finished, make sure that you use the 'submit' option in your application or else it will only be entered into your local library.

In general, iTunes works for Gracenote, while the free tool, Audiograbber (audiograbber.com-us.net) works for freeDB. But you can also check their websites for other options.

⯈SELLING OFFLINE

SELLING AT SHOWS

We cover the details of selling at shows in Chapter 9: Get Booked and Play Live. Show sales are not tracked at the Official UK Charts Company.

CONSIGNMENT

Most music stores, especially smaller independent stores, will let you sell your CDs on consignment. This means that they will pay you after the album is sold, rather than before.

Consignment helps you even if you don't sell a single CD. As we discussed in Chapter 3: Your Brand, you want to get your band name in front of as many people as possible. If music fans start seeing your CDs at stores around your area, they will begin to think that your band is significant (at least in the area) and are more likely to recognise your name the next time they see your poster.

Admittedly, this involves a lot of footwork for what might be only a small amount of exposure. And bricks-and-mortar music stores are disappearing rapidly as people turn to online stores or big-box retailers, who are not interested in consignment.

As we've said, give free copies to workers at the stores where you sell your CD. If any of them like your music, they'll probably promote it to people walking in the door. Give an extra one to the store itself so they can play it on the PA. People who work in CD stores are not doing it for the money; they love music and usually recommend their personal favourites to customers. Your CD, sitting in a consignment bin, won't sell itself. It needs to be heard and it needs other people to tell customers that it's worth buying. For inspiration, watch the movie *High Fidelity* and then read this section again.

Oh and while you're in the store, put up a poster for your album or an upcoming show, too.

Depending on where you reside, sales may be tracked by the corresponding charting authority (for instance, in the UK, the Official UK Charting Company) the store is monitored by. It's up to them to report sales of used or consignment discs.

GIRL SCOUTING

When we're just trying to make back the replication costs for making a CD, we employ a simple method we call 'Girl Scouting', based on the US organisation that has a yearly tradition of making their members, who are little girls, sell cookies. It's remarkably effective: who can say no? While you might not have a little girl on hand, every band member can at least be a salesperson.

The independent band version of this amounts to sending your band members and friends out of the door with a stack of albums to sell. When you mention your band to co-workers, friends, relatives or your dentist, throw in the fact that you've got copies of your latest album in your bag, in case they're interested. Throw in a 'friend discount' and you'll probably have yourself a sale.

Chapter 2: Your Network explains how important it is to credit everyone that had anything to do with your albums. This comes into play here, as anyone who is actually listed in the liner notes will usually agree to help sell the discs.

⇥ SELLING MUSIC ONLINE

ONLINE CD STORES

While some people want digital music, there are still some who prefer physical CDs. Online CD stores are the best way to handle this distribution, unless you want to set yourself up as an online merchant and deal with packing, shipping, and handling orders.

The good online CD stores focus on selling music, not selling their services to musicians. When you evaluate online CD stores, make sure that the front page of the website looks like a *store*, and not like an ad for musicians to sell their music. When you enter the site, imagine that you're a fan, not a musician. Ask yourself where you'd go to buy music. If the online store's front page mostly brags about being a great place for bands to sell music, avoid it.

If you use a store that seems indie-friendly, read the agreement carefully. Do not sign up for any services that takes any rights to your music. The music store is there to sell your music, but they should not get any more rights to it than a grocery store gets to the breakfast cereal it sells. Some stores try to take advantage of you. Don't let them. Also, there's no limit to the number of CD stores that your music can be sold on. So, don't agree to an exclusive deal unless you get a very clear benefit from it.

USING ONLINE STORES EFFECTIVELY

Once you decide which stores to use, use the following techniques to get the most out of your new storefronts:

1. **Make comparisons:** List major bands with a similar sound in the album description. Use the major labels' marketing dollars wisely by sending searches for those bands directly to your album pages.
2. **Feature quotes:** Make extensive use of good reviews in the description. These show your customers that people with acknowledged taste enjoyed your album. As we mentioned above, the movie listings page of your newspaper is full of quotes for a reason.
3. **Offer samples:** Make song samples available if the store allows it. If they don't, put song clips on your site, then link to those clips from the description in the online store.

4. **Link from your site:** Put links to all of your online album storefronts on every page of your band Website to drive traffic and make it as easy as possible to buy your music.

5. **Link to your site:** Link back to your own website from your storefronts so that they their customers can find more information about you and your albums.

CD BABY

In many ways, CD Baby (cdbaby.com) helped unleash the indie music movement. They are our top suggestion for an online CD store and all sales are tracked through the charting authorities. Their price structure is simple: there is a one-time setup fee and, from then on, CD Baby keeps the first US$4 of each CD you sell, and the rest goes to you. They handle the warehousing of your CD (they ask for a few copies and ask for more when you sell out), do all the shipping, and keep track of accounting – sending you cheques when you achieve a certain threshold (which you can set). CD Baby reserves cdbaby.com for music fans, so for more information about signing up as a musician head to cdbaby.net.

CD Baby was started by Derek Sivers, who created it to sell his own CDs. As a result, it's a very musician-centric company. Here is a short list of CD Baby's advantages:

1. **Comprehensive service:** Physical CD sales are handled seamlessly. CD Baby handles the credit card transactions, the shipping, the warehousing, and so on.

2. **Accounting:** CD Baby handles all the accounting with sales broken down by store, date, and sales price.

3. **Feedback from customers:** When customers buy a CD, they have the option to say where they found out about your music. This has been an invaluable source of information for us. You also get their email address.

4. **Presence in major record stores:** CD Baby has agreements with 'big box' chain stores in the United States such as including Best Buy and Wal-Mart. Your CD might not be available on the shelf, but it will be in their database if anyone searches on it. This means that a customer in the States can request to have your CD sent to their local store for pickup.

5. **Retail store fulfillment:** CD Baby has linked up with a CD distributor, and if any retailers request your album, they will ship it to them. (But it's up to you to generate the demand!)

6. **Helpful tips:** They offer suggestions on marketing and selling your music. Their regular emails feature surprisingly useful advice.
7. **Partnership with Amazon.com:** If you sell your CD through CD Baby, it will also be listed at Amazon.com (but not necessarily Amazon.co.uk).
8. **Fully-featured album pages:** CD Baby will provide song samples, statistics, and links to your website from your album pages.

Additionally, beyond offering worldwide physical CD distribution, they also handle digital distribution. See the next section for details about this service.

AMAZON.CO.UK/AMAZON.COM

Amazon (Amazon.com) also will warehouse and sell your CDs. Amazon takes a percentage of the sales price as part of its distribution deal, rather than a flat fee per disc at CD Baby. But Amazon.com gets enormous amounts of traffic, so there's a good chance of making sales there.

If you use CD Baby, they have an agreement in place to make your CD available at Amazon.com, so you won't need to deal with them separately. At the time of this printing however, this is not necessarily true of other Amazon stores such as Amazon.co.uk; however Amazon has announced plans to extend their stores into the UK, Germany, Austria, France, China, and Japan, though there is no date set.

PRINT ON DEMAND

As mentioned in Chapter 6: Your Albums and Merchandise, you can also print CDs on demand and sell it in an online store. See that chapter for details.

DIGITAL MUSIC RETAILERS & DIGITAL AGGREGATORS

Perhaps the biggest irony of digital music retailers like iTunes, Rhapsody, and Napster is that, even though many of them have opened their virtual shelves up to indies, they dislike dealing with them directly. Instead of going direct, you need to use a digital aggregator service. These services can come and go quickly, though, so we suggest you use them with caution.

Digital retailers typically take a percentage of each sale. For instance, iTunes charges 9 per cent, however all stores differ. Digital aggregators then usually take a percentage for their services (though not all do – see Tunecore, for example). The rest of the money not taken by these two services is then yours and is paid to you by the digital aggregator you use. For those musicians on a label, that's an additional party that takes a cut (depending on your contract and what rate you negotiated).

There's one problem with digital music retailers that you should be aware of before you use these services: timing. You often have no control over when your songs or albums become available for sale at the digital store. You may want to have a release party, and keep your album from being released ahead of time. Unfortunately the only way to ensure this is to submit your album to these services after your release is done.

CD BABY

Beyond selling your CD, CD Baby can also add your music to all the major digital music retailers. CD Baby does not charge any additional setup fees beyond the one-time setup fee for selling your CD. Instead, they keep 9 per cent of whatever the total amount they receive from the digital retailers. The rest is yours.

These digital sales are also tracked through the charting authorities. Again, to learn more about CD Baby's services head to cdbaby.net.

TUNECORE

Another service that can distribute your music to digital retailers is TuneCore (tunecore.com). They also will distribute your videos. For music, Tunecore charges a one-time setup fee per single or album, and a small charge per digital store you choose to be in – such as iTunes UK, iTunes US, iTunes Japan, Rhapsody, Napster, etc. These sales are tracked through the charting authorities. Videos are handled in a similar fashion, but Tunecore's fees are determined by the length of the video.

Unlike CD Baby, Tunecore does not take a cut of any sale; it lets you keep the wholesale price paid by these digital retailers. Instead, to maintain your presence at these online stores, Tunecore charges a yearly maintenance fee. Not paying the fee will result in the song or album being taken down.

To use Tunecore's service, you need to create an account. Doing so will allow you to upload your music and videos directly to them through your account profile. The back-end tools that Tunecore provides to manage this process are robust and easy-to-use. Their tools not only handle all the accounting for you, they also allow you to track and analyse your sales, upload new songs and videos into their system, track the status of your songs and videos as they become available at the digital retailers you selected, and access the many other services they provide.

Tunecore does not stop at digital distribution, however. They also have other services you can access a la carte such as CD print-on-demand, custom poster, fliers, and postcard creation, T-shirt, apparel, and merchandise creation and sales (via an embeddable widget), tour management services, ad-placement services, and more. For more information about their suite of services, head to tunecore.com.

REVERBNATION

ReverbNation (Reverbnation.com) will also distribute your music to digital retailers. At the time of this printing, for a one-time set-up fee, they will distribute your music to ten stores. Like Tunecore, annual maintenance fees will apply to keep your songs in the digital stores. Songs and albums can be uploaded directly to them through their online system. Additionally, because ReverbNation focuses on music promotion, they make it easy to include links to where to buy your music easy through their widgets (see Chapter 5: Your Web Presence for more details about their other tools and services). At the time of printing, digital sales are not tracked through the charting authorities. For more information about ReverbNation's digital distribution services, head to Reverbnation.com.

AMAZON.CO.UK/AMAZON.COM

Amazon.com has a program for selling digital music as well which are tracked through the charting authorities. Amazon takes a percentage of the sales price as part of its distribution deal, rather than a flat fee per disc at CD Baby or a yearly maintenance fee at Tunecore. If you use any of the digital aggregators above, you can get your music into Amazon.com. At the time of this printing, this is not necessarily true of other Amazon stores such as Amazon.co.uk, but they've announced plans to extend their stores into other countries in time, although there is no set date as to when.

DIGITAL AGGREGATORS

Digital aggregators differ in functionalities, features and price. Some of the ones we recommend are:

- **CD Baby (cdbaby.com)** CD Baby charges an initial set-up fee then 9 per cent for each digital sale. It automatically places your songs into a variety of digital retailers. If you expect to sell a low volume, but wish to maintain your presence at the various retailers without paying a yearly maintenance fee, this pricing scheme is advantageous.
- **Tunecore (tunecore.com)** Tunecore charges an initial set-up fee and then a yearly maintenance fee for each digital retailer that you want to place your songs in (you need to choose which digital retailers you want to be in given each one costs a fee). In return for the yearly retailer maintenance fee, you receive all the money from those digital sales minus the percentage the retailer takes.
- **ReverbNation (Reverbnation.com)** ReverbNation charges an initial set-up fee and then an annual renewal charge. It automatically places your songs into a variety of digital retailers. In return for the yearly maintenance fee, you keep all of the money from those digital sales minus the percentage the retailer takes.
- **Nimbit (nimbit.com)** Nimbit takes a percentage of each digital sale. It also allows you to upload your MP3s directly into their system. Nimbit has a widget-based merchandise table that you and your fans can be embed at your own websites.

WIDGET/APPLICATION-BASED STORES

These specialised digital music stores are usually compact embedded applications that you can easily add to your website. Even better, many of these services will allow your fans to insert your store into their websites as well. To encourage this, some of them even will share a cut of the sales with your fans. These stores often have additional features such as mailing lists, band bios, collecting email addresses, playing videos and merchandise fulfilment. Some widget-based stores are Nimbit (nimbit.com), Hoooka (hoooka.com) and Snocap (snocap.com). Each one provides different services, so you should read the feature lists of each to see what they provide.

RINGTONES AND MOBILE CONTENT PROVIDERS

Selling ringtones is not just for labels, it's also available to indie bands. A number of services have created the option of selling your songs or even parts of your songs to mobile phone customers. Keep in mind that mobile companies typically take a piece of the action, so your revenue is usually split three ways between the mobile service provider, the company selling the ringtones and you.

There are a number of mobile content providers such as Thumbplay, SendMeMobile and Myxer. While many of these work only with major labels, Myxer works directly with indie musicians (myxer.com). It's free to create an account and once you do, you can upload your music. Their online tools allow you to customise your ringtones using any part of the song you want (and allow your users to do the same if you choose). Once uploaded you can choose to sell it – keeping 30 per cent of each sale (20 per cent goes to Myxer and 50 per cent goes to the mobile phone company) – or give it away for free. Distributing and selling your ringtone is as easy as adding a widget to your site that sends the song directly to their phone number. But Myxer doesn't stop with your music, you can also upload images and videos or use their service to send text or image messages to your consenting 'fan list' such as a digital flyer announcing your next show.

SELLING DOWNLOADS FROM YOUR SITE

If you wish, you can also create a store to sell your own MP3s from your website, social networking or other Web presence sites. If you decide to go this route, you have a number of different services available. You should do a careful analysis of the associated costs and decide which service is the best for your own band. For example, some charge different rates based on the number of items you have to sell, the number of sales that you get or even the amount of MB space used by your digital items.

Most sites that sell digital downloads are made for people selling software rather than the very low cost and low margin MP3 files. For example, you need to make quite a few sales of MP3s at 79p in order to cover the monthly fee. Services that musicians have used to digitally sell music include E-Junkie (e-junkie.com) and Payloadz (payloadz.com). None of these services report to any of the charting authorities, however, so you should be aware of this before you decide to use them.

LEARNING MORE

To stay on top of all the new ways to get your music distributed and sold visit DIYMusicManual.com.

▶▶CHAPTER ELEVEN

GET PLAYED AND HEARD

When you think about getting your music heard, the first thing that probably comes to mind is radio. But radio simply isn't the best method any longer. In the post-net era, there are more ways to get heard than ever before. We're going to cover these methods below.

▶▶PREPARING TO GET HEARD

There are a few things you should get together before trying to get your music heard around the world.

PREPARE YOUR MUSIC

Have your music available in the following formats:

1. **MP3s:** Use these small, universally compatible files for free downloads on your own site, samples in your online store, submissions to music websites and social networks and elsewhere around the Web. (For MP3 encoding instructions, see Chapter 4: Your Website.)
2. **WAV files:** Use these large, high-quality files for podcasts, film, TV and other mediums. They aren't as easy to share but they offer the highest fidelity when it counts.
3. **CDs:** Have your music handy in physical form for selling online and at shows, marketing giveaways and other publicity and PR opportunities. No band member should ever leave the house without at least a couple of CDs, just in case.

PREPARE YOUR WEBSITE

Before you begin your campaign to get heard, prepare your website as outlined in Chapter 4: Your Website. As we've stated before, your website can make all the difference converting a one-time visitor to a fan.

For example, we were once mentioned on a blog of office humour after releasing an album of sarcastic songs about office life. Samples from the album were there on the site for the blog's readers to listen to and they were easy to find from the front page. If the songs hadn't been in place, that blog mention would have gone nowhere.

Some of the more effective ways to get heard are online. On the radio, the DJ might not even say the band's name. Online, the listeners request the song and actively listen. All your information and your online store is at their fingertips. Your website is a part of this process.

Before starting a campaign, make sure that your music, your store, your contact page and your press section are ready to go on your website. This is even true for offline campaigns. Your website will be the first place people will go for more information once you get their attention.

HOW TO TAKE NO FOR AN ANSWER

You're about to submit your music for consideration. This may leave you feeling a bit vulnerable. After all, what if they say no?

If you submit a song somewhere and they don't accept it, move on. There are many reasons why a venue or medium might not respond to your song, including: it got lost, it didn't fit their format, they forgot or any number of other reasons. The good news is that there are so many alternatives and this is a numbers game. You can't control it, so move on.

What you can control is your submission. Make the best music and craft the best publicity materials that you can and send them as far and as wide as you can. Don't use rejections as critiques. If you want feedback, go to other musicians or producers.

Most importantly, follow up. Most places that accept music submissions don't even tell you if they've decided against using your stuff. A well-managed follow-up can sometimes make the difference in getting your song played. Some of the methods we discuss in Chapter 12: Get Publicised will come in handy here. Many of our follow-ups have resulted in plays, so don't skip this essential step.

REGISTERING YOUR SONGS WITH A PERFORMANCE RIGHTS ORGANISATION

We suggest reading Chapter 7: Your Rights on Performance Rights Organisations (PROs) to learn how to get your music registered, so that the resulting plays on radio or elsewhere can generate income. Unless you're a big player or you're fairly well known, it's unlikely that you'll see any income but it still makes sense to get your music registered.

▶▶ GETTING HEARD OFFLINE

UK COMMERCIAL RADIO

UK Commercial Radio can be within reach of bands that make a serious effort to break in. Many of the radio stations cover bands local to their area but it is still an insular industry. Possibly the best way to get airplay is to hire a 'plugger' who will make the calls and follow-ups for you to get your music played. Best of all, a plugger probably already has connections at the stations that you wish to get airplay. You are buying their connections as much as their efforts when you hire one.

Each area's stations has their own quirks and local shows, some of which focus entirely on independent bands. You should research your local stations for the best ways to break in and gain more airplay.

DO YOU NEED A RADIO CAMPAIGN?

Getting your music *heard* is more than just getting played on the radio and a full-blown radio campaign might actually be a distraction from better opportunities that could spread your music further for the same effort. There are three major reasons to pursue radio:

■ Exposure
■ Boosting concert tour draws
■ Performance royalties

EXPOSURE

If your music is added to a station's rotation, you will potentially reach new fans. Most of the benefits of this airplay are somewhat indirect, however. Your song will get played but will the DJ announce the title correctly? The band name? Will he remember to announce anything at all? That doesn't necessarily help you make new fans. Unlike online mediums, you can't 'click' on the band name to go to the website or instantly buy a track.

When listeners decide to buy your music, they'll have to do a Web search on how they *think* your band name is spelled based on how the DJ pronounced it. And there's no good way to determine how many times you've been played even if you do get added to the rotation. It could be thousands. It could be once. Stations have no obligation to tell you. In comparison to websites, which track all downloads, you often have to listen to the radio station yourself to confirm if and when you get played.

BOOSTING CONCERT TOUR DRAWS

Timing your radio campaign to your tour schedule can be a great way to boost your draws. If coordinated with a fully fledged publicity campaign, listeners in the area will become familiar with you and your music and will be more likely to check out your show.

Posters in the area advertising your upcoming show are more likely to resonate with the community when timed to coincide with your music on the radio. Offering complimentary tickets to stations to give away to listeners will increase their incentive to play your band's music on the air, announce and advertise your show and have you come into the station to be interviewed and perform.

PERFORMANCE ROYALTIES

As discussed in Chapter 7: Your Rights, one additional benefit of radio airplay is that each play counts as a performance for the author/publisher. If you've registered with a PRO, you are eligible to earn performance royalties.

LOCAL MUSIC SHOWS

Although it's difficult to get added to a commercial radio station's main rotation, there are a few other opportunities. Some commercial radio stations have shows that feature local artists. For instance, in Chicago, we've been played on WXRT's Local Anesthetic with Richard Milne. Milne, like most local show hosts, will accept submissions from any local band. Often, as is the case with Milne, it's the host who decides what will get played. These shows can be a good way to get heard because they usually have large audiences and they love promoting local shows because it's something happening in their backyard. It helps to listen to these shows before submitting, since show hosts often prefer a particular genre or style.

Submitting to these shows is usually easy. Follow the submission guidelines on the station's website. Local music shows are usually flooded, so make sure you obey the guidelines carefully and, as with any radio campaign, follow up on your submission.

TALK SHOWS

Talk shows are another way to get played on commercial radio. If one of your songs is on a topic being discussed, they might just play it if it's brought to their attention. A play on a talk show helps make your music stand out more than had it been played in its standard music rotation.

There are, of course, no formal submission guidelines for talk shows. You will often have to find their contact information from their website. Sometimes the producer is a good person to approach. Other times, getting your music directly to the hosts works best. It helps if you're personally familiar with the show, allowing you to tailor the message. This happened to us when we sent our updated version of the traditional Irish song, 'Tell Me Ma' to Chicago morning radio talk show host Jonathon Brandmeier. All we did was write a short email about the song and how it might fit with the St Patrick's Day show and attached the MP3. We didn't receive any acknowledgement that it had been received but then, a few days later on that St Patrick's Day, he played our song.

RUNNING A RADIO CAMPAIGN

There are seven steps to running a successful radio campaign:

- Identify stations and shows
- Make a list and check it twice
- Call in advance
- Prepare your CD and press kit for submission
- Send it in
- Follow up to verify delivery
- Follow up to verify acceptance

If the purpose of your college radio campaign is to boost your draw for a tour, coordinate carefully to maximise the effectiveness of the campaign. This means planning ahead and building in enough time to get your music to each station, convince them to add your song and if possible schedule an interview or performance in-studio well before you pull up on campus in the van. Because this will seriously affect your planning, determine if this is one of your goals early on.

STEP 1: IDENTIFY STATIONS AND SHOWS

Your goal is to send your music directly to those people who will actually play it. There are *stations* that specialise in your style of music and also *specific shows*. You must identify both for your radio campaign.

In order to identify the stations, there are two free resources that you can use. These include the website for this book, DIYMusicManual.com as well as Yahoo.com, which has a listing.

For shows, you can use the DIYMusicManual.com site, where we list radio shows per station. You should submit your music directly to the person most likely to play it. To get in the general rotation, send it to the music director or the specific submission address they provide. If you want to get into a speciality show, find that DJ's address and send it directly.

STEP 2: MAKE A LIST AND CHECK IT TWICE

Once you've identified the appropriate stations and shows, the next step is: write it down. You need a comprehensive list of where and to whom you will be sending your music. A simple spreadsheet will do. Keep track of where and when you submitted your music and when you need to follow up. See below for our recommended headers.

INFORMATION TO TRACK DURING A RADIO PROMOTION CAMPAIGN

Since a radio promotion campaign takes weeks to pull off, you'll want to keep track of the following information in a table or database format:

- Radio station name
- Address
- Station submission guidelines for the particular radio station
- Radio station contact name
- Phone number
- Email address
- Notes about your call with the radio station contact to help trigger your memory when you later call to follow up
- If touring, to time airplay to when you'll be in the area, your personal deadline for when you need to have the station add your song to the rotation
- The date when you mailed the CD and press kit
- The date you need to call them to make sure the package was received and ask when it might be added to rotation
- The date when they tell you it will be added to the rotation
- A tick when it's confirmed your song was added to the rotation

---

STEP 3: CALL IN ADVANCE

Once you have your list, call to confirm the contact details, verify what kinds of materials they need and hype your music. You may want to skip this step but don't make that mistake. The key to any successful college radio campaign is making direct contacts and creating a personal connection with you and your music. Beyond giving you a leg-up against bands that simply 'submit and forget', you'll also be competing for attention with radio promoters who do this for their clients as a matter of course.

We'll discuss radio promoters in detail in the next section but remember that these paid professionals always use a call to hype their client's songs because it's their job to get the station to add them to their rotation. Airtime is limited and the difference between having your CD sit in a pile and getting it get added to the rotation is your ability to connect with someone at the station who will feel obligated not only to keep an eye out for your CD but to make sure it gets added. How you do this is ultimately up to you. This is one of the times where the Agent Strategy we discussed in Chapter 8: Get Noticed will come in handy.

STEP 4: PREPARE YOUR CD AND PRESS KIT FOR SUBMISSION

Prepare your submission according to the station's instructions. Unfortunately, most radio stations are still organised around the CD and don't accept MP3 or WAV files. So you'll have to do it the old-fashioned way and physically mail copies of the CD to your contact person's attention. Doing anything other than following instructions will probably result in your package being thrown out or, at best, seriously delayed as it's transferred between radio station staff.

Suggestions for preparing your CD include:

- **Put it in a standard jewel case:** If your CD is not already in a standard jewel case, put it in one. In general, CD libraries at college radio stations are based around the size of the standard jewel case, so thin cases or paper folders are inconvenient for them. (If you haven't had your CD manufactured yet and you're planning a college radio campaign, then this may be a deciding factor in how you package your CD.)
- **Remove the annoying plastic wrap:** If your CD is shrink-wrapped, remove it. Save them time and hassle.
- **Recommend 2–3 songs to play:** Label the case with the top two or three 'radio-ready' songs you definitely want them to hear. You don't want them losing interest in your CD by track three when track six is the best song on the album.

Unless otherwise instructed, your press kit should be simple – do not spend extra time and money on this. We talk about press kits in Chapter 12: Get Publicised. You can abridge the full kit for radio by limiting it to the bio and basic facts about the band (including the website). They're evaluating your music, plain and simple, and probably won't be reading your press kit on the air. If you include a positive press article or review about your music it might help but the only thing they'll really be interested in is the CD.

STEP 5: SEND IT IN

With prep out of the way, it's time to mail your package:

- **Write 'solicited material' on the envelope:** If you previously contacted someone at the station and they told you to send in your CD, write 'solicited material' in clear, easy-to-read print on the front and back of the envelope.
- **Write the date of your show on the envelope:** If you're touring and will be playing in the area, include the date of your show on the envelope. Adding a date tells the students that you're coming to town, which is an added incentive to promptly open the envelope, play your music and contact you for an interview an or on-air performance.

Be sure to mark the date you mailed the package on your spreadsheet and mark the follow-up date appropriately (allowing at least a week from the mail date, depending on your method of delivery).

STEP 6: FOLLOW UP TO VERIFY DELIVERY

After all the work you've done, you won't want to neglect this important step. On the follow-up date, call your contact to confirm that the CD arrived. This is a second opportunity to hype your music and the particular track you'd like them to play. If they didn't receive the CD or if they've already lost it, you'll need to re-send. If they did receive it, ask your contact when they're scheduled to evaluate it. Make a note of this date and mark it on your schedule.

STEP 7: FOLLOW UP TO VERIFY ACCEPTANCE

As soon as the second follow-up date arrives, call your contact once again to determine whether your music was in fact added to the station's rotation. This is not an odd question to ask. Stations receive this question regularly from radio promoters who need to report back to their clients.

Being included in the rotation does not guarantee that your music will be played. Unless you actually listen to the stations, you can never be sure if or when your music is played, since, as we said, at most stations it's the DJs who choose what to play from the songs in rotation. If they don't like your song, regardless of how it's labelled, they will skip it.

Doesn't this seem like a lot of work? It should come as no surprise that an entire industry sprang up around orchestrating these campaigns.

HIRING A PLUGGER

A large percentage of the music you hear on radio stations is chosen thanks to the work of radio pluggers. They offer three advantages over doing a college radio campaign yourself:

- **Existing contacts:** Pluggers know the stations and shows and have the necessary relationships in place.
- **Comprehensive service:** Promoters do all the work promoting, following up and verifying that your music has been added to the rotation.
- **Hype:** Promoters are good at schmoozing DJs and music directors and convincing them that your music is 'hot'.

Radio pluggers typically only accept clients whose music they feel is worthy of promotion. After all, their reputations are on the line when they try to get bands played. Pluggers tend to be tenacious, with the capacity for barefaced promotion that the job calls for. And, because they act as your agent, it's easier for them to hype your music as 'the best ever'.

One music director told us that, each week without fail, he'd get a call from the plugger describing 'hottest group ever' with 'the best song', insisting it be added immediately. Every week he'd have a new 'best song ever'. And although the tactic didn't work on this director, it always seemed to work with his junior music directors, who would approve the new song for rotation. They loved the attention this plugger gave them and how important it made them feel.

If you have the money, a radio plugger may be an option for you. Fees can range anywhere from £1,500 to £20,000 or more depending on:

- The scope of your campaign (there's a lot of college radio stations out there)
- The services you want (they'll charge you less if you do all the grunt work and mailing)
- The duration of the campaign

If you're going to spend money to promote your music, an alternative to a traditional radio plugger, whose campaign will be limited in time and scope, would be to calculate what you would spend and take that money to hire someone on your own. Find someone in your skill network with the right personality and skills to handle this process. One individual calculated that, for the amount of money he spent on a radio plugger for six weeks, he could have financed his own promotions person for six months. And unlike a radio plugger who has to allocate limited resources among many clients, a single part-time promotion person works for you alone. Of course, your promotion person won't have the established relationships in place that a radio plugger already has but with a little research even a newbie can be effective in this role. Just remember that your new hire will be competing against people who do this for a living.

LIVE MUSIC SHOWS AND IN-STUDIO PERFORMANCES

If you're touring or have a gig within a station's broadcast area, you should see if they have a live music show. Live music shows typically run during the day and feature in-studio performances and interviews with bands and musicians performing in the area that night or weekend.

Most stations are more than happy to have bands come in the afternoon before a show and play a few songs, give away a few tickets and get interviewed by the DJs. Beyond actively promoting your show and boosting your draw, doing in-studio performances is an excellent way to cement your relationships with the station staff and get to know them face to face.

Even if the station doesn't have a live music show, they may still want you to come in to do an interview, play some songs off your CD and give away some tickets. If you're on tour, you'll need to coordinate your radio appearances with your shows.

US COLLEGE RADIO

US college radio has long been friendly to international bands and is an excellent way to get your music heard to develop an international audience. It's quite different from student radio in the UK. US college radio works the way that most people think US commercial radio should work (but doesn't): you send them your music and, if they like it, they'll play it. It's wonderfully uncomplicated and far less expensive than dealing with commercial radio. They are always hungry for new, exciting music to play.

The people who control access to college airwaves are students. They're the DJs. They select the CDs. They read the news. They play the dead air. They run the station. These are the people you need to convince to play your music. Best of all, college radio is inclusive. Students host shows that run the gamut of styles and formats. No matter what kind of music you create, there's a college radio show that will play it.

But this doesn't mean it won't take hard work to get your music played. It requires time, effort and follow-up. The good news is that college radio is a medium within your arm's reach. Before spending your time and money, however, consider what you're going to get out of a college radio campaign. College radio has an undeniably smaller listenership than its commercial cousin.

HOW COLLEGE RADIO (USUALLY) WORKS

We can't say how all US college radio stations work but there are some common elements. Naturally, most college stations restrict staff to current students to make sure that as many as possible have the opportunity to work in radio. This includes the DJs as well as the music directors who decide what goes into their rotations. Because the music directors are students, you need to keep their motivations and schedules in mind if you want to convince them to play your music. Getting in touch with them will be at their convenience. Generally, student music directors keep irregular office hours and, because they're students, might be at class or in bed with a hangover when you call.

Typically, students who take part in radio are genuinely excited about new music. Most that we've met have unconventional tastes and prefer music outside of the mainstream – beyond commercial radio. Most love discovering something new – a new band, a new sound, a unique song – and sharing it with their listeners. Many are musicians themselves and love discussing music endlessly.

Many stations stick to a particular genre or style of music during daytime hours: alternative, rock, hip-hop and so on. They play a rotation of pre-selected music. Typically, it's the music director who determines what music to include in this daytime rotation, although some stations may let a committee of staff members decide. Like the music they play, music director personalities run the gamut. Some share music decisions with the DJs and staff, while others can be dictators. In true tail-wagging-dog fashion, some decide based on what charts in *CMJ*.

DJs, however, also have a say in what music is played, although it's typically limited. College DJs can technically play whatever music they want as long as they meet a certain number of plays of the pre-selected music. For instance, at KRUI, where one of the authors worked, the station divided music into heavy, medium or light rotation slots. CDs were physically labelled with red, blue and yellow stickers corresponding to how often a particular song should be played during the hour. DJs were supposed to play a certain number of songs every hour, favouring the heavy rotation songs and going down from there.

Even so, the college radio DJ actually controls which songs air and when. Contrast this with US commercial radio, where DJs are simply on-air personalities with no control over the music (despite frequent talk of a certain song being 'requested'). Music on commercial radio is decided by music directors and is typically programmed into computers beforehand.

After the daytime rotation, evenings and weekends are usually dedicated to radio shows that focus on a particular niche. These generally play music radically different from the kind featured in the daytime format, such as a thrash metal show on a station that normally plays country. Latin, punk, folk, jazz, alt-country, bluegrass, ambient or even children's music might be spotlighted.

Some of these programmes are long-established shows that have been inherited and handed down through the years from student to student. Others are the original invention of a particular student who received approval from the staff for their particular show format. The songs played on a particular show are decided by the student or students who control the show at that time. These shows tend to appeal to a limited, but targeted, college and college community audience.

CHARTING IN *COLLEGE MUSIC JOURNAL*

College Music Journal or *CMJ*, is to US college radio what *Billboard* is to US Top 40 commercial radio. It's an expensive industry magazine that tracks what's 'hot' on college radio. If your music is played often enough across multiple college stations, you have a shot at getting charted on *CMJ*. This can provide recognition by a trusted, objective authority that your music has momentum in the college market. This can generate interest in your band from the press and record labels. For many bands and labels, charting on *CMJ* is a major goal since it's considered a measure of grassroots attention.

Most campaigns that succeed at *CMJ* charting do so by paying radio pluggers to perform the intensive promotional work and follow-up necessary to get airplay in multiple college markets.

US COMMERCIAL RADIO

Commercial radio in the US does not work in the idyllic way still portrayed in some television shows. Generally, they don't accept unsolicited submissions. A commercial radio campaign can cost anywhere from tens to hundreds of thousands of pounds. Part of that money goes to 'independent promoters' who control access to the stations and block other music from getting added to the playlist. They can act as the gatekeeper and tollbooth for each station.

GETTING PLAYED ON US COMMERCIAL RADIO

Your best bet for getting into a commercial radio station's rotation would be to hire a US radio plugger (called a radio *promoter*) who specialises in commercial radio. But this isn't economically feasible for most indies.

There's always a balance between time and money for these activities and the amount of effort you would need to invest to get your music on commercial radio would probably be sufficient to become a professional radio promoter yourself. This is why most indie bands in the US avoid commercial radio altogether.

Even major label bands in the US usually get their start on college radio and try to get charted on *CMJ*, which is often a good springboard for commercial radio. If you wish to eventually get played on commercial radio, you should try charting on *CMJ* first.

US PUBLIC RADIO

US public radio is a great way to get your music played because the audience is much larger than that of college radio and it isn't as gated off as the commercial radio market.

A National Public Radio station will play the general NPR news feed and then add their local news at the end. Then, throughout the day, they will alternate local shows with some national ones.

Each programme has a producer of its own who makes decisions about the stories and music that are included.

GETTING PLAYED ON US PUBLIC RADIO

We suggest the following steps to get your music on public radio:

- Identify all of the programmes that you want to target (it's best to start with the local ones). Add each one to your spreadsheet, as discussed above.
- Go to each programme's webpage and find the producer's contact information and any submission guidelines.
- Craft and send a pitch that's tailored to each show's particular content. (Note that sometimes, you can get phone numbers or fax numbers. But other times you need to be content with an email.)
- Follow up!

We were able to get our debut album played on WBEZ, Chicago's public radio station, using this exact method. We found the email of the producer of 848, a programme on WBEZ, and sent a CD at their request. They played it on their show.

Keep in mind that producers may not get back to you, even if they play your music. A friend of the band once claimed to have heard us on public radio. Sceptical, we searched the radio station's site and discovered that, lo and behold, our song had been played after all – despite the fact that no one from the show told us.

SATELLITE, CABLE RADIO

Satellite radio works like satellite television, the signal beamed from orbit rather than from local towers. Satellite radio receivers are still mostly built into cars but there are also some portable devices available and their channels are also available to subscribers over the Web.

Satellite radio has been chipping away at terrestrial radio's listenership but it's still lagging far behind because it requires special equipment and a subscription fee. Initially, satellite held a lot of promise for indie bands but the format has became less friendly as it's matured.

Although some satellite providers have 'indie music' stations, those stations aren't attractive to listeners. People look for genres such as country, hard rock or classical. Your goal should be to get played on the genre that fits your music.

▸▸NON-RADIO OPTIONS

THEATRE AND COMEDY GROUPS

Theatre and comedy groups provide many opportunities to get played that are often neglected by bands. They can be a particularly good way to get heard. Audiences at a theatre show are really paying attention, as opposed to fans at a concert who are usually shouting or spilling beer on each other.

There are two good ways to get your music played in a theatrical performance. You can perform live as part of the show or get your recorded music played as a soundtrack for a scene or sketch.

The best part about getting your music played in a theatre is that your band will get mentioned in the programme. Your band name will appear with your website on a piece of paper that some people will take home. It's an instant flyer. You may also get an opportunity to present a mailing list and sell your albums.

If you're interested in getting your music in a theatrical performance, hook up with the local theatre community, improvisation community or sketch comedy community. (These are three distinct communities, if you can believe it, although there is always some crossover.) There are often many local artists who are putting on their own shows and you never know who might be looking for music unless you get involved.

We used this to good effect when we hooked up with a sketch comedy group and got a run of shows at the famous Second City, partly because they were able to promise a band with the sketch comedy (which made for a bigger show as well boosting the draw). The comedians turned out to be wonderful contributors to our skill and opportunity networks. Years later, they used our recorded music as part of yet another Second City show and then asked us to write a theme song to their TV show they created called *DVDGeeks. DVDGeeks* ended up getting picked up by a variety of television stations around the US resulting in our theme music being beamed into millions of viewers homes. Needless to say, these types of song plays have been great for our band CV.

It bears mentioning that music at a theatrical performance of any kind stands out, just as actors would at a concert. And we've found that these shows often have an easier time getting critical attention and mentions in the paper. It's a good way to get publicised and a good excuse for a press release.

FILM AND TELEVISION

Both independent and studio films are opportunities for indie bands. So are television shows. In fact, film and television production companies are starting to work with indie bands more and more because they are less expensive, easier to work with and easy to find, thanks to the Internet. To get played on film and television, you just need to make them aware of your music.

Fortunately, everything you do to get your band noticed contributes to this goal. Still, there are a few ways you can maximise the likelihood of getting your music on the small or large screen:

- **Your website:** Mention that your music is available for film and TV use on your website. That way, your site might come up in a search for 'film music'. Although it should be obvious that music can be used for anything at all, sometimes you have to draw producers a map. You might just give them an idea.
- **Film and TV schools:** With the Internet, you can make your music available to any film school in the world. If you have any film or TV schools in

your area, you can hook up with them more directly and provide your music for their use (usually just for exposure rather than money). And if the film takes off, it may create a lot of interest in your work.

- **Creative Commons:** There are sites based on the Creative Commons licence that makes music available to many types of creators, including film producers and television show producers. See creativecommons.org and Chapter 7: Your Rights for information about this.
- **Community television:** Some communities television stations have shows that need music. Given the copyright obstacles with using major label music, they are always on the lookout for pre-cleared alternatives.
- **Music aggregators:** TV, film and commercial producers sometimes rely on music aggregation services that act as middlemen between musicians and producers. We talk about this in Chapter 7: Your Rights.

MUSIC CONTESTS

From battle of the bands to songwriting contests, there seem to be countless places to 'compete' against other musicians to get your music judged and heard. While we have never seen music as a competitive activity, it can motivate some people. Below are a few of the opportunities that may come as a result of these contests. Some of these options cross into online options as well but we'd rather keep all of the contests in one place.

BATTLE OF THE BANDS

Battle of the bands contests are usually live, although many are appearing online by pitting bands' recorded music against one another. Some of these contests require a fee to participate but others are free. It's a simple enough concept: there's usually a group of bands, a way to judge the 'best' and a show that gives all of the bands a chance to perform. If held online, the 'performance' is usually a Webpage with the band's posted songs.

If you win one, it's something you can publicise. But even if you don't, you can at least expose your music to new listeners. So in spite of the fact that these are seen as competitive, it can be worthwhile, whether you win or lose.

SONGWRITING CONTESTS

Some contests focus simply on your ability to write songs. Songwriting contests have been around for quite a while and often require an entry fee to participate. In fact, that's the way a lot of these contests make their money – from the musicians.

There are innumerable songwriting contests you can enter, with perhaps one of the most famous being the John Lennon Songwriting Contest (jlsc. com). Some lists of songwriting contests can be found at Muse's Muse (muses-muse.com/contests.html) and The Craft of Songwriting (craftofsongwriting. com/contests.htm). Many of these songwriting contests offer prizes for first place, including recording gear, instruments, and, for some reason, record label contracts.

One notable and free songwriting contest that occurs weekly online is Songfight (songfight.org). Songfight typically posts a song title or titles on their website. Musicians have one week in which to write and record a song based on that title and email it in. Songs are made public for visitors to stream and download so they can vote on their favourite. The prize for winning is bragging rights for the week. If you enjoy a creative challenge, we recommend Songfight.

ALBUM CHALLENGES

The goal of an album challenge is write, record and produce an entire album in one month. Most album challenges were inspired by National Novel Writing Month (NaNoWriMo.org), which challenges authors to write a 175-page (50,000 word) novel within the month of November. And like NaNoWriMo, there's no contest or prizes at stake.

Three of the major album challenges that you can participate in are: the Record Production Month Challenge (rpmchallenge.com), February Album Writing Month (fawm.org) and National Solo Album Month (nasoalmo.org). The RPM Challenge and FAWM occur in February while the NaSoAlMo occurs in November alongside NaNoWriMo. Each are free to participate.

There are surprising numbers of musicians that take part in these challenges. According to Christopher Grenier and David Karlotski, two of RPM's founders, they've had musicians from all seven continents (yes, this includes Antarctica!). Karlotski states one of the purposes of the RPM Challenge is to 'get musicians back to why they do music in the first place: to create music for the sake of music and not focus on whether it's commercial or not'. In fact, that's what we found when we participated in the RPM Challenge ourselves. We had a blast writing the music and got two albums out of it, to boot. We also connected with other musicians on their website and discussion boards and even met a group of them in person at the Chicago celebration party, which was held simultaneously with many other cities all over the world.

One notable participant of RPM was Bob Boilen of the band Tiny Desk Unit. Boilen is a host and director of US National Public Radio's *All Things*

Considered. As a participant he highlighted RPM and some of the bands that participated on his show. Best of all, sites like RPM make their participants' music available free to the public year round on an online jukebox. So, it's yet another place to be heard.

▶▶GETTING HEARD ONLINE

As we mentioned in the introduction to this chapter, the online opportunities to get heard are often the most effective because they link directly to your website. The exciting thing about getting heard online is that any website at all can put your songs on their pages, not just music websites.

Ironically, music websites are probably the worst places to get played. They tend to be overcrowded and lack the necessary coherency to be a good place for listeners to find new music. We'll present many alternatives to music sites below.

FIND OUT WHERE THE PARTY'S AT

The difficult part about deciding where to spend your time and energy on the Web is determining whether a given website is popular or not. Most don't display their statistics, so you'll need to rely on other methods.

But just as important as the size of the audience for a particular website is the kind of audience. If you write songs about beer, for example, you'll want to target the most active websites and message boards about beer to promote your music. Even a modestly popular website can have a dramatic effect if its audience is mostly people who would probably enjoy your music for one reason or another.

WHO IS THE AUDIENCE?

The first thing to do with any website is work out what the audience is like. This comes into play in the indie music arena more than most. For instance, there are a lot of sites out there that say they're a great place for indie music to get heard, declaring all these benefits right on the front page. The problem is, as a listener, you wouldn't stay on a page that speaks directly to bands.

Amazon.co.uk, on the other hand, devotes its front page to selling to customers, although there are links for setting up your own stores there as well. YouTube.com also does a good job of balancing their front page between featuring the latest cool videos and explaining how to submit your own.

Think twice about signing up on any site that doesn't strike this balance.

Most likely, the sign-up agreements aren't fair to the musicians, because these sites aren't making their money off listeners and it's coming from somewhere.

GOOGLE PAGERANK

One of the quickest ways to judge a website's popularity is to install Google Toolbar (toolbar.google.com), available for Microsoft Internet Explorer and Mozilla Firefox. After installation, browse to any page to see its Google Page Rank on the green bar in the middle of the toolbar. PageRanks range from one to ten and are based on the number of sites that link to a website together with a host of other constantly shifting criteria.

PageRank is generally a good way to judge the popularity and trustworthiness of a site. A four or five is quite good, although these numbers change whenever Google tweaks its methodology. Keeping up with the latest changes to Google's PageRank on blogs about search engine optimisation (SEO) will help you interpret the numbers more effectively.

SEARCHES

You can use search engines to find out who is linking to a particular site. For instance, in Google, enter 'link:beatnikturtle.com' to see every site that links to ours. It won't take long to learn if the site is a scam, as posts complaining about it will be in the first few pages of results.

DESIGN

Often, it's possible to tell how good a site is simply by how well it's designed. If it has a lot of bad links or looks too simple, it probably won't be worth your time. People have to spend money to make sites look good and this is a reliable indicator of how seriously they take the endeavour. If they've commissioned a slick design, they've almost certainly spent some money doing SEO work to boost their Google PageRanks, which generates traffic. (See Chapter 4: Your Website for information more on SEO.)

MUSIC WEBSITES

While music websites come to mind first for getting heard on the Web, they're often the least effective online outlet. Most of them don't take a stand on what music is good, accepting songs from anyone who signs up for an account. These sites are often enormous, undifferentiated piles of music. Even a terrific song won't stand out in a chaotic mess like that.

Beware of music sites that feature terrible agreements for the musician, requiring them to give up irrevocable rights to their songs in return for the slight possibility that someone might actually listen to their music. Read any agreements carefully before signing up. There's often a provision stating that the agreement can change with almost no notice, so negative terms can be added in later or positive ones removed.

Also, remember to make sure that the site is targeting listeners and not indie bands. We've rarely seen the tradeoffs to be worth the trivial exposure that you can get from music websites such as MP3.com. Be very careful if you decide to use them and, if you do, mention popular groups with a sound similar to your own so that your music will come up in searches for those bands.

Part of the reason for the popularity of these sites (with musicians) is that they promise to generate interest in your music just by signing up. In our experience, interest comes from sending your music directly to the people who might be interested in it: reviewers, bloggers, podcasters, forum members and so on.

That said, a few sites that we've seen many musicians use to share their music (besides using MySpace.com) are Virb (virb.com), SoundClick (soundclick.com), alonetone (alonetone.com) and GarageBand (garageband.com) which give you a band page and a player to show off your music and other features.

NON-MUSIC WEBSITES

There's an entire Web full of sites out there and any of them can easily incorporate music. Rather than catalogue websites by the kind of content they normally feature, categorise them by topic.

We're not suggesting that you pitch just any site. You need to find the most popular ones whose topic is most directly related to your music. A post to the right message board or a mention on the right blog can mean a lot of listens for your songs.

To give you some ideas, as we mentioned previously, a few comments on the starwars.com message boards for our song 'Star Wars (A Film Like No Other)' brought a lot of people to our site. And our song 'Were All These Beer Cans Here Last Night' that was mentioned on Cheapass.com generated over 30,000 song plays. The song 'I've No Pants' found a home on NoPantsDay.com. And 'Why Don't You Drive?' – about those slow drivers that won't get out of your way – found its place on a popular trucking website.

Categorise your songs by topic, then find the most popular websites on each topic and figure out ways your music might fit in. Most sites have blogs and bloggers are always hungry for content on their chosen topic. Other sites have message boards you can post to. Still others have a news feed. Submitting your music may involve some sleuthing to find an email address and once you find one the submission itself should be informal, along the lines of: 'You might like this song about snorkelling.' If you can be on-topic to that extent, that's often all that you need to do.

Using a Web Flash player, you can give them the HTML code to embed your song directly in their blog rather than sending them a file. This has the advantage of letting you see the listening stats and may make it easier on someone who has a site and doesn't know how to play music from it. See Chapter 4: Your Website for details.

You should ask any site owner that does play your music to provide a link back to your own website, so that people who like the song can find you.

While this is one of the more informal ways of getting your music heard, because you are piggybacking on the popularity of each website and are using their interest in the topic to make your music heard, it can be one of the most effective tools at your disposal.

WEBCASTING

Webcasting uses the Internet to stream your music to people connected to an Internet radio station using a multimedia player. Unfortunately, it's been regulated into obscurity. The fees charged by the major music owners, as well as the rules and reporting requirements that webcasters have to deal with, are so prohibitive as to shut down most stations. Most webcasters today are terrestrial radio stations that are simulcasting their feed on the Internet. The other ones are usually affiliated with larger organisations like Live365.com, which handles the paperwork, some of the cost and the requirements that regulations in various countries have imposed on webcasting.

Webcasting started out unregulated, like most new technologies. The idea that ordinary people could basically make their own radio stations created a groundswell of interest in this new media. Unfortunately, the major copyright owners got together and set rates that were in many cases higher than those charged to terrestrial radio, along with difficult reporting requirements. These regulations quashed the initial excitement and put a stop to technological innovation.

A new agreement has been put in place since then that raised the rates significantly. Webcasters are now burdened with costs so high it will be unfeasible for a station to exist profitably.

Webcasting stations cover every genre. Many of them are friendly to indie bands. Submitting your music to Internet radio stations can get your music played and at least the payola problems that are present in commercial radio are largely nonexistent there.

Some Internet radio stations are explicitly devoted to indie music. While those stations are fairly easy to break into, we suggest you focus on stations that specifically cover your style of music. Because Internet radio is not closed to indies, why not try to get played alongside more popular songs in your style? The listeners that prefer indie-band-only stations are the listening avant garde, a much smaller audience than the general listening public. People often forget that indie music is not a style, just an indicator of whether a band is on a big label or not. There are indie bands in classical music as well as power punk but they don't necessarily mesh well on a radio broadcast. You're better off finding a station that matches your style to get your music heard by those who would probably like it.

Some sites to check out for Internet radio information are Live365 (live365. com), Shoutcast (shoutcast.com) and Radio Paradise (radioparadise.com).

PODCASTS

Because of the burdens placed on webcasting, podcasting has become the radio of the Internet. Podcasts are some of the best places for an indie musician to get played.

And people are listening. The rapid growth of podcasting has been stunning. If you were to search Google on 28 September 2004, for the term 'podcasts' you would have found 24 hits. On 28 September 2005, there were 100 million hits. Today, there are vast numbers of podcasts and the momentum and excitement over this new medium has only continued to grow.

Because podcasts are audio files, music and podcasting are a natural fit. Better still, many labels and label groups such as the RIAA actively deny podcasters the right to use their music. What does this mean for you? Podcasters are in need of music to play.

Podcasting is good for listeners, too. It provides a viable alternative for music fans tired of the increasingly homogenous music on radio. Podcasts are a place where music lovers and independent bands meet.

UNDERSTANDING PODCASTING

At its heart, podcasting is a very simple concept. Named from the enormously popular iPod, podcasting evolved thanks to the rise of blogs, the ubiquity of the MP3 format, the popularity of portable MP3 players and the cheap and easy availability of audio recording software.

To podcast, a person records an episode of their show, uploads the MP3 to the Internet and creates a link to the file from their blog. Thanks to the power of Really Simple Syndication (RSS), which we discussed in Chapter 4: Your Website, the podcast episodes can then be automatically downloaded and enjoyed by subscribers as new ones become available.

PROS

- Podcasters are always looking for music
- Free and easy to submit music
- Unregulated by the music industry
- Dedicated, niche audiences
- On-air mentions and hyperlinks to band website
- Episodes are archived indefinitely

CONS

- Smaller audiences than radio
- Less professional sound quality and shows
- No set rules for submitting music
- No set schedules for shows
- Podfading, i.e. podcasts stopping production on a whim

UNDERSTANDING THE PODCAST AUDIENCE

Podcasting is 'radio on demand'. It's easy, it's prevalent and most importantly people are listening. Podcast audiences tend to be small and, at this early point in the medium's development, tech-savvy but also very dedicated to the topic of the podcast or the personality doing the show. That said, some podcasts, such as *Keith and the Girl* (keithandthegirl.com) and Adam Curry's *Daily Source Code* (dailysourcecode.com) have consistently large audiences.

Podcasts put the audience in control. People can listen to episodes in their own time – not when they're broadcasted. Also, since episodes are simply audio files, they can listen anywhere on their portable MP3 players: in their cars, while working out or while commuting to work. They can pause a show and come back to it later without missing anything or choose to listen again at a later date.

Plus, since podcasters generally leave their old episodes up at their website, new listeners who discover a podcast at a later date can easily download earlier episodes. Best of all, listeners don't have to hunt around for the latest episodes – thanks to RSS their computers grab the new ones automatically.

UNDERSTANDING PODCASTERS

Podcasters are mostly amateurs, producing shows in their free time and with a shoestring budget simply for the love of it or for love of their subject. As a result, there are few rules or formalities when dealing with podcasters.

Production values vary greatly as well. Some podcasters use state-of-the-art recording and production techniques, with results that wouldn't sound out of place on the radio, while others sound like they recorded their show with a cassette recorder while cooking dinner. Some maintain rigorous schedules, updating their shows at the same time each week, while others upload new podcasts 'when they get around to it' or disappear all together ('podfade') due to lack of interest or more pressing commitments.

Thanks to copyright laws, most podcasters are not only happy to hear from indies, they are often in desperate need of 'legal' music to play.

PODSAFE MUSIC

Many podcasters want to play music but most popular music is controlled by major labels and label groups like the RIAA. Rather than allow podcasters to play their music, they have instead scared these potential advertisers away with legal threats. In other words, they have basically shut themselves out of this new music medium. Considering the fact that indies are usually locked out of every area that the music industry is in, this is a great opportunity. Since podcasters are not supposed to use major label music unless they pay for it and license it, they have generally turned to indie bands for music instead.

That's not to say that indie music isn't copyrighted – it is. It's just that indies are more likely to relax certain copyrights and allow podcasters to play their music. Some people think that podcasting works like radio when it comes to copyright but that is not the case. Because podcasts are downloadable audio files, there's no legal distinction between downloading a podcast with an RIAA song or downloading the song itself from a digital music store like iTunes.

Radio, on the other hand, is 'streamed' over airwaves and so copyright law has grown up to allow it special statutory exemptions to play music without even talking to the copyright holder who owns that music. Radio stations just need to pay Performance Rights Organisations for this privilege. But podcasters need permission from all of the copyright holders. While some podcasters, either out of naïveté or a sense of contempt for the RIAA, use whatever music they want despite the legal consequences, many prefer to do the right thing and avoid problems.

Unfortunately, obtaining permission to use a particular piece of popular music is not easy or cheap. As you know from Chapter 7: Your Rights, a podcaster needs to clear a variety of rights from various copyright holders. Not only would each copyright owner be likely to want money for these rights but the process would take weeks of effort, time better spent creating new episodes, grouting tiles in their bathroom, or, really, doing just about anything else at all instead.

To facilitate the use of music for podcasting, podcasters created the concept of 'podsafe' music. In essence, they ask musicians to license their music under a specific podsafe license – a licence that makes a few exceptions to the default copyright setting of 'all rights reserved' in order to allow podcasters to use the musician's music legally (and freely) in their podcasts. Issuing music under a podsafe licence also protects musicians as well, because it limits the rights that are granted.

It should come as no surprise that indie music makes up most of podsafe music. After all, indies can license their music any way they choose. With the right podsafe licence, you have the ability to grant podcasters a small exception within your umbrella of copyrights for a particular song. You can continue to sell your song and license it to others, all while letting podcasters freely play it on their podcasts to give you more exposure.

There are multiple podsafe licences but our favourite ones are issued by the Creative Commons (creativecommons.org), which are free to use and easy to understand, even though they are written by lawyers. They are flexible with regard to what rights you want to allow.

No matter which podsafe licence you decide to use, you should fully understand the rights that you are granting and those you are reserving. As with all legal matters, you should contact a lawyer with any questions.

PODSAFE COLLECTIVES

So, let's say you're a podcaster. You're aware of the legal issues of using copyrighted music in your podcast. You decide you want to add some podsafe music to your show. Great! Now, where do you get it?

Podsafe collectives are sites that host thousands of podsafe songs. Podsafe collectives are where musicians and podcasters meet. Musicians upload their music and get a profile page with an embedded player so podcasters can sample their stuff. Podcasters can then download and use whichever songs they want.

Podsafe collectives are a great way to make your music available to podcasters worldwide but note that each uses different licences. Some collectives are based on licences that are subject to change at the collective's discretion. We prefer podsafe collectives that use Creative Commons licences, such as PodsafeAudio.com.

PODSAFE COLLECTIVES

Use these sites to make your music available to podcasters for use on their shows.

- PodsafeAudio (podsafeaudio.com)
- Podsafe Music Network (music.podshow.com)
- OpSound (opsound.org)
- CCMixter (ccmixter.org)
- Magnatune (magnatune.com)

Submitting music to a podsafe collective is a passive way to get your music heard. It's easy to do and we recommend joining one. But to really get exposure, you'll need to actively submit your songs to podcasters.

MUSIC PODCASTS

Unlike commercial radio stations, music podcasts are usually happy to accept unsolicited music from independent bands. Most podcasters will announce the band name in the episode. The more professional ones will also post the band, album and website for each song in their podcast notes so that listeners can easily find and purchase the music. For this reason, getting on a music podcast can be even more effective than getting played on the radio. And because podcasts are archived, the episode will likely be accessible for future listeners for some time – the medium continues to promote your music long after it has been released.

These music podcasts offer excellent exposure for indies because their listeners are, by definition, fans of new music and podcasters are always hungry to find the freshest stuff for their audience. This doesn't mean that they have low standards. The best music programmes are typically very particular about what they will play, depending on their tastes. So if you submit a song to one and don't get chosen, don't get discouraged. Whether a particular podcaster finds your music appropriate is not something you can control. What you can do is make the best music you can and get that music to as many different podcasters as possible to increase your chances of connecting with people who enjoy it.

A few examples of well-known music podcasts include, C. C. Chapman's *Accident Hash* (accidenthash.com), Phil Coyne's *Bitjobs for the Masses* (indiemeltdown.com) and Brian Ibbot's *Coverville* (coverville.com).

THE UNIVERSE OF NICHES

Given that affordable and easy-to-use hardware and software has made podcasting accessible to the masses, it's no surprise that there are podcasters who cover any topic you can imagine: politics, comedy, education, religion, sports, self-help and so on. Almost every human interest is addressed by a podcast. It's hard to imagine a *radio* show about, say, crocheting but a search on PodcastAlley.com returns over twenty podcasts, with titles such as *Crochet Unraveled*, *CrochetCast* and *Crochet for Men*. The same holds true for music podcasts. Name a genre and there's a podcast that covers it – and ones that cover its sub-categories. Best of all, they're all looking for music to play. The podcasting world is a universe of niches and no niche is too small.

But podcasts aren't only talk shows. Sometimes podcasters produce a short-run series of podcasts on a particular issue such as a social, political, charitable or other cause. But that's all. Another trend is for authors to podcast their books in serial form. Notable authors who have done this include Scott Sigler (scottsigler.com), J.C. Hutchins (jchutchins.net), Tee Morris (teemorris.com) and Mur Lafferty (murlafferty.com). Once these podcasts run their course, the podcast ends. And yet all of these, as we will discover, need music.

The reason why podcasts are an effective way to get heard today is that listeners *request* to listen. While there is certainly something to be said for getting your music played on the radio and in other mass media, audiences actively download a particular podcast because of their interest in the subject matter being covered or the personality delivering it.

APPLYING THE STANDING-OUT STRATEGY

As we discussed in Chapter 8: Get Noticed, the Standing-Out Strategy tells us that submitting your songs only to music sites or, in this case, only to music podcasts, is not the best way to get noticed. Getting your music played on a non-music podcast, such as a talk show about football or a comedy show about politics, can introduce you to potential new fans in a more effective way. Think creatively about your music in relation to the podcasts that are out there. To the extent that your song fits a particular topic covered by a podcast, that song may represent the exact music that podcaster wanted to round out the show. Again, since podcasting is unburdened by formalities, it's all about asking – whether a podcaster adds your song is entirely at that creator's whim. You have to take that chance.

Just remember that some niches are very large, such as the boardgame niche that we mentioned previously, which had a website with over 600,000 unique visitors a month. Creative thinking about how your music and talents fit the needs of podcasters can get your music heard by many new ears. There are no set rules or boundaries and for indies, that's an advantage.

PODCAST THEME SONGS

Podcasts often have a theme song (or should). This identifies the podcast, establishes the brand and gets listeners pumped about the show. Some podcasters turn to indie bands for a song the band has already recorded. Others request a new song be created especially for them.

If you have a knack for this type of songwriting or have a song that naturally fits, most podcasters are very happy to receive an email from a band that wants to write a theme song just for them. Some bands do this for money and others will do it for exposure. The likelihood of a podcaster choosing your band to write a theme song is, of course, greater if you offer to do it as a favour.

If a podcaster uses your theme, you're likely not only to get a great mention (or multiple mentions over time), you'll also get a reciprocal listing of your band's site on their website as thanks. (It never hurts to ask for this just to make sure.)

We've done quite a few theme songs and each of them have given us a lot of great exposure. You can get an idea of the diversity of the audiences from this partial list:

- **Playing for Keeps** (playingforkeepsnovel.com), an award-winning serial Podiobook (book read by the author in a podcast) by Mur Lafferty. The series had over 20,000 listeners and eventually led to her getting a book deal.
- **Buffy Between the Lines** (buffybetweenthelines.com), a serialised podcast fan fiction audio drama written, produced and created by fans of **Buffy the Vampire Slayer**.
- **The Gigcast** (gigcast.nightgig.com), a Webcomic podcast.
- **Tor Books** (tor.com), audio interviews with renowned authors of science fiction and fantasy.
- **Give Us A Minute**, (joemurphymemorialfund.org). A charity podcast for the Joe Murphy Memorial Fund, to combat leiomyosarcoma and cancer in general.

When we do each of these themes, we are constantly overwhelmed by the amount of thanks and exposure we get, including many great comments in their discussion board and in person from fans. As you can imagine, this also generates theme song requests from other podcasters.

INCIDENTAL MUSIC, BEDS AND BUMPERS FOR PODCASTS

Listen to any commercial or public radio format and you'll notice that music – typically instrumental music – is used in a variety of ways to grab the attention of the listener and keep the show moving along. It's also used to introduce particular segments. Incidental music works well in radio but is often ignored in podcasts, yet this kind of music can really help a podcast sound more professional. If your existing music lends itself naturally to incidental music like beds (music played underneath talk) and bumpers (music played before or after talk) or you enjoy writing instrumental music, it's worth reaching out and exploring this option.

YOUR MUSIC AS A SPECIAL GUEST

Saturday Night Live is a popular, long-standing sketch comedy show in the US and yet, on each episode, they have a guest band perform twice. It breaks up the monotony of the sketches and gives the audience and talent a break from the format. Similarly, many 'talk' podcasts will feature a song or two, either because it's related to the subject matter or simply to break up the dialogue. Our music has received tens of thousands of podcast plays in this way.

As we discussed earlier, non-music podcasts are a very effective way to get your music noticed – more so than music podcasts, since yours is likely to be the only music on the show. Better still, non-music podcasters aren't inundated with song submissions and are usually equally excited about playing your music if it's a good fit for the show. Tapping a podcast in the right niche can build a strong connection with a lot of potential fans.

FINDING PODCASTS TO PLAY YOUR MUSIC

So now that we know how podcasters use music, it's time to find some to play your songs. There are a number of good podcast directories. Most podcasters voluntarily register with these sites because they want to advertise. See below for directories that feature a search engine as well as a category-based listing. Categories are a good way to find podcasts suited to your music.

In addition, some podcasters have organised networks of podcasts where they share resources, pool audiences and collectively market to the public. Examples of such networks include Farpoint Media (farpointmedia.net) and the Podshow Network (podshow.com). We suggest going to these network sites and finding podcasts that your music is suited for because these tend have large listenerships. And, we noticed that getting played on a podcast within a particular network usually led to other opportunities with additional podcasts within that network as word spreads about your band.

So what's the best way to approach a podcaster with the idea of using your music? For those podcasts that post submission guidelines, the approach is simple: just follow the instructions carefully. We talk about the best ways to send music to podcasters below. The ones that don't have a formal procedure to submit music are trickier. But remember, podcasters are just people. So all the common sense you learned while growing up continues to hold true here: being friendly and brief usually works great.

If you happen to have the same hobby or interest as a podcaster, it's best to start by pointing out your common interest and your admiration for their show and commenting on the particulars of a prior episode. Follow that by mentioning that you're a musician and that you might have some songs they could use on their show. They are often happy to accept at that point.

PODCAST DIRECTORIES

The following links are all podcast directories that can help you find the podcasts that may be a good outlet for your music.

- Podcast Alley (podcastalley.com)
- Podcast Pickle (podcastpickle.com)
- Podcast Net (podcast.net)
- The Podcast Directory (www.podcastdirectory.com)
- The iTunes Music Store (iTunes.com)
- Podiobooks (podiobooks.com)
- DIYMusicManual.com

PREPARING AND SUBMITTING YOUR MUSIC TO PODCASTS

Podcasters vary in how they want music submitted but one guideline is clear: they want it fast and convenient – through the Web, not sent through snail mail on a CD.

1. Make a quality recording
2. Choose the appropriate track

3. Encode the audio file correctly
4. Name the file using your band name and song title
5. Input ID3 tags in MP3s
6. Choose a licence for the music
7. Follow the podcast's submission guidelines
8. Send an email to the podcaster
9. Follow up

STEP 1: MAKE A QUALITY RECORDING

One submission guideline that is nearly universal for any quality podcast (and any band that takes itself seriously) is to use a quality recording of the song you are submitting. Everything that we talk about in Chapter 6: Your Albums and Merchandise holds true here.

STEP 2: CHOOSE THE APPROPRIATE TRACK

For music podcasts, you'll want to promote the song that would have the most appeal for listeners to that particular podcast. After all, you want them to be wowed enough to check out the rest you have to offer. Also, don't hold back your 'best tracks' from podcasters. Think of it like radio: would you want anything but your best track to be played?

STEP 3: ENCODE THE AUDIO FILE CORRECTLY

One way to completely mess up the first step is by encoding your audio file improperly. Bands often overlook this important step. Since a podcast will ultimately be made available in MP3 format, it's imperative that your audio file be encoded at the highest bitrate possible. Not all podcasters understand this point either. Some will happily add a band's MP3 to their show, only to compress the song a second time when they convert the finished podcast to MP3 format.

This has the unfortunate effect of adding digital pops and glitches (called 'artifacts') that distract and annoy listeners – no one wants to listen to an audio file that sounds like it is being played in between stations on an AM dial. Worse, although it's not technically the band's 'fault', the low quality of the audio reflects badly on the band.

Therefore, send an uncompressed WAV version of the song. These files are large, so use a large file transfer service like YouSendIt (yousendit.com) or ZUpload (zupload.com) to avoid clogging the podcaster's inbox.

STEP 4: NAME THE FILE USING YOUR BAND NAME AND SONG TITLE

Always name your audio files consistently. Although you are only submitting them to a particular podcaster, you never know where they may show up. Some podcasters may ask to make the song available directly from their website and it may end up in a huge folder of other song files. As a result, you want to make sure the file name is tagged correctly as outlined in Chapter 4: Your Website.

STEP 5: INPUT ID3 TAGS IN MP3S

As we discussed in Chapter 4: Your Website, the MP3 format comes equipped to handle a variety of information about the song through a tagging mechanism called ID3. You should fill in this information as we suggested there.

STEP 6: CHOOSE A LICENCE FOR THE MUSIC

As mentioned above, we suggest using a Creative Commons licence for your music in order to make it podsafe. A smart podcaster may ask about the licence, so be clear from the start which one you're using for the track.

STEP 7: FOLLOW THE PODCAST'S SUBMISSION GUIDELINES

This rule is simple: read each podcast's submission guidelines and follow them carefully. You don't want your music ignored just because you didn't follow their instructions. Most music podcasts have a preferred method of delivery, file format and information they need about the band (such as website, bio, etc.). Some want songs sent through email. More sophisticated or long-standing podcasts have FTP servers or other mechanisms. You don't want to start off on the wrong foot by causing more headaches for the podcaster. Follow their instructions. And, when it's not apparent what to do, ask for clarification *before* sending.

STEP 8: SEND AN EMAIL TO THE PODCASTER

Include the following:

- Band name and website
- Song title (and album, if applicable)
- Brief band bio and description of your music

Always keep this info short and to the point but be personable where appropriate. Be sure to spell the name of the person properly, as well as the name of the show. If a podcast has played your music before, remind them. You've passed their quality test previously, so they'll be more likely to play you again. This is especially important with music podcasts because they're inundated with submissions. When you wrap up, be sure to thank them!

STEP 9: FOLLOW UP

Keep track of every podcast you submit to. Track the name of the podcast, which song(s) you sent and the date of submission. Then follow that podcast to see if they play your music. Some never alert the musicians that they've used a particular song, so it may be up to you to see if you get played.

If you are played in a podcast, send a thank you email! Relationships with podcasters are a valuable collaboration. Maintaining that collaboration is the best way to keep getting played. For instance, one podcaster has featured our music a dozen times and continues to ask for more.

AUDIOBLOGS OR MP3 BLOGS

Audiobloggers, or MP3 bloggers as they are often called, are essentially free-lance music reviewers. The main difference between MP3 bloggers and traditional music journalists is that the former often provide the MP3 of the song being reviewed.

MP3 blogs are often distrustful of anything that seems like self-promotion. Although some accept submissions from bands, others are geared towards people who've otherwise discovered some music that they would like to talk about. If you find an MP3 blog that accepts submissions and reviews music in your genre and you can get a review, this can be a great source of quotes for your press kit and website. Readers of MP3 blogs are always looking for good new music, so a positive mention can get you some good exposure.

A good place to find audio blogs is to look through the site HypeMachine (hypem.com), which posts the latest audio blog entries from all sources in one place. Another is DIYMusicManual.com, which also has a list of audio blogs.

PLAYLIST SUGGESTION AND SHARING SITES

People use the Web to share many aspects of their personal lives and their musical tastes are part of this as well. Because of this, playlist sharing has become as much a part of social networking as micro-blogging. Essentially, everyone is their own radio station – broadcasting what they're listening to and sharing it with the world.

There are multiple sites that do this type of sharing and yet, surprisingly all work in very different ways to arrive at the same goal: introduce people to new music. We're going to cover two below, explaining their similarities and differences, as well as how to use them as a band. These applications are constantly evolving and we expect that this concept will continue to evolve, so we recommend keeping on the lookout for new tools when they appear.

LAST.FM

Last.fm (last.fm) tracks and shares the playlists of its users through a method called audioscrobbling. Scrobbling works like this: if a lot of the people who listen to They Might Be Giants also listen to Beatnik Turtle out of their own music collections, Last.fm will make an association between the two. This essentially uses the listening habits of their scobblers to decide which artists are similar to others. Once this is known, last.fm can suggest music to their listeners based on these associations. Basically, they can say 'hey, if you liked this artist, you may like…'. It's the perfect way to move listeners down The Long Tail of their niche of music to discover new artists they are likely to already enjoy but didn't know it.

Richard Jones, one of the founders of Last.fm, explained that the idea for audioscrobbling came out of his frustration with the standard ways to find new music. 'I wanted to figure out a way to discover artists I'd like without having to do all the work of culling through music magazines, music websites and doing all that research.' While Richard Jones approached the problem from a *fan* point of view, the implications audioscrobbling has for those of us *making* music is profound. Scrobbling can help answer the question: what other music do my fans listen to?

There are many ways to use this service as a musician. First of all, you can sign up for a label or artist account, create a profile and upload your music to their system so it can start being scrobbled by listeners and inserted in their playlists. While many services don't pay royalties on plays, Last.fm does if you choose to sign up. Information on this service is available at their website.

But getting your music scrobbled is only half of the service for musicians. They also provide additional statistics on your plays, including information about who's listening to your music, how many plays you're getting, whether your popularity is growing or shrinking and demographic information about your listeners, such as where they are located and their age groups. These tools can provide surprising insights into your music and your fans.

Finally, Last.fm has introduced a pay service for its playlists called PowerPlay. With PowerPlay, Last.fm can guarantee you a certain amount of plays of your song within their system. These targeted plays are not hidden from the listeners – Last.fm introduces any PowerPlay track as a 'sponsored track'. But they are still played to music listeners based on their own music preferences. Additionally, the PowerPlay tools that Last.fm provides allow you to know which countries are playing your song, if it was skipped and other useful statistical information about how well your PowerPlay marketing campaign is going.

IMEEM

Imeem (imeem.com) is a playlist-sharing social-networking site. You can upload songs, videos or other media to share it with friends. As a band, you can of course upload your own music in order to help share it with people. Users have the ability to create groups and share media among the groups.

Naturally, the more you appear on sites such as these, the more chances someone will recognise you. And if you participate as a user, you can increase the chances of getting your own music noticed. As we've said throughout this manual, while all of these are opportunities you need to question of how much you'll get out of each to decide where to spend your time. We do suggest at least exploring these types of sites.

MUSIC ARCHIVES

If you wish to give away some songs in order to get exposure, you may wish to use music archives in order to share your music. The most famous music archive is Archive.org (archive.org/details/audio). They make it especially easy to license your songs under a Creative Commons licence, should you want to use one. We recommend that you create an account just to check it out.

The downside to this service is that they tend to scale back the sound quality in order to save space and you may find that the songs that you upload may not sound good, so it's not a particularly good place to *highlight* your music.

LIVE MUSIC ARCHIVES

There has been a long tradition of trading live music performances that are recorded by fans. Naturally, with the Internet, the practice has gone online. Live music archives allow people to freely trade recordings of performances that fans attend.

There are some unique characteristics about these live music archives. First of all, they tend to be picky about sound quality and prefer music files that use lossless encoding. Secondly, they often insist on any files traded in their networks to be made freely available to all and traded for non-profit purposes only. And finally, they are usually very careful to only trade music from bands that allow it.

Perhaps the most well-known live music site is ETree (etree.org) which has software, resources and information about live music archives. If you're interested in finding out more about ETree, we suggest using their wiki (wiki.etree. org) to get the latest information or learn how to encode your own band's performances so that you can add it to this archive.

ETree's wiki has an interesting page that you should consider visiting called the Trade Friendly page (wiki.etree.org/index.php?page=TradeFriendly) where they provide lists of bands that allow the recording and trading of their music. For example, one such place that you can register your band is Bands That Allow Taping (btat.wagnerone.com). It's easy to create an account and register your band at BTAT if you want to encourage your fans to do this.

INTERNET CONCERTS

Want to go on a worldwide tour without leaving your basement? All you need is a Webcam, a decent microphone, a fast Internet connection, and, of course, a computer. Internet broadcasting sites make it possible to give people a concert no matter where in the world they are.

Treat a broadcast concert just as seriously as any other gig. It's possible that you'll get even more people watching than you might at a live show. Especially since most Internet broadcast services archive what you record for later viewing. This kind of performance can be just as important as your other live shows.

Plan for Web broadcasts exactly as you would any show, with the same level of attention to publicity. This technology represents a wonderful opportunity to play for thousands of people all over the world. Recommended resources to use are UStream TV (ustream.tv), Mogulus (mogulus.com) and GoTo Webinar (gotoWebinar.com).

PLAYING MUSIC FROM YOUR WEBSITE

As we discussed in Chapter 4: Your Website, playing music from your website is one of the best ways to distribute your music. By serving it from your own site, you have complete control over how the music plays, which of your songs and albums are featured and what other information visitors see while they listen.

Often people will link to your website from a blog or message board. Your music must be available there so that new visitors can listen immediately. Also, someone might hear one of your songs elsewhere and come looking for a further taste of your music. This process should be as seamless and smooth as possible. In fact, incorporating an 'Email a Friend' feature would help further spread your music by allowing visitors to easily send a link to a particular song or album page to one or more friends.

FILE-SHARING YOUR OWN MUSIC

The music industry tended to view file-sharing as the cause of rampant piracy and lost sales, but for indies, it has turned out to be an inexpensive way to get their music heard by new audiences. We recommend that you file-share your own music in order to get more exposure.

Even if you're file-sharing your music already, you may want to take a more structured approach to doing it for yourself. There are multiple file-sharing networks so you will need multiple programs to share your music on all of them. At this time, you will want to find programs to get you on to, at a minimum, Gnutella and ED2k but file-sharing networks can appear and disappear without warning in the ongoing war between the file-sharers and the industry. To see the latest networks, programs and techniques visit the companion site to this book, DIYMusicManual.com.

▸▸LEARNING MORE

To help you get your music out there and heard, head to DIYMusicManual.com. The community site maintains a complete and up-to-date list of all the new media in which you can get your music heard and out to fans. This includes listings of active music podcasts, MP3blogs, radio stations and more.

▶▶CHAPTER TWELVE

GET PUBLICISED

'Isn't it funny? One type costs everything and means nothing and the other costs nothing and means everything.'

James Ernest, president and founder of Cheapass Games on the difference between advertising and PR

The world appears completely different when you look at it through publicity-coloured glasses. You start thinking about the press angle for everything you do as a band. You see potential press releases for every achievement. You'll start thinking about everything your band does three to four months in advance, because that's the lead time most media outlets need.

Like it or not, every form of entertainment relies on the media to get people interested in it. While it would be great to just focus on playing music, musicians don't have that luxury if we want to get our music heard by as many people as possible. As Ariel Hyatt of Ariel Publicity (arielpublicity.com) said, 'I don't care what business you're in, big or small, unless you spend 40 per cent of your time on promotion and marketing, you're dead in the water.' And although the Internet has made it much easier to communicate and get some attention, it's really only added another layer to your publicity campaigns, one you can worry about a little closer to the event itself.

Publicity can be a large and mysterious world, so we're going to cover the parts of it that are important for musicians and break it into steps so you can conquer it.

THE MYTH OF 'THE MAGIC BUZZ BUTTON'

By now you should realise that getting your band and music heard takes work and perseverance. Publicity works the same way. And yet, some musicians still think that there's a shortcut. Jim DeRogatis, music editor for the Chicago Sun-Times and co-host of National Public Radio's *Sound Opinions* and author of multiple books, said, 'There's this perception that there's some mystery button that gets pushed and buzz starts. It's this magic, elusive thing that every group is trying to get. But buzz just means that people are excited about the band and are talking about it.' As Gavin Mikhail said, getting noticed requires patience and diligence since buzz is the result of 'a long, slow burn'.

But initial publicity and chatter about a band is rarely organic. It needs a push to get it started. Money and orchestrated PR campaigns are usually the only way to speed up this process. We'll talk about how to wage these campaigns yourself below. Eventually, you can get to a point where people have heard of you and things will grow organically.

▶▶ THE TRADITIONAL MEDIA AND NEW MEDIA

The Long Tail doesn't just apply to music. It's changed everything that delivers content. In journalism, the Web has enabled more coverage of topics outside the mainstream or ones that weren't as friendly to advertisers. Citizen journalists can cover subjects unhindered by political or financial influence or by a specific publication format or schedule. These Web-based reporters have short-circuited the process of journalism, forcing the older model to play catch-up.

Some people distinguish between 'new media' and 'traditional media'. We will offer a definition here of each term but keep in mind that the Long Tail is a continuous spectrum, not a set of discrete camps. That's why you should always research your media outlets carefully before submitting and never take their requirements for granted. We will refer to press contacts as journalists whether they have a radio show, podcast, TV show, blog or magazine or newspaper column.

THE TRADITIONAL MEDIA AND NEW MEDIA

Media	Submission Guidelines	Examples
Traditional media	Generally have formal submission guidelines, prefer press releases and require three to four months of lead time.	Newspapers and newswires, televised news and talk shows, radio programmes and magazines.
New media	Generally have informal submission guidelines, prefer personal messages to press releases and don't require long leads.	Blogs, podcasts, video blogs and other websites.

PUBLIC RELATIONS

If you have the notion that reporters find stories by pounding the streets and investigating, you might need to change your thinking before going forward with your campaign. You should also drop any illusions about journalists covering you just because you're playing good music. Although they occasionally do find stories the old-fashioned way, the reality is that most of the articles you read are based on press releases.

What this means is that, if you want the traditional media to pay attention to you, you should get the stories directly into their hands via releases. It also means that you will be competing with professional PR people who do this for a living. It probably sounds tough. And it is time-consuming but you *can* do this yourself. You do have one thing going for you: journalists are always looking for a good story and you can give it to them.

▶▶GOALS OF A MEDIA CAMPAIGN

If getting press is so difficult, is it even worth the effort? It's a question you have to ask since there are definitely other worthwhile things you could do with your time – including working on music. Overall though, we think it makes sense for bands to invest the effort in coordinating a full-scale press campaign or spend the money on a good publicist.

Here's what a press campaign can do for you:

- Boost your draw for your upcoming performance or tour.
- Bring more visitors to your website.
- Get your music played.
- Sell albums and merchandise.
- Establish your band with the media, who will not only share your story with the public but also be more likely to write about you in the future.
- Generate press clippings that will help you get better shows and more attention in the future.

All of these benefits help everything you do as a band. And since a band's worth is often measured in popularity, a press campaign is a natural tool that can get it for you. Certainly, labels understand this and spend a lot of their money for big album launches on publicity.

Finally, consider what the movie industry does when it wants a film to succeed. Marketing budgets equal to half or more of a movie's production costs are not unusual. For example, *Spider-Man 3* cost US$258 million to make and had a marketing budget of US$150 million. This marketing budget went towards advertising the movie on billboards, buses, television, radio and magazines. And all of it coordinated and timed to display just before the release. While you don't need to spend half of your money and efforts on PR, this should give you an idea of how important it is to plan a comprehensive publicity campaign for your band and follow through with it.

▶▶PR CONCEPTS

Think publicity, always. Everything your band does should be considered material for press releases. When you're planning anything from a performance to an album launch, ask yourself: is this sufficiently newsworthy? If necessary, alter your plans to make your new project even more press-friendly. While some musicians just focus on music, remember that music is entertainment. And entertainment and publicity go together like peanut butter and chocolate.

Not all press releases have to be about momentous events. Some announcements we've sent out include:

- Our music video getting 5,000 views.
- Hitting the halfway point in our Song of the Day project.
- Launching a new album.
- Releasing a song about *Star Wars* near the first film's thirtieth anniversary.

Each of these has a decent angle but some are obviously juicier than others. For instance, we sent out a press release announcing that we reached the half-way point of our Song of the Day project knowing that it probably wouldn't be covered as a story. But, by talking about the project, we gave them a reason to anticipate the press release we would be sending when we finished it at the end of the year, a story we did want them to cover. In other words, the press release was more about priming the journalists than the story itself. When we sent out the final press release, the journalists were already familiar with who we were and the story itself.

You may also wonder how a press release about getting 5,000 views of a video is newsworthy. First of all, the press release just might make someone curious enough to actually play it (and this kind of press release is usually just an email, so the link is right there). Second, we used the announcement as an excuse to mention other projects that we were doing at the time, including the Song of the Day and early notice of our forthcoming album, about which we were going to send an official press release the following month. Third, the release creates yet another impression of our band name and logo on the recipient. The more familiar the press is with our name, the more likely it is that they'll cover us in the future.

PR IS AN ICEPICK

Remember as you're putting together your campaigns that each release should send a *very* targeted message to each audience. Don't try to be everything to everybody. This is true not only for PR but in marketing your band and your music everywhere.

Bob Baker (thebuzzfactor.com), who we consider to be *the* music marketing guru, said it best, 'You need to find your most defining aspect. You need a sharp focus. If you try to break through a wall, you can't get through if you use a board. But you can if you use an icepick.'

When you market yourself to the media, fans or on Web presences, you should take a stand and sharpen your message to focus on just one defining feature in order to break through.

PR IS A CROCK POT, NOT A MICROWAVE

The Internet has made us impatient. We expect information and gratification immediately. Unfortunately, PR takes place in people-time rather than Internet-time. Even successful PR campaigns take months, even years. The goal of your campaign is twofold: getting coverage for your upcoming event, as well as spreading the word about your band in the long-term.

The first press write-ups in a PR campaign are hard to get because you have nothing to build on. But once you have some press clippings, it will become easier to get more stories. This means you need to start small. For your first campaigns, target local newspapers, blogs and anything else that seems to be within your arm's reach. Use those initial press clippings to get mentions in more widely read or prestigious outlets.

IT'S STILL ABOUT WHO YOU KNOW

Press coverage conveys two benefits. One is the clipping itself and the other is a new press contact who now knows you, liked your story and is likely to cover you in the future. Send thank you notes to every journalist who mentions you and do your best to get to know them personally. Professional publicists personalise press releases to some journalists because, by establishing a personal connection, they can get more of their stories covered.

IF THE MEDIA DIDN'T COVER IT, IT NEVER HAPPENED

The media is like a public memory. If you had an event and the press never covered it, it's as if it never happened. Because of this, you should try to get at least some kind of clipping about every major event that you do, even if it's only a mention on a blog. It's the best way to establish a public 'memory' of the history of your band.

TIMING IS EVERYTHING

Traditional media isn't generally interested in something that has already happened – they want to know about the news before it happens, so that they have the necessary lead time to break the news the moment it does.

Traditional media outlets like news shows and magazines generally have articles slated three to eight weeks ahead of time. This means that, if you want the press to pick up a story, you need to give them a press release early enough to allow them to cover it.

New media outlets, on the other hand, tend to publish news immediately. They don't keep a backlog of stories. Writing to a blogger about an event months in the future doesn't make sense to them. They want to know about an event just before it happens or on its release. Put the dates you plan to approach both traditional and new media outlets on your band calendar.

THE TWO WAYS TO GET COVERAGE

A PR campaign boils down to a two-pronged strategy: sending out press releases to try to convince journalists to write a particular story and making it as easy as possible for the press to cover you if they decide to do so. There are also a few things you can do to increase the likelihood that journalists *spontaneously* write stories about you:

- Write clear press contact information on your website, so it's obvious whom reporters should ask about interviews and so on. Also, provide all the tools they would need to write a story, like bios, fact sheets and images.
- Get blogs to write about you. Both traditional media journalists and new media watch blogs for story ideas.
- Piggyback on events that are already being covered by the press. For instance, you might offer to perform at a noteworthy charity event.
- Add 'If you are a member of the press and want a free CD, write to us at …' to all of your Web presences, so that you welcome them to get your music if they want it
- Brainstorm and execute projects that are unusual or interesting.

When we began our Song of the Day project, we only announced it to our fans. But word about it spread as people blogged about it, generating a lot of interest and sending more people to the site. In another instance, Todd Martens at *Billboard* magazine wrote about our band because he read about us on Lawrence Lessig's blog (lessig.org) and Caryn Rousseau of the Associated Press wrote about us after reading a short blurb about us in a Chicago happenings blog called Gapers Block (gapersblock.com). None of these stories began as a press release but at the same time they weren't entirely spontaneous because the seeds were planted in other media.

A JOURNALIST'S SECRET PLEASURE

If there's one thing that journalists love to do, it's get a scoop on breaking news. They want to be the first to break the story. Giving them the scoop as to what your band is up to works especially well if you know a journalist personally and can give them an exclusive before sending the press release to others. Keep in mind that this can also work against you, because sometimes other outlets will lose interest if the news is already released. If you do this, you need to keep track of which stories are under wraps and which have been released. This is a technique for more established bands since what they do tends to be newsworthy.

IMPROVING PRESS RELEASES 1000 WORDS AT A TIME

While you might be tempted to simply send text, your press releases will be more much effective if you add images. Janelle Rogers of Green Light Go Publicity has over twelve years of experience as a publicist, ten of which were spent working for major labels. Her advice is, 'People make decisions visually first, before listening or reading.'

CONSISTENCY AND PERSISTENCE

Rogers says that the most important qualities of a media campaign are consistency and persistence. Both of these qualities will establish you as a serious source of news for journalists. So, you need to send quality press releases on a regular basis. Once you develop relationships with the press, you can send more direct and informal messages.

But Rogers warned us that there's a fine line between persistence and pestering. Journalists in both new media and traditional media can become annoyed when someone gets on their case to write a story. Rogers gave us some rules of thumb to help avoid stepping over that line:

- **No means no, but...**: If you get a 'no', accept it but remember that it just means they won't print *this* article at *this* particular time. They still might pick up a future release, so don't take them off your list.
- **It's the second email that counts:** According to Rogers, one journalist told her that he would only start paying attention after the second email, even when coming from a professional publicist. Even when coming from *her*, in fact. So when you send email press releases, wait a week and then send a follow-up if you don't hear back. You always have an excuse: spam filters sometimes eat emails, so it's acceptable to confirm whether they received the first email.
- **Never send an old story**: Persistence does not mean sending reworded versions of old stories to the same outlets. Make sure that every new release covers new news. It's okay to refer to older events in a new release, as long as there's new content or a new angle.

TWO STEPS FORWARD, ONE STEP BACK...

When you get major press coverage, your site will immediately get a huge number of visitors over a short amount of time, perhaps a day or so. And after that initial burst of traffic, your site will go back to normal but with a slightly higher uptake in the number of regular visitors. People will often read a news story or find a link on a bulletin board and click through for a closer look. After checking that one page and satisfying their curiosity, most will leave. Only a few will be hooked enough to stick around.

You will see this behaviour again and again as you do your publicity campaigns, so don't be surprised when you get these bursts and then a drop in traffic afterwards. Your best bet for keeping people coming back is to have constantly updated content, as we discussed in Chapter 4: Your Website.

Jonathan Coulton had this experience throughout his 'Thing a Week' project as certain songs got coverage. For instance, he recorded a unique cover of the song 'Baby Got Back', which had him deluged with listeners. The majority just downloaded the song and went on their way. But after the visits cooled off, his Web statistics indicated he gained a few more regular visitors than before. We noticed the same trend with our Song of the Day project.

FOLLOWING SUCCESS

One of the simplest ways to work out where to get coverage is to study bands with similar music who are a step or two ahead of you in terms of popularity and success. Simply perform a Web search on those bands to find out where they've received press attention. Read the articles and look at the angles the media took. Note which particular journalists covered them and make a list of potential press contacts. These journalists are much more likely to cover your band than the ones found in entertainment writer listings. You might also consider adding search engine alerts for new entries, so that you can jump on opportunities when they appear.

Also, don't forget to piggyback off the other band's name in your subsequent press releases.

▶▶ THE PRESS KIT

When a journalist receives a press packet from you, he or she will ask two questions: Who are these guys and what do they want from me?

The press kit answers the first question. Your press release answers the second. The good news about your press kit is that you can use it over and over again with any release that you send out.

ONLINE PRESS KITS VS PAPER PRESS KITS

Paper press kits have been a mainstay of publicists for years and they still do come in handy from time to time when you want to send someone a CD. But your online press kit will be used far more often.

You will need a press section of your website to hold your online press kit, organised in a way that makes it easy for the press to get your information. Think of a journalist on a deadline who wants a photo of your band or needs a fact such as the date your band was founded. Make it easy for that person to get those basic facts quickly and without hassle.

We recommend turning each part of your press kit into PDF documents, which are the easiest type of files to read and print. You should also put up all of the content as Web pages, so that visitors can read it quickly when they visit your site.

We suggest hosting this on your own website but there are also sites such as Sonicbids (sonicbids.com) which specialise in hosting an online press kit and also provide methods to submit your materials directly to talent buyers, bookers, TV, radio, film and more.

MAKING A PRESS KIT

PRESS KIT GROUND RULES

Here is your basic strategy for a professional press kit:

- Keep the format consistent for all pages of the kit.
- Use your logos, stories, images and letterhead you created in Chapter 3: Your Brand.
- Studies have shown that you only have about six seconds to hook someone's attention with your press kit. It should be visually arresting and it should give them the information they want quickly.
- Put your contact information on every page. Include the name, email, phone number and website for your press contact.

Don't ignore the last rule. Whoever is reading your kit should be able to contact you at a moment's notice. Should they print out or get a paper version of the kit, they may lose the front page, so put your contact information on every single one.

PRESS KIT COMPONENTS

Here are the components of a press kit:

1. Band bio
2. Band photos
3. Press clippings
4. Info sheet
5. Song samples (online press kit only)
6. Press releases (online press kit only)

We are going to talk about each of these in separate sections below.

BAND BIO

There are two kinds of bios you can create: one intended for the press; the other intended for bookers. These differ.

The band bio for the press should always fit on one page and feature a picture of the band. This bio should tell a story that tickles the reader's interest, giving them just a flavour of the rest of your press materials. Don't make this a history of the band. The band bio for bookers should provide a history of the band, as well as each musician, so that a potential booker can see how much experience the band collectively has.

We will post examples of good band bios at DIYMusicManual.com to give you a place to start.

BAND PHOTOS

As we've said, the visuals can be the deciding factor between a kit that is read and one that gets discarded. The very best photos tell a story and stay true to the band's image. Avoid the standard pictures of the band in front of a brick wall and try to stage photos that are distinctive and memorable. According to Janelle Rogers, who has seen countless press kits, some of the most effective band photos have been candid shots taken by one of the band's friends. Journalists will often look at the band photo before listening to the music and it can colour their perceptions of what they hear.

Band photos should be 20 x 23cm in size. For an online press kit the photo should be in JPEG format at 300 DPI (dots per inch) resolution. At your website, you should provide thumbnails of your band photo at your Press/Booking page so that people don't have to download each large image file just to see what it looks like. If you can, provide multiple photos because different circumstances and promotions call for different types of shots. What might work for a booker might not be appropriate for publication in a newspaper.

PRESS CLIPPINGS

There is nothing more effective in your press kit than press clippings. They provide real-world, objective validation of your band's success. Also, journalists hate missing a story and the right clippings can make them feel like they've been missing out on something great. Use these guidelines to make your clippings sheet:

■ Choose the best of the best.

■ Your clippings page should be no more than two pages, front and back.

■ Take the best quotes or snippets from the clips and put it in a list on the sheet.

■ Feature articles should be included whole. (Which could make them longer than two pages but by that point, you now have a feature article which warrants it.)

■ Reviews and fan quotes are both fair game.

INFO SHEET

Since your bio is a story about your band, you will need a separate info sheet that lists details like when your band was founded, your discography, what your music sounds like and other details a journalist might need for his story. This should be no more than two pages long.

Here's a list of everything that you should consider adding to fact sheets:

■ **Blurb:** A one- or two-sentence blurb about your band and its music.

■ **Basic information:** Band name, websites, genre, similar bands you sound like, date founded, hometown.

■ **Discography:** List each album, the date released and a descriptive blurb. For our info sheet, we include thumbnail images of our album covers.

■ **Band members:** Instrumentation and list of band members.

■ **Radio plays:** If you have any radio play, indicate where and when.

■ **Live show info:** Lists venues where your band has played live and any tours you've done.

■ **Press:** You may wish to list the publications and media coverage that you have received in one place. Unlike the clippings page, this is just a list of the media outlets, articles and dates.

■ **Upcoming projects:** You should list the projects that you are currently working on.

This takes longer than you'd think, because it calls for brief, targeted writing. The trickiest part is keeping the information up to date. Review your info sheet monthly and keep adding new information to it as you get more press, plays and exposure.

SONG SAMPLES (ONLINE PRESS KIT ONLY)
Pick three of your strongest songs and add them to the online press kit. Use an embedded flash player so they can just hit play if they want to hear what you sound like. If you have multiple pages in your online press kit, keep the player on the left or right side of every page.

Your goal is to give the press samples of every type of media you create: text, photos, music and video. Find the best of what you have of each and put it on your pages to give them a taste. Do not set music or video to play automatically on these pages, because you don't want to annoy people who just want your bio or photo.

PRESS RELEASES (ONLINE PRESS KIT ONLY)
You should include your prior press releases in your online press kit so the press can reference what you've done before.

⏩ THE TRADITIONAL MEDIA

Traditional media are still rooted in formalities and these formalities truly distinguish a traditional media campaign from a new media campaign. Because the rules for approaching traditional media seem obscure and difficult, many musicians don't even bother trying for coverage. It's true that the new media is getting more and more effective for getting the word out but a good media campaign should embrace both kinds.

Traditional media will need an official press release and your press kit. Informal emails that tickle their interest will, at best, get them interested enough to ask you for the full package. But the good news is that they are now usually willing to accept an emailed submission. The only time you will need their physical address is when you send them a CD.

THE FITTING-IN STRATEGY
The key defining factor of a traditional media outlet is its target demographic. Outlets are acutely aware of who their audience is and what they are interested in. This isn't surprising, considering most of these media companies

make their money from advertising and their success rests on their advertisers knowing what demographics are being targeted. This means that traditional media outlets are looking for perfect-fit stories for their demographic.

While we talked about the Standing-Out Strategy in Chapter 8: Get Noticed, when you deal with the press, the goal is to fit in. You need to break out of thinking how the press should pay attention to you and instead concentrate on solving problems for each journalist. Journalists are interested in:

- **Finding relevant stories:** Journalists are always on the lookout for interesting stories that will be appropriate for their demographic. People buy kickboxing magazines to read about kickboxing. People check the local newspaper when they want to do something fun, like see a band over the weekend.
- **Hitting deadlines:** Journalists are tasked with filling a certain amount of space before their deadline. To be safe, they usually build up at least a one month buffer of stories and it can be even as much as three- to four-months.
- **Getting the facts:** Journalists need all the information to flesh out the story, including facts and photos. Research takes time and if it takes too much time, they may cut their losses and skip the story altogether.
- **Capturing the zeitgeist:** Journalists want to write stories of the moment: identifying and articulating the latest trends.

The more you can meet their needs, the more coverage you will get. This might mean that you write targeted press releases to particular media outlets based on their focus and demographics. If you send a general press release, keep the above goals in mind when you write it and give outlets enough story hooks to take your story in different directions for their own needs. And always consider piggybacking on a story that is big at the moment.

NEVER MAKE THEM WAIT

Never make a journalist wait if they get in touch with you for a story. They have deadlines. If they are calling you about a story, they need the information now. If you make them wait, you might miss out on a chance for publicity.

▸▸ THE NEW MEDIA

The new media is informal, fast and usually inconsistent in the quality department. These online outlets are mostly run by people who are simply covering what they personally love. Generally, they won't write their stories or record their podcasts ahead of time like the traditional media does. In fact, they don't often have a regular release schedule in the first place. New media journalists are usually skeptical of the traditional media and love to cover topics that the traditional media won't. In fact, that is a big reason for the existence of the new media.

And of course, one of the topics that the traditional media ignores is indie music. In fact, many new media proponents argue that traditional media are keeping good indie music from the people who want to hear it. (And who are we to argue?) In short, being an indie band is an advantage, not a disadvantage, when it comes to new media.

Ironically, new media journalists have a special disdain for anything that looks like promotion. For example, here's the start of a blog review of our fifth CD, *All In A Day's Work*. We sent an email to the Office Humor Blog, (officehumorblog.com) because the album seemed to be a perfect fit. Indeed, the writer liked it. But take a look at how they started the review:

> Last week I received an email from a person representing a band called Beatnik Turtle – a band that apparently has an office-themed album coming out August 7. Normally I'd write off such an email as some sort of spam but I decided to check out the Beatnik Turtle website to see what they have to offer and I'm glad I did.

The traditional media would *never* start an article admitting that an email from a representative of the band caught their attention. But the writer in this case was not only telling the story of how he found out about it, he was also disclosing the fact that he found out about it from the band itself in the interest of transparency.

So the traditional media expects you to send them unabashedly self-promoting materials but usually ignores them. The new media, on the other hand, would love to write articles about you but *doesn't want to get anything that seems like promotion!*

That's not the only irony. The traditional media writes supposedly neutral or unbiased articles based on these press releases. The new media, in spite of rejecting outright promotion, usually takes a *personal* or biased point of view of news, events and entertainment (most are even written in the first person just like the above blog).

HOW THE NEW MEDIA WORKS

Unlike the traditional media, the new media often doesn't feel as obligated to please their audiences because they aren't usually trying to sell anything to them. They cover topics because it's their passion, not because they are trying to hit a particular demographic or drive sales for their 'advertising department'. This gives the new media an authenticity that is lacking in the traditional media and that is often the appeal for their audience.

The new media usually doesn't have a backlog of news and doesn't feel pressured to meet deadlines. They often cover stories immediately when they show up. But because they print news whenever they want, they often have a bigger appetite for news than the traditional media.

The exceptions, of course, are the largest and most popular examples of blogs and new media, in which case, they tend to act more like the traditional media lining up stories ahead of time and possibly receiving press releases. They have an income stream to protect, as well, so that may influence their stories.

THE FITTING-IN STRATEGY (REPRISE: THE NEW MEDIA REMIX)

Just as you have to fit in to the traditional media's needs, you will also have to fit in with the new media in order to get covered. But the process is entirely different.

A new media journalist wants stories that are personally interesting to them. Their interests are easy enough to discern by looking at the topics covered by the site. Most bloggers and podcasters find their stories on their own. In fact, the best way to convince one to cover you is to encourage them to make the story their own and find their own unique spin.

In general, the new media loves covering niche stories, ones outside the mainstream. They love poking fun at the traditional media and they also become attached to stories about bucking the system. As an indie, you will often have these stories. For instance, one of our fans blogged about how he was frustrated by the digital rights management (DRM) restrictions that Napster imposed on his music and used our album as an example. This was a number of years ago, when the music industry did not release any of its digital downloads in DRM-free formats. We dislike DRM as well and only made our music available on Napster through CD Baby, which put us on every digital music store. So, we sent the blogger DRM-free versions of all of the songs he'd bought. Naturally, the blogger was very pleased with our response. We blogged about this and sent a link to our blog entry to Stanford law professor Lawrence Lessig. The fact that we were giving our music out without restrictions was highly relevant to him. He picked up the story and then so did other blogs.

While traditional media pitches need to be formal, the opposite is true for the new media. Some do accept press kits but sending one is usually a mistake. In fact, if you're *lucky*, they'll ignore it. If you're not, they will publically criticize you for your shameless self-promotion.

Here are a few ideas for getting new media coverage:

▪ Send a short email consisting of nothing more than 'Hey, I thought you might like this', with a link to a blog entry or song, using a non-band account.
▪ Get someone else, preferably a fan of the site who has suggested material in the past, to send an email to on your behalf.
▪ If the site accepts comments or features a message board, find a way to relate your song or story to the discussion at hand. Since site owners usually read their own website comments, this is an authentic way to give them the idea for a story.
▪ Tell the site owner that you're with a band and that you love their blog or podcast or video show. Add that you think that they may like your song, album or story. While this is self-promotion, it's also a meeting of equals that new media types sometimes appreciate. This also opens the possibility of cross-promotion, which we talked about in Chapter 2: Your Network.

Remember that the new media will cover stories soon after they learn about them. Some will post stories within a week, some the same day. And, of course, some are unreliable and won't cover a story even if they say they will.

▸▸WRITING PRESS RELEASES

Press releases are mostly used with traditional media but while you are unlikely to send the new media your releases, they may end up going to your site to research you and may end up reading them.

Press releases work best when they incorporate current trends in pop culture. It's easier for journalists to sell their audience on a story they are already familiar with rather than a completely new one.

Press release writing can be difficult. You might find yourself laboring over each word. We find it to be the most demanding kind of writing that we do. Here are the basics:

- **Length:** It should be short – one or two pages.
- **Contact information:** Add your publicity contact information at the top of each page. Include a name, phone, email and website.
- **Release date:** If there's a date that the story should be released (such as the release date of an album) put it at the top. Otherwise, add 'FOR IMMEDIATE RELEASE'.
- **Headline:** The headline, often written in all caps, should be designed to catch the journalist's attention. It's a good idea to use salting here.
- **The lead:** This is the first sentence or two of the press release. There are two types. A news release should answer the questions, Who? What? When? Where? Why? and How? A feature story should have a hook that is attention-grabbing or amusing.
- **The press release text:** Tell your story briefly, succinctly and make it as compelling as possible. Aim it at your audience's interests as you write it and read it out loud several times to make sure that it's punchy. Use small words and subject-verb-object sentence construction for more impact.
- **Call to action:** Your story should have a call to action.
- **Mention recent and future projects:** Near the end of a press release, it's a good idea to mention recently finished projects as well as future ones. You never know what the press will pick up on.
- **Envelope teasers:** When you mail the press your materials write further information on the envelope itself. For instance, Carla Ulbrich, folk musician, always writes a special note if she'll be in town such as 'Playing in your area at the Riviera on March 12!'

If you'd like sample press releases to start from, we've posted some examples at DIYMusicManual.com.

▶▶INTERVIEWS

If your press release hits home, you might be called for an interview. How well your interview goes will depend partly on your personality and partly on preparation. Interviews are much like stage performances. You need to practise for them just as you'd practise for a show. The difference is, you will never be exactly sure what questions they'll ask. Here are some techniques that will help you prepare.

WHAT TO EXPECT OUT OF AN INTERVIEW

By the time you're contacted to do an interview, they'll usually have an idea of the story that they want to tell. Most of the time, they are interviewing you to fish for original quotes that will match their story and perhaps fill in some details that weren't covered in your press release or press kit. It's rarer to get a feature story, where a journalist will interview you to learn what you're really about. Your goal during the interview is to give journalists what they're looking for while subtly blending in the points you want to get across. It's a delicate balance.

In a written piece, you'll be lucky to see more than two actual quotes from a one-hour interview. Clearly, you don't have much control over these stories, except for how you answer questions and the points that you manage to squeeze in. After your first interview or two, you will probably be frustrated by the fact that most journalists get at least one thing wrong in every article that they write. They will misspell your name, get your website wrong, get the story out of order or take something you said out of context. Combat these problems with talking points, soundbites and other techniques we talk about below.

TALKING POINTS

Talking points are just a list of the points you want to cover, with short, paragraph-length statements ready to go for each point. You will usually have two types of talking points handy for interviews. One consists of answers to basic questions like 'Who are your influences?' and 'Where do you get your ideas?' The other includes points that you want to introduce to the interviewer, like your latest projects and anything that your band will be doing over the next few months. If the interview seems to be getting off track, you should try to pull it back to the talking points, because that will be the strongest material.

SOUNDBITES

Soundbites are short packaged quotes, no more than three or four sentences long. The shorter they are, the better. You want to prepare soundbites before interviews because print journalists are looking for them. But they're especially useful for radio and TV interviews. If you give a journalist a good soundbite, they are more likely to use that rather than something you said off the cuff which might not reflect positively on you.

FACT SHEETS AND FOLLOW-UPS FOR INTERVIEWS

We talked about the fact sheet in the press kit section but it comes into play again after an interview. Journalists often wait until the last minute to get in all the little details such as basic information like the date you were founded, your website address, the number of band members you have and so on. If they have to look it up, they may get the information wrong. Your fact sheet is the best way to help them get the facts right.

Offer to send journalists a fact sheet once the interview is finished in case they don't have one. Also, send up a follow-up email after every interview to thank them and to clarify anything that you think was unclear. These two steps may save you a lot of grief in the future. It will also help cement your relationship with them, which is an even more important objective.

ANECDOTES AND STORIES

Janelle Rogers from Green Light Go Publicity says that one of the most important things to prepare for an interview are stories to tell about the band. Be specific and engaging with these anecdotes, as it gives journalists hooks to write about. For radio and television, it's the stories that can make an interview truly memorable.

▸▸PRESS CAMPAIGNS

Press campaigns can be as simple as sending out a press release and as complicated as a highly orchestrated mailing campaign simultaneously promoting a tour and a new album. No matter what you are trying to do, stick to these steps.

- Determine your goal.
- Prepare a targeted press list.
- Plan the timing of the campaign.
- Update your press kit.
- Write a press release or multiple releases if different media outlets call for different angles.
- Send email press releases first.
- If there is a CD, send physical press releases after email press releases have been out for a week.
- Send email to the new media straight after your project is released to the public.
- Send follow-up emails for your campaign and use trackback to check the results.
- Send thank you messages to any media outlets that cover you and keep track of them.

STEP 1: DETERMINE YOUR GOAL

Your most effective press campaigns will have well-defined goals. Goals help determine which media outlets to target and how to best schedule your campaign.

Some example goals include:

- Get articles written about a CD release party.
- Get a review of your album.
- Get coverage of a big charity show.
- Get attention for a music video.
- Increase your draw for an upcoming tour.

These are, of course, just examples but the point is that they don't always have to be big goals. Any goal will help determine the later steps.

STEP 2: PREPARE A TARGETED PRESS LIST

Each media outlet will respond to different aspects of your stories. Music journalists will be concerned with your music and your influences, the local paper will want to know about your latest shows and so on. You may need different press releases for each of these targets and they will each have different deadlines, so plan carefully.

Your press list is simply a list of the submission contacts at each outlet. If you haven't worked with that outlet before, you will have to do research to find the right person. This is where publicists have an advantage, because they have already gathered a large database of contacts and can put together press lists for new campaigns quickly. In fact, many publicists will send an email with personalised notes to each contact in order to raise their response rate.

As you generate your list, keep in mind that you shouldn't send every press release to every outlet. In fact some of your press releases will go to just a handful of outlets.

STEP 3: PLAN THE TIMING

Once you have a press list, work out what their normal lead time is and plan your campaign accordingly. If they need a three-month lead and you know that your CD release party will take place on a certain date, you'll know when to send them your press release. If you're targeting new media, you can probably send messages out just a week or so before major events and immediately after the release of an album.

STEP 4: UPDATE YOUR PRESS KIT

Before you send out your press materials, it's a good idea to look over your fact sheets, bios, clippings and other materials. Details change quickly with bands and it's worth your time to make sure everything is up to date. Very often, we'll find that our fact sheet mentions future events that have already taken place. We also often find information to add, such as new places where our music has been played.

STEP 5: WRITE PRESS RELEASES

As discussed in the section above, write a press release. The press releases should be targeted for each type of outlet to be most effective.

STEP 6: EMAIL PRESS RELEASES

Most outlets prefer email press releases. You can improve the chances of getting your email read by creating a compelling subject line and a punchy lead. The subject line might be the only thing a journalist reads before they delete your email. Again, we recommend salting your subject line to create an expectation that can only be met by reading the body of the message. Provide links to your online press kit in the press release. Links to songs and especially videos are also recommended.

STEP 7: SNAIL MAIL CDS

You should only spend the money to send a paper press release when you have a CD to promote. You'll need paper versions of your press kit, your press release and a pitch letter.

The pitch letter should summarise the press release, salted just enough to get the journalist interested in reading more.

STEP 8: SEND EMAIL TO NEW MEDIA CLOSE TO DEADLINES

As we said, you'll get better results out of the new media when you contact them close to the event that you want covered. This will probably go out months after you send materials to the traditional press.

STEP 9: SEND FOLLOW-UP EMAILS AND USE TRACKBACK

Remember our lesson: some journalists won't even read your release until the second email. Wait about a week and send a second email to any journalists who haven't already responded (use the spam filter excuse!).

After your campaign begins, track your progress by searching for your band name in search engines and watching the referrers page of your website stats.

STEP 10: SEND THANK YOU MESSAGES

If you get a story covered, send a thank you but don't expect a reply. You want to use each successful article to build a relationship with the press. The more you know them personally, the more articles they are likely to write about you.

▸▸PRESS CAMPAIGN TIPS

YOUR EXPECTED RESPONSE RATE

According to Janelle Rogers, you can send 100 emails out for a campaign and get only ten responses or less. Publicity, unfortunately, is a numbers game. You'll need to take the responses you do get and do as much with them as you can.

PR NEWSWIRES AND PRESS SERVICES

Newswires accept all types of press releases and blast them out to all of their subscribers. Many publications rely on these wires as sources of fresh stories. When we were covered by the Associated Press, for example, the story went to many publications and newspapers in different parts of the country picked it up. Newswires are a particularly good place to get coverage because of this.

Some newswires are free to submit to such as the Music Industry News Network (mi2n.com) while others are for-pay. Whether to use them or not depends on what your goals are. Newswires want press releases. There's no need to send the full press kit. Any press releases that are sent on a wire should have a call to action to reach your press contact for more information, so that they can make a request.

For a complete list of current free and for-pay newswires to use for your publicity campaigns, head to DIYMusicManual.com.

THE TWO MAGIC WORDS

When it comes to any physical mail you might send, there are two magic words: SOLICITED MATERIALS.

Use them when you can.

If you manage to get in touch with a journalist and they tell you to send your materials, that's an invitation to use those magic words on your envelope. These words will move your press release to the top of the stack since they're expecting it. If you do send a press release that was solicited, be sure to write this on the envelope and in the cover letter.

WEB TRACKBACK

One problem with the press is that they rarely tell you they've written a story about your band, even if you sent them a press release. The only way you'll know if they've written an article is if you discover it for yourself.

To track mentions of your band, you should use the Web trackback techniques that we discussed in Chapter 4: Your Website. First of all, after a press release is sent out, you should do regular searches on your band name in the major search engines. Second, you should track your Web statistics and watch the referrer list carefully. You might discover articles that have linked to your website that the search engines have missed. Even better, you will be able to see how many people come to your site from each link, so you can learn which articles are the most effective.

▶▶INTERNET CAMPAIGNS

As we discussed in the Web presence chapter, the Web has evolved from a broadcast, to a conversation and finally to a collaboration. While publicity is usually about *broadcasting* a message to as many people as possible, it doesn't have to be limited to that.

DIGITAL POSTERS

Make a digital version of your posters. There are actually many places where you can 'post' these on the Internet. The most common use is as a comment on MySpace. Again, think of it like a billboard on a busy road. Colourful posters get people's attention more than a plain text message.

After creating a digital poster, upload it to your website and then link to that image within your post to the message board, wall or comment since many boards don't allow you to upload images but will let you insert one that is hosted elsewhere. This has the added bonus of allowing the image to be tracked in your Web statistics, so you can learn which posts and posters are the most effective.

NEWS AGGREGATORS

As stated in Chapter 5: Your Web Presence, sites such as Slashdot, Fark and Metafilter are key targets for Internet campaigns. The best part about of these sites is that they don't always post news stories. They can, and often do, post links to songs, videos or whatever link takes their fancy, especially if it's related to one of their interests. They are always happy to send their users to something entertaining.

Although many of these sites choose stories from user-submitted links, it's ultimately an editor who decides what gets posted. It's never possible to tell exactly why an editor picks what they do, because most of these editors are fickle. Your best bet for getting a mention is to find an angle that would appeal to the editors. Follow each news aggregation site for a while until you have a feel for their interests before submitting.

FAN NETWORK CAMPAIGNS

Your fan network is the most persistent and genuine way to get your press campaign under way. If your fans are willing to help you, they can put your name in places that you haven't even thought of. The Brobdingnagian Bards found early on that their fans were a very effective part of their campaigns after they'd been given a little direction. To coordinate them, they used email to give their fans three simple steps to follow in order to help get the word out:

1. Post the band name and URL around the Web.
2. Link to our blogs.
3. Tell a friend. Or, even better, a couple of friends.

Giving your fans a more targeted direction can make your campaign all that much more effective. For instance, Gavin Mikhail discovered that a segment of his fan network was actively promoting him online at various sites. However, there was no rhyme or reason to where they were enthusiastically plugging his name and music. So, Mikhail reached out to them and together they came up with an effective campaign targeting sites and fans of artists that his music is similar too. The result of this coordination worked tremendously.

Giving something in return when you're working to organise and motivate your fan network is effective. Mikhail helped motivate his fans for a particular campaign by giving them something in advance for their help: two free songs from his website. It's essential, he advised, that you realise what a service your fans are doing when they help promote you in this way. As he noted, many musicians make the mistake of simply writing to their fans or posting on Facebook and MySpace walls to 'go vote for me', 'tell your friends about my new album' or 'buy my stuff'. This type of focus actually has the opposite effect of motivating your fans. As we discussed in Chapter 2: Your Network, fans want to be treated as people – not promotional tools. They're doing it because they're a part of your team.

Beyond email, there are a host of street team management tools you can use to coordinate your fans. Collaboration tools and services we discussed in Your Web Presence chapter such as Yahoo Groups (groups.yahoo.com), Google Groups (groups.google.com) and Ning (ning.com) can help you organise and manage your street team. Additionally, there are a number of services that will handle street team management on your behalf or already have a legion of 'fans' ready to work for you. For a listing see DIYMusicManual.com.

▸▸HIRING A PUBLICIST

Now that you've been on a tour of what you need to do in order to publicise your band, you might be feeling overwhelmed. As we discussed in Chapter 2: Your Network, do-it-yourself does not mean that you have to do it alone. Publicity is one area where finding or hiring someone to help makes a lot of sense. If you're thinking of hiring a publicist, these are some of the key services they can provide:

- Help you assemble a press kit and bio.
- Brainstorm, plan and implement press campaigns.
- Find angles to your stories that fit with what the media are looking for.
- Write press releases.
- Give you ready-made press lists appropriate to each press release.
- Send your press releases under their letterhead, which gives it a better chance of getting noticed.
- Put together your press clippings for your press kit.
- Follow up with media after your campaigns.
- Set up and coordinate interviews.

And keep in mind that there are many kinds of publicists. While some focus on the traditional media, Ariel Hyatt (arielpublicity.com), who we mentioned earlier, runs a service called CyberPR, that can assist with managing new media campaigns. This service finds the kinds of connections that make sense for your band and your music that we talk about in this chapter, such as determining your most appropriate niches to target, assessing your and your band's own interests for possible PR angles and other appropriate connections that can help you get covered in the new media.

Further, she has relationships with many podcasts, blogs and other new media within her Web service, giving them access to new music and bands. Considering that the new media is often turned off by press releases, CyberPR presents your music and your story in an appropriate way, helping you to make the kind of authentic connections that you need to make, should you want help with doing this kind of campaign.

If you decide to use a publicist, don't just pay them and expect them to do everything for you. You should do the following in order to get the most out of a publicist:

- Tell them all of the events that you have planned for the next year at least. This includes CD release shows, major concerts and anything else that will need a lead time for the traditional press.
- Inform them of any newsworthy event. Remember that these can be very small things, such as a music video getting viewed over 5,000 times.
- Give them all of the press contacts you've developed on your own. They will make better use of every connection that you have.
- Make sure that they have copies of all of your press materials.
- Give them high-quality MP3s of your best songs. The media outlets that accept music will sometimes ask for an MP3 before the entire album.
- Make sure to give them enough lead time for any story that has to go to the traditional press. If a story missses the deadline window, there might be nothing a publicist can do for you.

▸▸LEARNING MORE

If you want to learn more about publicity, we recommend *Public Relations for Dummies* by Eric Yaverbaum, Robert W. Bly, Ilise Benun and Richard Kirshenbaum and *Guerrilla Music Marketing, Encore Edition* by Bob Baker. Additional information and resources can be found at DIYMusicManual.com.

▶▶CONCLUSION

When we wrote this book, we hoped to achieve what one reader of the original online version emailed us to say, 'I get it. A dog-eared copy in every battered instrument case, eh?' And that image stuck with us throughout the writing of the book. It kept us focused on our goal to write a book that real musicians like ourselves would use in the real world and would refer to often.

No one knows where the music industry is headed. As Jim DeRogatis said, 'If anyone says they know what it will look like in five years, they're lying.' And he's right. But no matter what happens to the industry, we do know one thing: musicians will always be able to do it themselves. In fact, there are new opportunities to connect with fans and get your music out there appearing on a daily basis. The amazing thing is that they are within your arm's reach.

We hope that the *Manual* will help you recognise when these new opportunities appear and that you take advantage of them for your music. But remember that you're never alone. We'll be keeping up with these opportunities as well as all the latest tools, gear, sites and resources at DIYMusicManual. com, where you can join us and a community of other motivated musicians.

We'd love to hear any suggestions, ideas and comments. You can get in touch with us by mailing *contactus@DIYMusicManual.com* or going to the website and using the contact form.

But enough reading about music. Now go out and make it.

After all, there's no better time to be a musician.

▶▶ACKNOWLEDGEMENTS

No book is created by just the authors and this book is no exception. We'd like to thank our agent Rick Broadhead for realising our potential. We wouldn't be writing this if it weren't for him. Thanks for all the guidance and encouragement.

Thanks to everyone at Ebury for their help, knowledge and support in bringing this *Manual* to life. Special thanks to our editor, Ken Barlow, for believing in the work in the first place and for helping turn a couple of musicians into authors who write good.

We'd like to thank everyone involved in Beatnik Turtle. Without the band, there'd be no book. In no particular order, we'd like to thank everyone involved in the band and with TheSongOfTheDay.com: John Owens, David Hallock, Chip Hinshaw, Tom Susala, Mike Hernandez, Mike Combopiano, Chris Joyce, Ryan Lockhart, John Lisiecki, Matt Scholtka, Caroline Bruno, Cheyenne Pinson, Dana Huyler, Ted ('Hi, my name's Ted and this is my song about ants') Blegen, Alison Logan, Steve Owens, Dugan O'Keene, Eric Elmer, Jerry Waggoner, Danielle Wetle, Tom Hordewel (and his alter ego Tom Beeyachski), Mike Holmes and everyone else who has been a part, past and present.

We'd like to especially thank Tom Roper for picking up and running with TheSongOfTheDay.com when we had to turn our attention to researching, doing, interviewing for and writing the book. Sure we'll write a book and do 365 songs in the same year, what's so hard about that?

There are many who helped make this *Manual* a reality but don't know it. These have been our advisers and mentors – people who have helped pioneer the areas that made it possible for musicians to do it themselves and inspired us. These include, in no particular order: Lawrence Lessig, Derek Sivers, Janis Ian, Eben Moglen, Bruce Schneier, Richard Stallman, Steve Albini and Eric Boehlert.

We also want to thank everyone we interviewed for the *Manual*. In no particular order we'd like to thank: Chris Anderson (thelongtail.com), Derek Sivers

(sivers.org), Jim DeRogatis (jimdero.com), Jeff Price (tunecore.com), Norman Hajjar (guitarcenter.com), Simon Wainwright (hopeandsocial.com), Roo Pigott (hopeandsocial.com), Mark Wordsworth, Peggy Manning (fistralpr.co.uk), Holly Anderson (eventful.com), Sharon Howell (lewispr.com), Richard Jones (last.fm), Todd Martens, Mur Lafferty (murlafferty.com), Fletcher Lee (leeproductionsinc.com), Patrick Faucher (nimbit.com), Matt Scholtka (scholtkadesign.com), Michael Freeman, Ariel Hyatt (arielpublicity.com), Bob Baker (bob-baker.com), Mike Dolinar (getmadbaby.com), James Ernest (cheapass.com), Scott Alden and Derk Solko (boardgamegeek.com), Christian Ward (last.fm), J.C. Hutchins (jchutchins.net) and Brian Austin Whitney (jpfolks.com).

We'd also like to thank all the talented indie musicians we talked to: Hope & Social/Four Day Hombre (hopeandsocial.com), Gavin Mikhail (gavinmikhail.com), Jonathan Coulton (jonathancoulton.com), Brad Turcotte (bradsucks.net), Grant Baciocco (throwingtoasters.com), Andrew McKee and Marc Gunn (thebards.net), George Hrab (georgehrab.blogspot.com), Carla Ulbrich (carlaulbrich.com), Peter Shukoff (nicepeter.com), and Yvonne Doll of The Locals (thelocals.net).

Additionally, we'd also like to thank the editor of the precursor to this book, *The Indie Band Survival Guide*, Brad Weier, for his excellent work as well as Erik Balisi for his initial help. We'd also like to thank all the musicians who emailed us after reading the online version. Their advice, insight and questions helped make this *Manual* all the better.

And lastly, we'd like to thank everyone who has been part of Beatnik Turtle and TheSongOfTheDay.com past and present as well as the friends, family and fans of Beatnik Turtle.

▶▶RANDY WOULD LIKE TO THANK...

I want to give my heartfelt thanks to my parents, Glenn and Susan Chertkow, for their support. Thanks to the GamesNight people for keeping the games going during my absence. Also thanks to my D&D group for taking on an entire army without your cleric.

Thanks to my sister and brother-in-law Heather and John Cumings and niece Chloe. Thanks also to Grandma Alaine Klein and Grandpa Eddie Klein for the encouragement. Thanks to my good friends Tony Downing, Dana Huyler, Steve Levy, Jay Kline and Bradley Trenton Malloy Quinn for the personal support. Also, thank you to the Pegasus folks for the research, banter, distractions and senseless violence, including Shannon Prickett, Andrew Crawford, Tom Shekleton, James Tripp and Jessica Firsow.

I want to thank everyone who has worked with me in music, David Bloom, the perfect set group and Berklee College of Music. And especially my departed and much-missed sax teacher, Frank Schalk and Paul Maslin at PMWoodwind (pmwoodwind.com) for his excellent saxophone advice. Also, thanks to New Trier's music department, especially James Warrick and Jim Thompson.

I need to say a special thank you to Quinn Obermeyer for his understanding while I wrote this book. And also to Zin Fooks, for his wisdom, camaraderie and for helping me get through this major project. Spasibo. Also, thanks to the rest of the team at my day gig for filling in and for mostly mocking me while I did this book: Jim McCafferty, Dan Noah, Shawn Delaney, David Matuszewski, Matt Obermeyer, Scott Soto, Andy Franklin and Tommy Carter.

And thanks to Jason for co-writing this. Working with you on this project, as well as all of the others, has been a pleasure.

And, finally, to Peggy: I'm sorry. You can have Jason back now.

▶▶JASON WOULD LIKE TO THANK…

First and foremost, a big thanks is owed to my wife, Peggy Mahoney, for all her love, support, encouragement and understanding as I put long hours into the *Manual* and Beatnik Turtle. I'm lucky to have a wife like you and Liam is lucky to have you as his mom. I love you both.

The reality of it all is that everything contained in this *Manual* stems from Beatnik Turtle. And everything about Beatnik Turtle stems from my parents, Jim and Jean Feehan, who, for some reason, allowed me to build a home studio years ago in their basement. Little did they know their decision made on a whim would result in countless musicians traipsing through their home at all hours of the night, instrument cases banging up their walls and a never-ending stream of Beatnik Turtle music soundtracking their lives as they struggled to complete the crossword, do the dishes or watch TV. Despite their inconveniences, they've constantly worried more about us than themselves ('did you guys eat?'). Although they may still have no idea what the hell we're doing with Beatnik Turtle, *The Indie Band Survival Guide* or the *DIY Music Manual*, they certainly are proud nonetheless. And I'm proud to call them my parents. Thanks Mom and Dad. I love you.

I'd like to thank the rest of my family, including my brother Jared Feehan, my cousins John and Jeff Franzen and my grandparents William and Ester ('Sick of Sandwiches') Grommes. I'd also like to thank my fun and supportive in-laws, Joe and Collette Mahoney, as well as Chris and Moira Waldron for all their support, advice and encouragement throughout this process.

▶▶ABOUT THE AUTHORS

RANDY CHERTKOW

Professionally, Randy Chertkow is an Information Technology specialist with over fourteen years of experience in enterprise-class Fortune 100 companies. He has a Bachelor's in Business Administration in Information Systems from the University of Iowa and a Master's of Science in Computer Science: Data Communications, with a secondary concentration in Artificial Intelligence from DePaul University, where he graduated with distinction. Randy has played music all his life, including jazz, rock and classical music. His instruments include baritone, tenor, alto and soprano saxophones, flute, B♭ and bass clarinet, guitar, bass and anything else he can get his hands on. He started at the challenging New Trier High School Jazz programme and went on to study jazz at Berklee College of music and then completed a Perfect Set course at the Bloom School of Jazz. He writes, records and performs with Beatnik Turtle as well as performing with theatre companies around Chicago. Randy also writes Sci-Fi and fantasy (dreamofanotherworld.com) and about computer topics (effectivemonitoring.com).

JASON FEEHAN

Professionally, Jason Feehan is a practising corporate lawyer who works for a multinational executive search firm. He has a Bachelor of Science in Political Science and Psychology from the University of Iowa and a JD from Chicago-Kent College of Law. He plays guitar, keyboards, sings, records, engineers and produces. He founded Beatnik Turtle in 1997, growing it from a four-piece band into an eight-piece rock machine with a full horn section and a recording studio all its own. Unfettered by a formal music education, he often learned to play instruments as he wrote the music and used nearly anyone in arms-reach who could play or said they could play a musical instrument. He is a very prolific songwriter and has written close to a thousand songs, three of which are actually not too bad.

BEATNIK TURTLE

The authors' band, Beatnik Turtle (*BeatnikTurtle*.Com) is a horn-powered pop-rock band based in Chicago. They have recorded eighteen albums, released over 400 songs and successfully completed a Song of the Day project where they released one song for every day of 2007 at its website, TheSongOfTheDay.com. They've written music for TV shows, commercials, films, podcasts, theatre (including Chicago's Second City) and have licensed music to Disney/ABC Family.

▶▶RESOURCES

Visit DIYMusicManual.com for an up-to-date and fully comprehensive list of Resources.

Allen, David, *Getting Things Done*, London: Piatkus, 2002

Anderson, Chris, *The Long Tail*, London: Random House Business Books, 2007

Avalon, Moses, *Confessions of a Record Producer*, San Francisco, Backbeat Books, 2006

Baker, Bob, *Guerrilla Music Marketing, Encore Edition*, USA: Bob Baker, 2006

Beall, Eric, *Making Music Make Money: An Insider's Guide to Becoming Your Own Music Publisher*, Boston: Berklee Press, 2007

Frauenfelder, Mark, *Rule the Web!*, New York: St Martin's Griffin, 2007

Gibson, Bill, *The S.M.A.R.T. Manual to Mixing and Mastering Audio Recordings*, Boston: Course Technology, 2006

Gladwell, Malcolm, *The Tipping Point*, London, Abacus, 2002

Goldberg, Justin, *The Ultimate Survival Guide to the New Music Industry: Handbook for Hell*, Los Angeles: Lone Eagle Publishing, 2003

Goldstein, Jeri, *How To Be Your Own Booking Agent: THE Musician's and Performing Artist's Guide to Successful Touring*, Charlottesvill, New Music Times, 2000

Kirchenbaum, Richard, Eric Yaverbaum, Robert W. Bly and Ilise Benun, *Public Relations for Dummies*, Hoboken, John Wiley & Sons, 2006

Krug, Steve, *Don't Make Me Think: A Common Sense Approach to Web Usability*, Berkeley, New Riders, 2005

Lessig, Lawrence, *Free Culture: How Big Media Uses Technology and the Law to Lock Down Culture and Control Creativity*, Creative Commons licence at free-culture.cc

Levine, John R., Margaret Levine Young and Carol Baroudi, *Internet for Dummies*, Hoboken: John Wiley & Sons, 2007

Moglen, Eben, 'Freeing the Mind: Free Software and the Death of Proprietary Culture', http://emoglen.law.columbia.edu/publications/maine-speech.html

Morris, Tee and Evo Terra, *Podcasting for Dummies*, Hoboken: John Wiley & Sons, 2008

Morris, Tee, Evo Terra and Ryan Williams, *Expert Podcasting Practices for Dummies*, Hoboken: John Wiley & Sons, 2007

Owsinski, Bobby, *The Mixing Engineer's Handbook*, Boston: Course Technology, 2006

Passman, Donald S., *All You Need to Know About the Music Business*, London: Penguin, 2007

Ratcliffe, Mitch and Steve Mack, *Podcasting Bible*, Hoboken: John Wiley & Sons, 2007

Stim, Richard W., *Getting Permission: How to License and Clear Copyrighted Materials Online and Off*, Berkeley: NOLO, 2007

Taylor, Joe, *Host Your Own Concerts*, USA: Lulu, 2004

Walch, Rob and Mur Lafferty, *Tricks of the Podcasting Masters*, Indianapolis: QUE, 2006

▸▸WEBSITES

BLOGS
Blogger (blogger.com)
Livejournal (livejournal.com)
Wordpress (wordpress.com)

BLOG PINGS
http://api.feedster.com/ping
http://rpc.pingomatic.com/
http://rpc.technorati.com/rpc/ping

BLOG SEARCH ENGINES
Google Blog Search (blogsearch.google.com)
Technorati (technorati.com)
Micro-Blogging
Jaiku (jaiku.com)
Pownce (pownce.com)
Tumblr (tumblr.com)
Twitter (twitter.com)
Utterz (utterz.com)

▸▸CONTESTS/ CHALLENGES

ALBUM CHALLENGES
February Album Writing Month
(http://fawm.org)
National Solo Album Month
(nasoalmo.org)
The Record Production Month
Challenge (rpmchallenge.com)

LIST OF SONGWRITING CONTESTS
Muse's Muse (musesmuse.com/
contests.html)
The Craft of Songwriting
(craftofsongwriting.com/contests.
htm)
John Lennon Songwriting Contest
(jlsc.com).
Songfight (songfight.org)

▸▸COPYRIGHT

Creative Commons
(creativecommons.org)

AUSTRALIA/NEW ZEALAND
Australasian Mechanical Copyright
Owners' Society: AMCOS (apra.
com.au)
PPCA (ppca.com.au).

UK
UK Copyright Service
(copyrightservice.co.uk)
The Intellectual Property Office (ipo.
gov.uk)
Mechanical Copyright Protection
Society: MCPS (mcps-prs-alliance.
co.uk)

Office of Public Sector Information in
the UK (opsi.gov.uk)
PPL (ppluk.com)
Video Performance (vpluk.com)

▸▸TRADE MARK

AUSTRALIA
IP Australia (ipaustralia.gov.au)

EU
Office for Harmonisation in the
Internal Market: OHIM (oami.
europa.eu)

NEW ZEALAND
Intellectual Property Office of New
Zealand (iponz.govt.nz)

UK
Intellectual Property Office (ipo.gov.
uk)

▸▸EMAIL

EMAIL LIST SOFTWARE
EZine Director (ezinedirector.com)
PHPlist (PHPList.com)

OPEN SOURCE LISTSERV
Mailman (gnu.org/software/
mailman/)

▸▸MERCHANDISE

STICKERS
Stickerguy (stickerguy.com)
BandWear (bandwear.com)

T-SHIRTS
Cafepress (Cafepress.com)
Spreadshirt (spreadshirt.com)

Zazzle (zazzle.com)

OTHER MERCHANDISE
Branders (branders.com)
PRstore (prstore.com)

▶▶PLAYING LIVE

BOOKING
Eventful.com

HOUSE CONCERTS
HouseConcerts (houseconcerts.com)

INTERNET CONCERTS
GoTo Webinar (gotowebinar.com)
Mogulus (mogulus.com)
UStream TV (ustream.tv)

INVITATION SOFTWARE
Evite (evite.com)

MUSIC FESTIVALS
Festivals.com (festivals.com)
UK: Efestivals (efestivals.co.uk)

US COLLEGE BOOKINGS
Association for the Promotion of
    Campus Activities (APCA.com)
National Association for Campus
    Activities (NACA.org)

▶▶MOBILE/PHONE

CONTENT PROVIDERS
BroadTexter (broadtexter.com)
Myxer (myxer.com)

SKYPE
Skype (skype.com)

▶▶MUSIC AGGREGATORS

NOMA Music (nomamusic.com)
Sonicbids (sonicbids.com)
Taxi (taxi.com)
WildWhirled (wildwhirled.com)

▶▶PODCASTS

PODSAFE COLLECTIVES
CCMixter (ccmixter.org)
Magnatune (magnatune.com)
OpSound (opsound.org)
PodsafeAudio (podsafeaudio.com)
Podsafe Music Network (music.
    podshow.com)

PODCAST DIRECTORIES
DIYMusicManual.com
iTunes
Podcast Alley (podcastalley.com)
Podcast Pickle (podcastpickle.com)
Podcast Net (podcast.net)
Podiobooks (podiobooks.com)
The Podcast Directory (www.
    podcastdirectory.com)

PODCAST SYNDICATION SITES
Liberated Syndication (libsyn.com)
Podpress (podpress.org)

▶▶MUSIC ARCHIVES

Archive.org (archive.org/details/
    audio)

LIVE MUSIC ACHIVES
ETree (etree.org)
Wiki (wiki.etree.org)
Trade Friendly page (wiki.etree.org/
    index.php?page=TradeFriendly)

▸▸ MUSICIANS

Andrew McKee and Marc Gunn (thebards.net),
Beatnik Turtle (beatnikturtle.com)
Brad Turcotte (bradsucks.net)
Carla Ulbrich (carlaulbrich.com)
Gavin Mikhail (gavinmikhail.com)
George Hrab (georgehrab.blogspot.com)
Grant Baciocco (throwingtoasters.com)
Hope & Social/Four Day Hombre (hopeandsocial.com)
Jonathan Coulton (jonathancoulton.com)
Peter Shukoff (nicepeter.com)
Yvonne Doll of The Locals (thelocals.net)

▸▸ MUSIC STORAGE AND SHARING SERVIVES

Amazon's S3 (aws.amazon.com/s3)
Box (box.net)

▸▸ PR NEWSWIRES AND PRESS SERVICES

Music Industry News Network (mi2n.com)

▸▸ RECORDING

COLLABORATIONS WITH OTHER MUSICIANS ONLINE
eJamming (ejamming.com)
JamGlue (jamglue.com)

HOME RECORDING
Audacity (audacity.sourceforge.net)

SAMPLES AND LOOPS
Acid Planet (acidplanet.com)
ccMixter (ccMixter.org) (free material licensed under Creative Commons)
Drums On Demand (drumsondemand.com)
East West Samples (eastwestsamples.com)

VIRTUAL MUSICIANS FOR HIRE
DrumsForYou (drumsforyou.com)
ESession (esession.com)
Session Players (sessionplayers.com)

▸▸ SALES

DIGITAL MUSIC STORES
CD Baby (cdbaby.com)
iTunes (apple.com/itunes; apple.com/uk/itunes)
Nimbit (nimbit.com

ONLINE CD STORES
Amazon (amazon.com; amazon.co.uk)
CD Baby (cdbaby.com)
Tunecore (tunecore.com)

SELLING DOWNLOADS FROM YOUR SITE
E-Junkie (e-junkie.com)
Payloadz (payloadz.com)

WIDGET/APPLICATION-BASED STORES
Hoooka (hoooka.com)
Nimbit (nimbit.com)
Snocap (snocap.com)

▸▸ SEARCH ENGINES

Google.com
   Alerts: google.com/aletrs
   Submit link: http://google.com/
   addurl/?continue=/addurl
Live.com
   Alerts: alerts.live.com
   Submit link: http://search.msn.
   com/docs/submit.aspx
Yahoo.com
   Alerts: alerts.yahoo.com
   Submit link: http://search.yahoo.
   com/info/submit.html

PAGE RANK
Google PageRank – Google Toolbar
   (toolbar.google.com)

RSS
Feedburner (feedburner.com)

▸▸ SHARING SITES

MUSIC-SHARING SITES
Alonetone (alonetone.com)
Imeem (imeem.com)
Garageband (garageband.com)
Last.fm (last.fm)
Virb (virb.com)

PHOTO-SHARING SITES
Flickr (flickr.com)
Photobucket (photobucket.com)
Webshots (webshots.com)

VIDEO-SHARING SITES
Blip TV (blip.tv)
YouTube (youtube.com)

▸▸ SOCIAL NETWORKING

Bebo (bebo.com)
Facebook (facebook.com)
MySpace (myspace.com)
Ning (ning.com)
Reverbnation (reverbnation.com)

MESSAGE BOARDS
CD Baby (cdbaby.org)
DIYMusicManual.com
Just Plain Folks (jpfolks.com)
Velvet Rope (velvetrope.com)

MESSAGE BOARD PROGRAMS
BBPress (BBpress.org)
PHPBB (PHPBB.org)

OTHER BANDS AND MUSICIANS
Just Plain Folks (jpfolks.com)
The Funny Music Project or The
   Fump (thefump.com).

SOCIAL-BOOKMARKING SITES
Non-Voting Sites:
   Delicious (del.icio.us)
   Magnolia (ma.gnolia.com).
Voting Sites:
   Digg (digg.com)
   Reddit (reddit.com).
   StumbleUpon (stumbleupon.com)
   – toolbar based

VIRTUAL WORLDS
Second Life (secondlife.com)
   Streaming services within Second
   Life:
   IceCast (icecast.org)
   ShoutCast (shoutcast.com)
There (there.com)

⟫STREAMING

Flash Music Players (Streaming)
JW MP3 Player (jeroenwijering.
    com/?item=jw_mp3_player)
Wimpy Player (wimpyplayer.com)
XSPF Web Music Player (musicplayer.
    sourceforge.net)

UPLOADING MUSIC TO YOUR WEBSITE

PC:
    WS-FTP (ipswitch.com)
    WinSCP (winscp.net)
MAC:
    Transmit (panic.com/transmit)
    Cyberduck (cyberduck.ch) are both
    good choices

VIDEO PLAYERS

Blip TV (blip.TV)
YouTube (youtube.com)

⟫SURVEY SITES

Free Online Surveys
    (freeonlinesurveys.com)
MisterPoll (misterpoll.com)
SurveyMethods (surveymethods.
    com)
SurveyMonkey (surveymonkey.com)
Zoomerang (zoomerrang.com)

⟫WEBSITE

CONTENT MANAGEMENT SYSTEMS

Movable Type (movabletype.com)
WordPress (wordpress.org)
Plugins (wordpress.org/extend/
    plugins/)

DONATIONS, SPONSORSHIPS AND MEMBERSHIPS

AMember (amember.com)
PayPal (paypal.com)

WEBHOSTING

FreeWebs (freewebs.com).
Hostbaby (hostbaby.com)

WEB STATISTICS

AWStats (awstats.sourceforge.net)
Mint (haveamint.com)
Webalizer (mrunix.net/Webalizer)

⟫WEBCASTING

Live365 (live365.com)
Radio Paradise (radioparadise.com)
Shoutcast (shoutcast.com)

▶▶INDEX